DEBATING THE
REAGAN PRESIDENCY

Debating Twentieth-Century America
Series Editor: James T. Patterson, Brown University

DEBATING THE
REAGAN PRESIDENCY

JOHN EHRMAN and MICHAEL W. FLAMM

ROWMAN & LITTLEFIELD PUBLISHERS, INC.
Lanham • Boulder • New York • Toronto • Plymouth, UK

ROWMAN & LITTLEFIELD PUBLISHERS, INC.

Published in the United States of America
by Rowman & Littlefield Publishers, Inc.
A wholly owned subsidary of The Rowman & Littlefield Publishing Group, Inc.
4501 Forbes Boulevard, Suite 200, Lanham, Maryland 20706
www.rowmanlittlefield.com

Estover Road
Plymouth PL6 7PY
United Kingdom

British Library Cataloguing in Publication Information Available

Library of Congress Cataloging-in-Publication Data:

Ehrman, John, 1959–
    Debating the Reagan presidency / John Ehrman and Michael W. Flamm.
        p. cm. — (Debating twentieth-century America)
    Includes bibliographical references and index.
    ISBN 978-0-7425-6139-7 (cloth : alk. paper) — ISBN 978-0-7425-6140-3
(pbk. : alk. paper) — ISBN 978-0-7425-7057-3 (electronic)
    1. United States—Politics and government—1981–1989—Sources. 2. United
States—Politics and government—1981–1989. 3. Reagan, Ronald. I. Flamm,
Michael W., 1964– II. Title.
    E876.E343 2009
    973.927—dc22   2009000106

Printed in the United States of America

♾ ™ The paper used in this publication meets the minimum requirements of
American National Standard for Information Sciences—Permanence of Paper for
Printed Library Materials, ANSI/NISO Z39.48-1992.

CONTENTS

Documents

INTRODUCTION

Few serious observers now doubt that Ronald Reagan was the most important and influential president of the late twentieth century. Yet most would not have predicted the outcome in 1981, when he took office at a time of national crisis and self-doubt. At home, the economy suffered from high inflation and unemployment, with no relief in sight. Abroad, it seemed as though the United States could not contain an increasingly powerful Soviet Union. Many prominent intellectuals speculated that America's governing institutions could not cope with the challenges of the era. Others dismissed Reagan as a man of modest intelligence whose conservative ideas were, at best, outdated and, more likely, inadequate or irrelevant for dealing with the country's serious problems.

Eight years later, however, the country and the world were vastly different. Reagan had presided over an economic revival and, as the result of a wave of technological innovation, the ways in which most Americans lived and worked were rapidly changing for the better. After more than four decades, the Cold War was effectively resolved, with the United States the clear winner. Reagan's success brought him a landslide reelection in 1984, enabled him to hand the White House to his chosen successor, George H. W. Bush, in 1988, and made conservatism the dominant force in national politics. Little wonder that Reagan left office in 1989 with the highest approval rating of any president in the last half of the twentieth century, or that in 2007, three years after his death, a Gallup Poll named him the second-greatest president in American history.

Nevertheless, the Reagan presidency remains the subject of heated debate. Domestically, critics contend that his economic policies left millions behind, fostered growing inequality, and created budget deficits of historic proportions. They also assert that his social policies often led to discord, especially on issues like abortion and AIDS. Internationally, Reagan's detractors claim that he committed serious misdeeds as part of the Iran-Contra scandal. They also argue that in Central America and the Middle East, his focus on anti-Communism exacerbated the problems of violence, poverty, and terrorism. In general, moreover, Reagan's critics have long asserted that he gained popular approval mostly by deceiving the American people through the use of sophisticated public relations.

John Ehrman is a historian and an authority on modern American conservatism and the Reagan years. In his essay on domestic politics and policy, he seeks to answer the central question of the 1980s: How was Reagan able to implement untried policy ideas and move the center of gravity in American politics from the middle to the right? His answer, based on a careful examination of the economic data as well as other evidence, is that Reagan gained popular approval for his policies because they brought real benefits to most Americans. Ehrman first explores the sources of Reagan's political beliefs in his personal background and the conservative movement. Then he shows how Reagan put those ideas into practice as president. In Ehrman's view, Reagan was a shrewd politician who chose his battles carefully. His most important domestic objective was to reduce the federal government's economic role, and so he left intact the major social programs of the New Deal and Great Society rather than try to cut them back in politically draining—and probably unwinnable—battles that would have endangered his main goals. Ehrman also devotes considerable attention to the reasons why opposition to Reagan was often ineffective, and he concludes that his Democratic and liberal opponents had difficulty comprehending the nature of the changes Reagan had brought to politics and the economy. Therefore they could not develop successful tactics or alternative policies that had popular appeal.

Michael Flamm is a historian who has studied and taught the Reagan era for more than twenty years. In his essay on foreign affairs, he emphasizes the president's active and assertive role—contrary to the popular perception that Reagan was a passive and disengaged leader. Flamm also examines the sources of the president's abiding anti-Communism as well as his blend of pragmatism and principle, which at times led him to defy the expectations of both liberals and conservatives. In the Middle East, Flamm notes that Reagan's efforts to spread freedom and peace enjoyed little success, while his attempts to curry favor with Iraq and Iran ultimately backfired. In Central America, the White House fostered democracy in El

Salvador and Nicaragua, although it came at a high cost in human suffering and, after the Iran-Contra scandal erupted, political support. Finally, the author acknowledges the essential part Reagan played in bringing the Cold War to a peaceful end, but he suggests that the president must share substantial credit with Soviet leader Mikhail Gorbachev.

The economic crisis and presidential election of 2008 may mark the end of what many now call "the age of Reagan." Nevertheless, he has dominated American life for almost three decades—only Franklin Roosevelt had a similar impact—and the legacies of his presidency will remain influential for years to come. The controversies surrounding his record are unlikely to disappear soon, and the authors do not claim to have produced the final word on the man or his moment. But John Ehrman and Michael Flamm offer a judicious account of a turbulent time when changes at home and abroad generated both opportunities and anxieties. In a balanced appraisal reinforced by historical perspective, they explore the successes and failures of Ronald Reagan, a towering figure whose enduring legacies continue to cast a large shadow over American politics and society in the twenty-first century.

DEBATING THE REAGAN PRESIDENCY: DOMESTIC POLITICS AND ISSUES

John Ehrman

For a generation, Americans have lived in a country shaped by Ronald Reagan. From his inauguration in 1981 until 2008, it was a place where the influence of free-market ideas was central to almost every economic and social policy debate, where rapid technological change became the norm, where prosperity was almost uninterrupted, and where the government hesitated to undertake major new programs. No American born before the early 1960s has any adult experience of a different political, economic, or social environment, and no one born since the early 1970s has any meaningful memory of life and politics before Reagan. Even with the shocks of the economic and financial crises of 2008 creating a demand for larger, activist government, it is not at all clear that Reagan's legacy will be completely undone. Without question, therefore, he has to be ranked with Franklin Roosevelt as a president who reshaped politics, economics, and society, and who still affected national politics long after he had departed from Washington.

This evaluation undoubtedly would surprise many political observers who watched Reagan during the 1980s, however. Until Reagan was elected president in 1980, American politics had been dominated by the moderate liberal coalition that FDR had built. Even after the election, critics continued to dismiss Reagan as a political lightweight, skilled as an actor but lacking the national-level political experience he would need to enact his conservative proposals and govern successfully. His opponents also viewed him as having limited intellectual capacities, citing as evidence what they viewed as his apparently simplistic and rigid beliefs in limited government and the benefits of the free market, as well as his embrace of unproven

1

conservative policy ideas. Reagan defied such views, however, and not only governed successfully for two full terms—becoming the first president to do so since Dwight Eisenhower, almost thirty years before—but also moved American politics clearly to the right. Perhaps the most telling measure of Reagan's success is that for twenty years his successors embraced, or at least did not try to reverse, his policies of keeping taxes low, minimizing federal regulation of the economy, and tolerating unpredictable social changes driven by technological innovation and economic change.

How Reagan was able to do this is a fascinating story. At its highest level, it is a narrative of how ideas guide politics and are put into practice

President Reagan's official portrait, 1981. (Courtesy of the Ronald Reagan Library.)

as policy. It is also an example of how ideas interact with complex social and economic forces to shape events. But it is also a story about people, including the politicians who make decisions and then must cope with the consequences of their actions, and the ordinary people who are affected by events and, in turn, take actions of their own. Moreover, many aspects of this tale remain controversial and provoke arguments not only about the Reagan years, but also about how Americans should face current and future issues. Considered as a whole, his presidency tells us a lot about how American politics operated in the 1980s, and how the events of the Reagan years continue to shape our political and personal lives.

RONALD REAGAN

Ronald Reagan was born on February 6, 1911, in the small town of Tampico, Illinois. His father, Jack, was a shoe salesman who drank too much and moved his family around Illinois to pursue opportunities that never seemed to work out. His mother, Nelle, was a religious woman who introduced Reagan to acting in plays at her church, the Disciples of Christ. The family settled in Dixon, Illinois, in 1920, where Reagan spent the remainder of his youth before going to Eureka College, a school run by the Disciples, where he was graduated in 1932. Reagan in many ways was a gifted young man. He was handsome and athletic—he rescued seventy-seven people during his summers working as a lifeguard—and his intelligence and remarkable memory enabled him to go through school with a minimal amount of effort. Reagan also had an excellent speaking voice and delivery and was determined to break into radio, which was the dominant mass medium of the time. Through a combination of perseverance and luck he landed a job as a sports announcer for a station in Iowa in early 1933 and quickly became a popular baseball broadcaster in the Midwest. Next, he turned his ambitions toward the movies and, while in California to cover spring training in 1937, took a screen test at Warner Brothers. The studio signed Reagan to a $200 per week contract, and he went to work learning the craft of acting. Reagan proved to be a good actor and, propelled by his success in such major films as *Knute Rockne—All American* (1940) and *King's Row* (1942), as well as by his marriage in 1940 to a rising actress, Jane Wyman, seemed about to become a major star.

World War II derailed Reagan's career. He had joined the U.S. Army Reserve while living in Iowa and was called to active duty in April 1942. Reagan spent the war in Hollywood making training films, but the public forgot about him and, after his discharge in July 1945, the studio was un-sure of how to use him. Reagan's postwar films flopped and his marriage to Wyman—whose career took off after the war—fell apart. Although he married another actress, Nancy Davis, in 1952, Reagan seemed to be a washed-up actor with limited prospects. In 1954, however, Reagan's career rebounded. General Electric needed a host for a new weekly television show it was sponsoring, *G.E. Theater.* GE offered the role to Reagan, with a salary of $125,000 per year, and he immediately accepted. His contract also required Reagan to spend sixteen weeks per year touring GE plants, giving motivational speeches to the company's employees. Reagan hosted *G.E. Theater* and toured for the company until 1962. During that period he became a nationally recognized figure and gained invaluable experience in crafting speeches, speaking to crowds, and withstanding the demands of constant travel.

The postwar decade also was a critical time in Reagan's ideological de-velopment. Well before the war, Reagan had been deeply interested in poli-tics and current affairs, and he had been an ardent supporter of Roosevelt and the New Deal. After the war, Reagan still was on the left wing of the Dem-ocratic Party and was politically active in the Screen Actors Guild (SAG). Like many liberals during the 1930s and the war years, Reagan had been tolerant of Communists because they appeared to be allies in the struggles for civil rights and social justices at home and against Fascism abroad. During the late 1940s, however, Communists and Communist sympathizers were working to take control of SAG and other Hollywood unions, and their tactics included violence and intimidation. Appalled by what he saw, and directly involved in the struggles after he became president of SAG in 1947, Reagan became deeply opposed to the Communists and a supporter of President Harry Tru-man's strongly anti-Communist liberalism. That same year, Reagan agreed to serve as an informer for the FBI, reporting on Communist activity in Holly-wood, and in the fall of 1947 he testified to the House Un-American Activ-ities Committee on the Communist threat. Reagan's terms as president of SAG eventually proved to be important beyond making him an anti-Com-munist. The job involved Reagan in brutal factional disputes with other Hol-lywood unions, long talks on complex financial issues, and brought him un-der attack from all sides at various times. Nonetheless, Reagan won favorable deals for the union and gained invaluable experience negotiating in a difficult environment that he later put to use as president. "I got to know a thing or two about negotiating when I represented the Screen Actors Guild in contract talks with the studios," he said in the late 1980s. "After the studios, [Soviet leader Mikhail] Gorbachev was a snap."[1]

His years with GE also made Reagan a committed conservative in domestic affairs. This was a complex transformation, with several influences working on Reagan. One was his personal financial situation, in which his high income made him subject to the top marginal tax rate of more than 90 percent. Another was his prolonged exposure to GE executives and their views of the superiority of free enterprise and opposition to government regulation. This was not a matter of absorbing a simplistic orthodoxy, however. GE's top executives, with whom Reagan spent a great deal of time, were men with well-developed understandings of how American politics worked, which they used to maneuver against the company's opponents in Washington, DC, and the labor movement. His contact with ordinary workers, many of whom were socially conservative, also helped push Reagan to the right. Finally, Reagan had long been a voracious reader and during this time read widely in conservative political philosophy. The result of these influences was that, by 1960, Reagan had completed the transition from liberal to conservative. At the core of his ideology was a sincere belief that God had chosen the United States to show mankind what free people could accomplish, and that lowering taxes and minimizing the role of government in economic and social affairs would liberate the people's creative energies.[2]

Scholars have only recently begun to appreciate the sophistication of Reagan's conservatism. Throughout his career, Reagan's liberal critics derided his views as outmoded and unsophisticated—in a typical comment, historian Robert Dallek claimed in 1984 that Reagan held his views because of emotion, not because he had thought them through carefully. But, as political scientist Hugh Heclo and historian John Patrick Diggins since have shown, Reagan's views had deep roots in American intellectual history and political philosophy. Heclo has pointed out, for example, that Reagan's belief that the United States was God's chosen country originated with the Pilgrims and that, when Reagan quoted John Winthrop to describe America as a "City on a Hill," he was carefully appealing to Americans' traditional views of themselves as a people with a redemptive mission. Similarly, Heclo notes, Reagan always was careful to differentiate between the American nation, which he saw as a virtuous association of free people, and the government, which he believed had to be restrained in size and power lest it escape from its role as servant of the people and become their master. Diggins, for his part, emphasized Reagan's optimistic outlook. For Reagan, according to Diggins, the United States was "always in a state of becoming, as the land of tomorrow." This point of view reinforced Reagan's belief that a large government served only to restrain the energies of the people.[3]

By the early 1960s, Reagan had become a popular figure among conservatives. He campaigned for Republican presidential nominee Richard Nixon in 1960 and continued speaking on the conservative circuit after Nixon's defeat. With his delivery polished during his years with GE, Reagan delivered a consistent message calling for a strong stance against Communism abroad and cutting back the size of government at home. On October 27, 1964, Reagan delivered his standard address—known as The Speech—to a national television audience on behalf of Arizona senator Barry Goldwater, the Republican candidate for president. Reagan's address brought in record levels of campaign donations and, when Goldwater lost badly to President Lyndon Johnson a few days later, Reagan became the new leader of American conservatism.

Following Goldwater's defeat, many politicians and pundits assumed that the conservative movement was finished. During the next two years, however, growing racial and campus unrest, disappointment with the results of Johnson's ambitious social programs, and doubts about the war in Vietnam and liberal foreign policies began to create a backlash against liberalism. In this atmosphere Reagan, propelled at first by conservative businessmen and activists, ran for governor of California against the liberal incumbent, Pat Brown. Reagan based his campaign on the need to restore order in California, especially on university and college campuses, and he proved to be a smart candidate and deft campaigner. Brown and the Democrats, for their part, tried to portray Reagan as a political amateur, rigid ideologue, and intellectual lightweight, but they badly underestimated the strength of voters' disillusionment with liberalism and the impact of Reagan's charm and speaking skills. On November 8, 1966, Reagan defeated Brown by almost a million votes.[4]

After an uncertain start, Reagan proved to be a strong, effective governor. When he took office in January 1967, Reagan inherited an unexpectedly large budget deficit that Brown had hidden with accounting tricks. Reagan first tried to close it simply by ordering all state departments to cut their spending by 10 percent and finding one-time savings in the budget. This approach failed miserably, however, and soon he was forced to support tax increases. Reagan did so reluctantly but skillfully—he ensured passage of the tax increase by appealing to Californians with a series of television advertisements—and used the legislation as an opportunity to start reforming California's regressive tax system, and he worked with the Democratic leaders that controlled the state assembly to make the requisite deals. Reagan also learned from his early mistakes. In the summer of 1967, he fired his finance director and replaced him with Caspar Weinberger, a lawyer and former state legislator, who from then on ran an orderly budget process. Reagan also dismissed his inept chief of staff and replaced him with attorney William Clark. Clark and his successor, Edwin Meese, established a smoothly running system for bringing Reagan the essential information he needed for decisionmaking in short memos. The memos forced the staff to define and discuss issues sharply and then to present Reagan with clearly defined options. Reagan, in turn, made his decisions quickly—"he has turned out to be a man of some strength who likes to make decisions and makes them easily," noted the *New York Times* in December 1967—and then relied on his staff to carry them out. This remained his operating style until he left the White House.[5]

Once the tax crisis was over and the staff system was in place, Reagan went on to additional successes. Faced with continuing campus unrest, he worked hard to keep California's state colleges and universities open and resisted the temptation to seek punitive budget cuts; indeed, Reagan increased spending on higher education and strengthened the system by replacing weak administrators. He also won the support of environmentalists by supporting conservation efforts. Reagan easily won reelection in 1970, and in his second term he focused on welfare reform. Again working with the assembly's Democratic leadership, he obtained a package that tightened eligibility and instituted work requirements, but also raised benefits for the truly needy. California's welfare caseload fell by about 20 percent in the following years. Overall, during his two terms Reagan made progress toward his goals of limiting government and taxes, ensuring that the government ran smoothly, protecting valuable institutions, such as California's state universities, and reforming the state's finances. In August 1974, as his second term was closing, the *Los Angeles Times* reported that Reagan was leaving office with some 70 percent of Californians giving him a positive approval rating. Conservatives, while lamenting that Reagan had not done more to reduce the size of California's government, praised him nonetheless for his dedication to conservative principles and proving that conservatism could work as a governing philosophy.[6]

Part of the reason for Reagan's success was his ability to project an alternative personality. Almost everyone who knew or worked with Reagan commented on how remote and unknowable he was and how few friendships he had. Since his early days in radio, however, he had built a public image as an easygoing, good-humored, likeable man—"he has a remarkable immunity to the slings and arrows that ordinarily afflict people in public office," observed one California Democrat in 1967. In public, he used his warm, affable persona to good effect throughout his career. Amid the conflicts that wracked America in the 1960s, many politicians gave in to the temptation to attack the counterculture in bitter terms. Reagan, in contrast, scored his points while also drawing a laugh, as when he described hippies as people who "act like Tarzan, look like Jane, and smell like Cheetah." Over the years, these and many other similar stories helped soften Reagan's image, made him seem like an accessible, ordinary figure, and did much to make him personally popular, even when he was in serious political trouble.[7]

Reagan's success as governor led to speculation about a possible run for the presidency even before he left office in 1975. Indeed, discussion of a Reagan candidacy had begun during his first year as governor, and he made a half-hearted run at the Republican nomination in 1968. Reagan spent 1975 touring and speaking around the country and, having grown dissatisfied with President Gerald Ford's moderate policies, declared himself a candidate that November. At first, Reagan's campaign was poorly organized, and he lost the early 1976 primaries to Ford. He recovered, however, by attacking what he claimed to be Ford's willingness to return the Panama Canal to Panamanian control and won a series of major primaries during the spring. When the primaries ended, neither Ford nor Reagan had enough delegates to win the nomination, and both campaigns worked feverishly for several weeks to secure a majority. Ford, with the advantage of incumbency, won the battle and Reagan, with an eye toward the future, campaigned hard for Ford in the fall. Ford lost a close election to the Democratic nominee, former Georgia governor Jimmy Carter, but on the Republican side Reagan was the clear winner. Not only was he still the leader of America's conservative movement, but it now was much larger and more energetic than after the Goldwater defeat. Reagan resumed traveling and speaking, wrote a newspaper column, and delivered daily radio addresses, and he was the obvious favorite for the Republican nomination in 1980.[8]

Reagan's pre-1980 career proved to be excellent preparation for the presidency. A naturally optimistic man to start with, he generally had achieved his goals—his only failures were the end of his movie career and the loss to Ford—in the ruthlessly competitive worlds of Hollywood and California politics. As governor of California, he had quickly learned how to lead a large polity (California became the most populous state during his tenure), as well as the art of dealing with legislative opponents and the importance of choosing his staff on the basis of competence rather than just ideological purity. Reagan also possessed considerable intelligence and, though he liked to hide it, a capacity for hard work. Those who worked closely with Reagan or who followed him closely, such as political reporter

Lou Cannon, were impressed by his self-discipline and professionalism. Opponents who knew Reagan only superficially, like Pat Brown, often dismissed him at first, only to learn the hard way that Reagan could quickly outmaneuver them by using the skills he had mastered during forty years of public life.[9]

REAGANISM: IDEAS

As Reagan prepared for the 1980 presidential campaign, it was clear that American liberalism was in serious trouble. The style of liberalism that had emerged from the New Deal and immediate postwar years had emphasized using Keynesian policies to enable the government to guide economic growth by manipulating taxes and budgets, establishing new social welfare programs, expanding the rights of minorities and women, and firmly opposing Soviet expansionism abroad. The Democrats, with a coalition of Southern whites, blacks, northern ethnic and urban voters, and organized labor, had dominated national politics until the late 1960s. Conservatism, in contrast, was a weak and politically marginal movement during this period. Indeed, liberalism's dominance was so great that social scientists often denied that true conservatism existed in the United States and simply dismissed those on the right as people who suffered from psychological problems.[10]

After Johnson's landslide victory in 1964, however, the Democratic majority began to shrink. The Vietnam War split liberals on foreign policy, with some anti-Communist liberals becoming Republicans. Southern whites, upset with the Democrats' support of civil rights, began drifting toward the GOP. In the north, socially conservative and working-class voters disturbed by urban unrest and unhappy with liberal support for affirmative action, abortion rights, and other cultural shifts, began to move away from the Democrats. More troubling for the Democrats, however, was the economy's performance in the late 1970s. American economic problems had been growing since the early part of the decade, and by the Carter years productivity growth was anemic, unemployment hovered between 6 and 7 percent and, worst of all, the inflation rate continued to rise, exceeding 13 percent in 1979. Carter tried several policies to deal with the problems, but only succeeded in looking helpless. The voters, for their part, issued a warning to Carter and the Democrats in the 1978 elections by handing fourteen seats in the House, three in the Senate, and six governorships to the Republicans.[11]

The economy's problems made voters and government officials open to policy experiments that further undermined liberalism's political strength. Since the early twentieth century, and especially since the New Deal era, liberals had supported government regulation of such major industries as telecommunications, finance, railroads, and interstate trucking. Perhaps the best known example of how such regulation worked was in the airline industry, for which the government set fares, allocated routes, forbade the establishment of new carriers, and kept existing firms from going bankrupt. Economists had long understood that these restrictions on competition imposed increased costs and inefficiencies but, because the system seemed to work well enough, there was little support for change. In the troubled economic environment of the late 1970s, however, economists, consumer advocates, and politicians began to push for changes to the status quo; even though major firms in each industry predicted that deregulation would bring disaster, the brokerage industry was deregulated in 1975, the airlines in 1976, and interstate trucking in 1980. In each instance, prices fell dramatically, new companies entered the industries, and firms were forced to make their operations more efficient even as they rushed to offer new products to attract consumers. In the airlines' case, for example, by late 1978 more than half of passengers were flying on discounted tickets, while airlines added new routes and established frequent flier programs to attract and reward customers. For the airlines themselves, the increased traffic led to the establishment of new carriers and much greater profits for the industry. Perhaps even more important than the economic benefits of deregulation were its political results, for these experiments provided concrete evidence that, despite dire predictions to the contrary, reversing or abolishing long-entrenched liberal policies could bring significant benefits to customers and companies alike.[12]

A case similar to economic deregulation took place in the political arena in California in 1978. Inflation had been driving up property values in the Golden State to the point where some homeowners found that their property tax bills had doubled in a few years, even as their incomes grew much more slowly. A conservative activist named Howard Jarvis started a drive to cut property taxes with Proposition 13, a ballot initiative that would roll back assessments, limit property taxes to 1 percent of market value, and limit future increases. In all, Proposition 13 promised a tax cut of about $7 billion. Liberals strenuously opposed Proposition 13, predicting that its passage would force state and local governments to slash budgets for schools, public safety, and a host of other programs, as well as dismiss more than one hundred thousand employees. Despite the warnings, the voters passed Proposition 13 on June 6 by a two-to-one margin, and soon found that its opponents' predictions were wrong. While some services were cut and a relatively small number of public employees lost their jobs, California's economy was prospering and total state tax receipts continued to rise. The state, as a result, was able to help localities make up for lost revenue by redistributing some of its budget surplus and charging fees for services that had been free. For conservatives, Proposition 13 showed the potency of tax cuts as a political issue, and the Republican Party, using a bill introduced in 1977 by Rep. Jack Kemp (R–NY) and Sen. William Roth (R–DE) to cut income taxes by 30 percent, made tax reduction its leading policy proposal. For voters, the Proposition 13 experience further discredited liberal warnings that adopting conservative policies would lead to disaster.[13]

Liberalism's problems stood in stark contrast to the growing success of conservatism in the late 1970s. Until the 1970s, the conservative movement had rested on the two basic principles of anti-Communism and support for free-market economics. Conservatism became more complex during the 1970s, however, as disaffected Democratic voters joined the movement. Many of these voters still supported major government programs established during the New Deal and Great Society eras, but were socially conservative and repelled by the cultural changes of the 1960s and 1970s. Conservatism was helped, in addition, by the growth of the Christian right. Conservative Christians, many of whom had either been Democrats or had not participated in politics, were deeply troubled by such developments as the legalization of abortion, outlawing of prayer in public schools, growth of the gay rights movement, and other evidence of what they viewed as the moral decline of the United States. Led by such figures as the Rev. Jerry Falwell, the Christian right claimed to represent thirty million to sixty million evangelical or fundamentalist Protestants and theologically conservative Americans. Conservative Christians not only had the potential to bring millions of new voters to the Republicans, but also to provide vital organizational support for conservative candidates.[14]

As the conservative movement grew, it needed an idea that could appeal to its increasingly diverse supporters. Supply-side economic theory filled this role. In large part, supply-side economics restated classical economic and libertarian principles that emphasized the roles of producers and consumers, rather than government management, in the economy. A journalist, Jude Wanniski, interpreted the ideas of two professional economists, Arthur Laffer and Robert Mundell, to bring supply-side economics to the attention of politicians and the public. Writing first on the op-ed pages of the *Wall Street Journal* and the conservative policy journal *Public Interest*, and then in his book *The Way the World Works* (1978), Wanniski declared that supply-side policies of tax cuts, expanded deregulation, monetary restraint, and a return to the gold standard, would stimulate economic activity and simultaneously solve the problems of unemployment and inflation. Wanniski and other supply-side advocates claimed, in addition, that deregulation would lead to a new wave of technological innovation while increased economic activity would generate enough additional tax revenues to cover the costs of the tax cuts. Supply-side advocates also sometimes portrayed the theory in religious terms, emphasizing that it offered faith and hope for the future.[15]

Supply side offered something to each segment of conservatism. For free-market conservatives, who had long sought to reduce taxes and regulation, supply-side writings provided updated theoretical ammunition; for newer arrivals in the conservative movement, supply side promised prosperity without the need to cut popular government programs. Supply side gave Christian conservatives a moral justification for tax cuts and deregulation. For conservative politicians looking at the lessons of deregulation and Proposition 13, supply side offered a set of politically popular proposals. Not surprisingly, Republicans rushed to declare their support for supply side. Ronald Reagan, who had supported taxes and deregulation for more than two decades and viewed the government as restraining innovation, told the *Wall Street Journal* in May 1980, "I believe in the supply-side model."[16]

Reactions to the rise of supply-side economics foreshadowed many of the political debates that were to take place during the Reagan presidency. Supply-side advocates had staked a bold claim with their predictions that a self-financing tax cut would bring prosperity and end inflation. Liberal journalists mocked this—writing in the *New Republic*, Michael Kinsley labeled the "notion that cutting taxes for a tiny minority can benefit everybody" as a "malignant growth." Liberal economists were more polite, but just as skeptical. Walter Heller, who had been chairman of the Council of Economic Advisers (CEA) under Presidents Kennedy and Johnson, wrote in 1978 that economic history did not support supply siders' claims and, in fact, he predicted that their proposals would "sweep away all hopes of curbing deficits and containing inflation." Conservative economists supported tax reductions and regulatory reform but believed supply-side proposals and claims were too extravagant. Nixon's CEA chairman, Herbert Stein, wrote in 1979 that "the promises, and the assumptions underlying them, are dangerous," and one neutral researcher dryly noted that supply side used "economic models that are seriously flawed." As the Reagan years unfolded, each of these groups argued their positions consistently: supply siders never yielded in their claims, liberals denigrated Reagan's performance, conservatives supported him cautiously, and academic economists tried to understand what was really going on.[17]

The 1980 election made clear the stakes that were involved in these debates. The Democrats stuck with Keynesian economics and Carter ridiculed supply-side proposals as tax "rebates for the rich, deprivation for the poor and fierce inflation for all of us." Despite Carter's poor economic performance, however, voters were not convinced that supply-side policies would succeed, and the campaign remained close until the last week of October. Then, in a televised debate with Carter, Reagan famously asked the voters, "Are you better off than you were four years ago?" Most concluded they were not and decided to try the supply-side alternative. On November 4, Reagan took 51 percent of the popular vote, and won forty-four states and 489 electoral votes. (Representative John Anderson, a liberal Republican from Illinois, ran as an Independent and won 5.7 million votes but no states.) In Congressional races, the Republicans picked up twelve Senate seats, taking control of the upper chamber, and gained thirty-four seats in the House, although the Democrats still hung on to their majority. The results, however, were not an unqualified endorsement of supply side or conservatism. As decisive as the election had been, Reagan's victory in the South and among some key electoral groups, such as blue-collar workers, had been narrow. Polling results, moreover, made it clear that voters had rejected Carter far more than they had embraced Reagan. Consequently, if he did not deliver on his promise to restore prosperity, or failed to govern effectively, the electorate had shown they would throw Reagan out of office in 1984 as well.[18]

REAGANISM: TAXES AND BUDGETS

Throughout his presidency, Reagan's critics often charged that he achieved his political successes largely by providing myths that people wanted to believe in. Journalist Haynes Johnson, for example, wrote soon after Reagan left office that Americans in the 1980s had been hungry for reassurance and were happy to believe Reagan's tales about the power of old-fashioned capitalism to solve their problems. Historian and social critic Garry Wills provided the most sophisticated version of this critique when he wrote that Reagan succeeded by selling sentimental myths about the American past and the country's goodness, which his policies would bring back. Reagan, Wills wrote in 1987, "combines an infantile repressiveness of story with the utmost sophistication of special effects." The portrait of Reagan as myth maker has endured, but it is an inadequate explanation for his success in implementing his policies. Reagan succeeded not because he fooled anyone but, rather, because he carefully selected his advisers, worked hard, and maneuvered skillfully.[19]

In the transition period between his election and the inauguration on January 20, 1981, Reagan began to apply the lessons of his California experience to his presidency. Indeed, Reagan's stands as the best-executed transition in recent history (and was the model that Barack Obama followed in 2008). In 1967, Reagan had learned the importance of choosing his top staff for their competence rather than ideological purity and now, to the surprise of the large number of observers who had expected Edwin Meese again to become chief of staff, Reagan instead chose James A. Baker III for the top White House position. Baker was a lawyer from Texas who managed Ford's effort to round up delegates after the primaries in 1976 and then ran his friend George H. W. Bush's campaign for the Republican nomination in 1980; when Bush lost to Reagan in the primaries and accepted the vice presidential spot on the ticket, Baker joined the Reagan campaign and proved to be a master strategist. Many of Reagan's longtime staff and associates distrusted Baker because of his service to Ford and ties to Bush—the latter a moderate Republican who, during the primaries, had called the supply side "voodoo economics." Even though Baker was not a supply-side believer, however, he was more conservative than most people realized, and he had little difficulty shifting his loyalty to Reagan. "My leader called me to his service because he wanted to change things . . . and he thought I could help," Baker later wrote.[20]

Joining Baker was a tightly knit group of senior advisors to Reagan with whom, unlike other White House chiefs of staff, Baker initially shared power. Reagan appointed Ed Meese as counselor to the president and placed him in charge of domestic policy. Also in this group was Michael Deaver, a close personal friend of the Reagans, who watched over media events. Meese, however, was famously disorganized and Deaver had little interest in policy, so Baker gradually gathered more power into his own hands. Finally, working closely with Baker was David Stockman, a young congressman from Michigan and a dedicated supply sider who Reagan appointed to be director of the Office of Management and Budget. He had the critical job of culling through the federal budget, looking for programs to be cut.

Baker deserves credit for many of the successes Reagan enjoyed during his first term. Reagan, as in California, generally gave broad instructions and then left to his subordinates the details of turning these into legislation and policy. Baker's job was to oversee this process. The Texan was an extraordinarily skilled administrator who tolerated dissent, kept competing factions working together, and ran one of the most effective White House staffs in modern times. Baker's most important step was to form early in the administration the Legislative Strategy Group (LSG). Chaired by Baker and including Meese, Deaver, and other high-level White House aides, the LSG met almost every day to settle policy questions and develop and implement strategies for moving Reagan's legislation through Congress. To accomplish this, Baker later wrote, meant that the LSG "did the grunt work" of reviewing polling data to determine trends in public opinion, tracking support in Congress and key constituencies, and doing any "necessary cajoling, hand-holding, and trading."[21]

Baker also oversaw the implementation of a new type of presidential media strategy. There was little point in the administration having a message, Baker believed, if it did not make a concerted effort to sell the message to the public. Working with Deaver and Communications Director David Gergen, Baker and the LSG formulated a "line of the day," which was the administration's daily central message. Every morning, the White House passed the line to cabinet departments and agencies, to ensure that the administration spoke with one voice. The White House focused the daily press briefing on the message and did its best to make the message irresistible to television news shows, and thus have the networks spread it to the entire country. "We had to think like a television producer," wrote press spokesman Larry Speakes, and provide a "minute and thirty seconds of pictures to tell the story, and a good solid sound bite." As part of this strategy, Deaver practiced his specialty of placing the president in settings that provided additional images for television to use; Reagan, with his formidable performance skills, almost always shined at such events, which enhanced his ability to communicate directly with the American public. The White House did its best to find other ways to circumvent the filtering of effects of television and radio news shows and speak directly to the public, most notably with the institution of Reagan's Saturday morning radio addresses, which he started broadcasting in the spring of 1982.[22]

Critics complained from early in the Reagan years that the White House was manipulating the media to ensure favorable coverage. Baker's operation was able to "regulate to a remarkable degree the nature of the news," was one typical observation, and journalists saw clearly that the administration's approach enabled it to set the terms of debate in Washington. The criticisms were accurate, but also missed the point. Baker, Deaver, and Gergen were using tools—polls, radio, and television—that had been available to, and exploited by, presidents for decades. Their breakthrough was to use them in a way that was more sophisticated, centralized, and, combined with Reagan's skills, more effective than in any previous administration. There also were limits to what they could do—none of their marketing skills, for example, were able to prevent Reagan's public approval ratings from sliding during the recession of 1981–1982 or the Iran-Contra affair. Ultimately, moreover, the criticisms were empty. Its success made the Reagan media strategy the new standard for presidential political communications. Indeed, every administration since Reagan has done its best to copy his approach, and to this day presidents continue to broadcast radio addresses almost every Saturday morning.[23]

Reagan and Baker moved quickly to put this machinery to work to push through the supply-side program of tax and budget cuts. Unlike when he became governor in 1967, Reagan was prepared to start work immediately after his inauguration. He also understood that success would depend on focusing on this one priority and not wasting his energies on a large number of legislative initiatives, as Jimmy Carter had. Thus, Reagan's effort to enact his program defined his first year in office and was so important that he made a critical decision to put off attempting to enact any of the social changes that conservatives hoped for so as not to distract from his economic program. Stockman and other economic advisers worked furiously, starting in December 1980, to develop the administration's specific budget proposals. Reagan, in turn, opened the campaign in his inaugural address, when he spoke in his customary terms of the need to limit government so that the "creative energy" of the people who "dream great dreams" could be unleashed to restore prosperity. Reagan continued with this theme in an address to Congress on February 18, 1981, when he described the crisis of inflation and unemployment but declared that it "is within our power to change this picture, and we can act with hope." Reagan proposed a 30 percent cut in income taxes in three annual increments of 10 percent, a wide range of tax cuts for business, and $49 billion in social-spending reductions that Stockman had identified. In the only area of the budget slated for a spending increase, Reagan proposed adding about $140 billion in new defense spending through 1986 to fulfill his campaign pledge to restore American military strength. Overall, Reagan promised, his program would not only cut inflation in half but also spur investment, create thirteen million jobs by 1986, raise the growth rate for GNP to 4 to 5 percent per year, and put the federal budget in surplus by 1984.[24]

Behind the scenes, Baker and the LSG worked nonstop to plot strategy, count votes, and make the deals that would turn Reagan's proposals into law. The LSG also worked closely with Reagan, providing him with memos that named members of Congress he needed to call to gain their support and their main concerns; Reagan, White House records show, made the calls and then returned the memos to the LSG with handwritten notes on the results of the conversations. Simultaneously, Deaver and Gergen orchestrated the media effort. "Almost no news item, no speech, no trip, no photo-op whatsoever was put on the President's schedule during 1981 unless it contributed to the President's economic program," Speakes later wrote.[25]

In the midst of this, on March 30, 1981, a disturbed young man named John Hinckley tried to assassinate Reagan as he left a speaking engagement in downtown Washington. Reagan was seriously wounded but, in large part because he was in excellent physical condition, recovered quickly. Popular relief that the president had survived—it was the first time that a president had survived wounding by an assassin—as well as admiration of his bravery as he bantered with the doctors in the emergency room, increased Reagan's popularity ratings. The White House made good use of the bounce. Reagan was at his rhetorical best when he spoke to Congress on April 28, the eve of an important vote. "We have much greatness before us," he said, as senators and representatives cheered his recovery. "All we need to do is act, and the time for action is now." Even as the increase in popularity dissipated during the summer, Reagan still was able to take advantage of the goodwill from the spring. Most important, on the evening of July 27, he spoke from the White House to ask voters to tell their senators and representatives to vote for "hope and opportunity." The next day, the Capitol was flooded with phone calls and mail supporting Reagan.[26]

In contrast, Democrats were confused and divided. With the loss of the Senate and presidency, Speaker of the House Thomas "Tip" O'Neill (D-MA), became the Democratic leader in Washington. O'Neill remained faithful to the ideals of the New Deal and Great Society, but he failed to develop a strategy to oppose Reagan. Instead, O'Neill believed that he only had to wait for Reagan's policies to fail and the voters to come back to the Democrats. At the tactical level, O'Neill badly underestimated the strength of the White House effort as well as Reagan's personal political skill. It also did not help Democrats that O'Neill, who was overweight, dressed badly, and came across on television as a caricature of liberalism, was badly outclassed by the White House media operation. Thus, in April 1981, while the LSG and Reagan were working to defeat Democratic counterproposals,

O'Neill went to Australia and New Zealand on a two-week junket. "We had momentum," one Democrat complained bitterly. "Then Tip goes off on a junket for two weeks. Meanwhile, the White House is at work, they put on a real campaign, and we had only a half-baked effort." To add to the Democrats' problems, about forty Southern Democratic congressmen—so-called "Boll Weevil" Democrats—understood the implications of Reagan's popularity and the growing strength of the Republicans in their districts, and therefore often sided with the president instead of their own leadership. "What's happening to me in Washington?" O'Neill asked plaintively in May, as Reagan's proposals moved through Congress. "I'm getting the shit whaled out of me."[27]

Reagan got almost all of what he had asked for. In August 1981, with the Boll Weevils providing crucial votes in the House, Congress passed the Economic Recovery Tax Act (ERTA), which cut income taxes by 5 percent starting in October, and an additional 10 percent in each of the following two years. The top income tax rate fell from 70 percent to 50 percent and, when the start of automatic adjustments of income tax rates for inflation (known as indexing) and business tax cuts were added in, the bill was expected to reduce taxes by some $750 billion during the following five years. On the spending side, the accompanying budget bill sliced about $130 billion from federal spending over three years. The significance of Reagan's victory was clear. The tax cut was the largest in American history. The press proclaimed a "Reagan revolution," and declared that he had achieved mastery over Congress and Washington politics. Conservatives were elated. "Fundamental change is possible," proclaimed *National Review*, as it celebrated the reversal of the hitherto "leftward course of economic policy in the United States." In just six months, noted the *New York Times* rather more glumly, Reagan had reversed fifty years of politics and policy by "cutting back sharply on the growth of social programs." Political journalist E. J. Dionne saw more of the same in the future, predicting that the tax cuts would "eventually force a deficit-minded Congress to make even more spending cuts."[28]

Reagan's triumph was short lived, however, and the twelve months that followed the passage of ERTA did as much as the tax and budget cuts to define Reagan's conservatism. Starting on Election Day 1980, Federal Reserve Chairman Paul Volcker had begun tightening interest rates to combat inflation; unlike in previous failed efforts during the Carter years, Volcker did not back off as rates increased to painful levels. In July 1981, just as ERTA was about to be passed, the economy slipped into recession. Stockman's projections for a budget surplus had assumed a healthy economy and additional spending cuts in the coming years. In the weeks after ERTA became law, however, it became clear not only that a recession had hit—which would further reduce tax revenues—but also that cabinet secretaries and Congress were fighting hard against more cuts to favored programs. Reagan and Secretary of Defense Caspar Weinberger, moreover, were determined that the defense budget would not be cut. (In fact, defense spending rose from $155 billion in 1980 to $279 billion in 1985.) Rather than surpluses, Stockman's projections now showed deficits of more than $100 billion per year, and stock and bond prices plunged. August, noted the *Wall Street Journal*, had begun with "White House elation over the president's tax-cut victory, but [was] ending with a sense of despair."[29]

Through the fall, pressure built on Reagan to stop the growth of the deficit by canceling some of the tax cuts. Not only did Democrats call for reversing Reagan's policies, but some twenty-five northeastern and Midwestern Republican congressmen, calling themselves "Gypsy Moths" and fearing defeat in the 1982 elections, pressed for cuts in defense spending and a moderation of the tax reductions, as did Senate Majority Leader Howard Baker (R-TN). As the recession deepened (unemployment peaked at almost 10.8 percent in December 1982, making the slump the worst since the Depression) and estimates for the deficit continued to increase, the credibility of supply-side claims lay in ruins. Even Stockman, who had been a passionate believer in supply-side theory, admitted that many of his

Press conference, July 28, 1982. (Courtesy of the Ronald Reagan Library.)

assumptions about taxes and the budget had been wrong. "There was a certain dimension of our theory that was unrealistic," he admitted to journalist William Greider, and no one in the administration "really understands what's going on with all these numbers." Democrats immediately seized upon Stockman's confession. Stockman was acknowledging "what I and other critics have been saying for six months," crowed Tip O'Neill. But Reagan insisted that he would not agree to any type of tax increase. "We stick with our tax program; we go forward with the reduction in tax rates . . . I have no plans for increasing taxes in any way," he said at a press conference in mid-December."[30]

The question of what to do about the deficit set off a vicious fight inside the administration. Stockman, realizing that additional spending cuts, even if Congress agreed to them, would be too small to have much effect on the deficit, began to press Reagan to increase taxes. James Baker agreed, and the two joined forces. Secretary of the Treasury Donald Regan, backed by supply-side believers who served under him in high Treasury Department positions, tried to convince the president to stand firm. Outside the administration, supply siders, led by Jack Kemp and the editorial page of the *Wall Street Journal*, also urged Reagan not to panic but, rather, to hold the line and wait for the tax cuts to bring prosperity. In the spring of 1982, however, with the recession getting worse and deficit projections still growing, Reagan gave in. In March, he authorized Baker to start negotiating a modification to ERTA with congressional leadership.[31]

The next several months almost repeated the experience of 1981. Baker and the LSG managed the administration's efforts, with Reagan again lobbying members of Congress. The Democrats were led by O'Neill—performing much more effectively as he worked from a position of strength and began to master the types of media maneuvers that Deaver used—and drove a hard bargain. Eventually, the White House and Democrats hammered out a package that combined a $98-billion tax increase with spending cuts of $17 billion. At the crucial moment, on August 16, Reagan again spoke to the nation to build support for the legislation, although this time he had to shore up support among Republicans rather than overcome Democratic opposition. Again, too, Reagan won the final vote as Congress passed the Tax Equity and Fiscal Responsibility Act of 1982 (TEFRA) on August 20. Just as the 1981 tax cut had been the largest ever, TEFRA was the largest tax increase in American history.

Supply siders viewed TEFRA as disaster for the Reagan revolution and their hopes for achieving conservative goals. Even before the negotiations began in March, the most committed of the supply siders began to resign from the administration, bitterly accusing the moderate Baker and turncoat Stockman of leading Reagan away from the true faith. Reagan, editorialized the *Wall Street Journal*, needed "committed advocates backing him in his crucial struggles," not his own staff working against him. Supply siders also forecast disaster if Reagan gave in to Stockman and Baker. The struggle, declared Jack Kemp in June 1982, was not just about taxes but also about the "future of democratic capitalism" and Western civilization. But in their fury and rejection of compromise, supply siders missed an important point: the core of the 1981 tax cuts remained intact. TEFRA did not raise individual income tax rates or repeal indexing; instead, most of the revenue increases came from higher excise taxes, changes in depreciation rules, and other adjustments that fell on business but that most individual taxpayers (and voters) did not notice. This would be the case, too, when later Reagan tax increases, in 1984 and 1986, spared individuals but pried revenues from the dark corners of the tax code.[32]

Another point the supply siders did not understand was that Reagan, far from betraying conservatism or being manipulated by Baker and Stockman, had shown how conservatism could succeed in national politics. Reagan took the long view of politics, never viewing it as an all-or-nothing contest, and understanding that the American political system rewarded negotiation and compromise. As in California, he maintained his goal of limiting government, but he seldom went beyond the limits of popular support. Indeed, the former union negotiator read the polls carefully and made all-or-nothing stands only when he was sure he would win, and generally was willing to shift tactics and accept partial victories—or retreats—if circumstances demanded. "Die-hard conservatives thought that if I couldn't get everything I asked for, I should jump off the cliff with the flag flying—go down in flames," Reagan said in 1985. "No, if I can get 70 or 80 percent of what it is I'm trying to get, yes I'll take that and then continue to try to get the rest in the future."[33]

Two additional cases from Reagan's first year in office show how he chose his battles carefully. The first, and most famous, was his decision to face down the air traffic controllers when they went on strike in August 1981. The controllers' union, the Professional Air Traffic Controllers Organization (PATCO), had been pressing for several years for substantial pay and benefit increases, even though its members were better paid than most government workers; by the summer of 1981, PATCO's leaders were threatening a strike, even though it was forbidden by federal law. When the controllers walked out on August 3, Reagan denounced the strike as illegal as well as an assault on public safety. He also declared that any controller who was not back on the job in forty-eight hours would be fired and never rehired by the federal government. PATCO stood firm, but Reagan was as good as his word and fired 11,300 of the 17,000 controllers. The Federal Aviation Authority, which had made detailed contingency plans to continue traffic control operations and thereby keep the nation's airlines flying, used the remaining controllers, supervisors, retirees, and military controllers to operate the air traffic control system for the two years it took to train a new cadre of controllers. Polls showed that the public agreed with Reagan on the safety issue and overwhelmingly supported his handling of the strike (there was also little sympathy for PATCO's well-paid, white-collar membership). PATCO, for its part, was bankrupted by fines, decertified as the controllers' union, and disappeared in 1982. The strike was a singularly important moment in Reagan's presidency, for he had shown that when he felt an important principle was at stake and the public would back him, he would take a maximalist position and act decisively.[34]

More typical of Reagan's tactics, however, were cases such as the Social Security uproar in the spring of 1981, when he backed down rather than fight over an issue he did not view as critical or where a defeat would place other priorities at risk. That spring, as Stockman sought additional budget savings, he convinced Reagan to agree to a package of cuts in Social Security that would save some $24 billion per year. The cuts also would prevent a looming financial crisis for the system, which was running out of money because benefits, indexed to inflation in the early 1970s, had risen beyond the system's ability to pay. Democrats, looking for a way to fight back against Reagan, quickly denounced the plan as an assault on the government's most sacred social program—O'Neill called the proposal "despicable"—and Congressional Republicans wanted no part of it. Reagan, seeing a distraction from the main tax and budget battle and sensing that a political disaster loomed, backed down. That fall, he appointed a bipartisan commission headed by Alan Greenspan to find a way to keep Social Security from going broke. Greenspan's commission engineered a compromise plan that increased Social Security taxes, raised retirement ages, taxed some recipients, and thereby pushed the system's fiscal problems into the next century.[35]

This became a pattern for the remainder of Reagan's presidency. Even as Reagan spoke out against many liberal institutions and programs, he never again risked his popularity by attacking the great middle-class entitlement programs of the New Deal and Great Society. Similarly, he never ventured beyond his anti-abortion rhetoric to work actively for the overturning of *Roe v. Wade*, or seriously tried to end affirmative action. Although conservatives were often disappointed by his aversion to bold moves, Reagan avoided becoming bogged down in fights that he could not win or where victory would come at a disastrous cost. As a result, he was able to maintain a commanding position in Washington, and his major victories were overwhelming and proved enduring. Succeeding administrations, for example, have moved income tax rates up and down, but only within a narrow range and there has been no serious effort to restore taxes to their pre-ERTA levels. Indeed, from the time Reagan took office until the passage of Medicare reform in 2003, the federal government did not institute any new major social programs.

The tax and budget struggles of 1981 and 1982 foreshadowed yet another important aspect of Reagan's presidency. From the fall of 1981 until he left office, the deficit was the dominant issue in domestic politics. In 1980, the deficit had been $74 billion, then an astonishing figure, and a major issue in the campaign. Under Reagan, however, the deficit reached a peak of $221 billion in 1986 (see table 1 on p. 64). The deficits brought a rapid growth in total federal debt, from $995 billion in 1981 to $2.8 trillion in 1989, and annual interest payments more than tripled. Each year, Reagan and Congress argued over the budget, with neither side willing to accept more than marginal changes in spending and taxes, and each blaming the other for the lack of progress and continuing deficits. The stalemate persisted, moreover, despite popular disapproval of the deficits and well-publicized worries by professional economists and lay commentators about their long-term effects on the economy.

The inability of Congress and the Reagan administration to reduce the deficit should not be surprising, however. The deficit was, for most voters and politicians, an abstract concept and number. The complexities of federal tax and budget procedures made answering even the most basic question about the deficit—how big was it?—into an enormous undertaking, both in theory and in terms of practical measurement. In addition, despite the fears that it was hurting the economy, no one could say for certain how much it affected overall economic performance while, year after year, predictions that huge deficits would cause an economic catastrophe failed to come true. In contrast, any serious effort to reduce or eliminate the deficit through tax increases and budget cuts would not be an abstraction but, rather, a painful reality for taxpayers, beneficiaries of government programs, and members of Congress. Thus, in the absence of a disaster, inaction became the preferred alternative for policymakers and the public. Taxes remained low, spending went on, and the deficits remained high.[36]

REAGANISM: DEREGULATION

The Reagan administration's political approach to implementing the second ideological pillar of the supply side, deregulation, was the same as with taxes and budgets. Since his conversion to conservatism, Reagan had been deeply committed to reducing the government's role in regulating business and economic outcomes, and he made this an important goal for his presidency. "Adding to our troubles is a mass of regulations imposed on the shopkeeper, the farmer, the craftsman, professionals, and major industry," he told Congress when he introduced his economic package in February 1981. This view, and the additional point made by economists in the administration that much of the government's regulatory structure was outdated and "no longer serves the interests of the contemporary economy," shaped regulatory policy for the remainder of the 1980s.[37]

As serious as he was about deregulation, Reagan was careful not to take large political risks on the issue. The administration consistently backed away from efforts to dismantle popular regulations or those that had been accepted by corporate America. Thus, for example, the administration initially cut the budget for the Environmental Protection Agency (EPA), appointed poorly qualified managers to its top positions, and let its staff shrink. After scandals revealed that many of the agency's most important programs had been crippled, however, the administration restored the EPA's funding and appointed William Ruckelshaus, the agency's original head in the early 1970s, to be its chief and rebuild its programs with a restored budget.[38]

The administration also allowed political expediency to trump its commitment to free trade. In May 1981, rather than take on additional battles while it was working to pass tax and budget cuts, the administration gave in to demands from the auto industry and its congressional supporters for protection against Japanese imports. The United States forced Tokyo to agree to "voluntary export restraints" that limited the number of cars Japan would ship to America. The result was to create an artificial shortage of Japanese cars, which economists estimated raised their prices up to $2,500 per vehicle, and also enabled U.S. automakers to increase their prices; in all, the quotas may have transferred as much as $10 billion from consumers to the Japanese auto manufacturers, and billions more to Detroit. The administration acted in the same way in September 1984 when, two months before the presidential election, it placed import quotas on steel to protect U.S. manufacturers who had been losing billions of dollars and dismissing tens of thousands of workers. Here, too, later studies found that the main effect of the quotas was to raise the price of steel and retard badly needed innovation in the industry.[39]

Deregulation fared better, however, when the administration could build on preexisting policies or the actions of others. In areas that had been deregulated during the 1970s, the administration followed a hands-off approach and let events take their course. In the financial industry, for example, expanded competition for customers and their money led brokerage firms to start offering services, such as checking, that previously had been provided only by banks. The banks responded by offering brokerage services, and both groups worked to develop additional financial management services. Airline deregulation continued as well. Amidst fierce competition, new airlines appeared and went broke frequently, all airlines scrambled to offer new routes and services, and fares continued to drop. With more people able to afford to fly, passenger traffic rose steadily—it increased by more than 50 percent from 1980 to 1988—albeit with the drawback that airplanes and airports became more crowded and uncomfortable.[40]

Deregulation of the nation's telephone system was another success, and also one that resulted largely from decisions made outside the Reagan administration. Since the 1920s, AT&T held a monopoly on national long-distance and local telephone service. Under legal pressure, the monopoly began to crumble in the late 1960s and 1970s, and in 1981 AT&T agreed with the government to be broken up. Starting on January 1, 1984, the company was split into seven regional firms, all of which had to allow any long-distance carrier to connect to their networks. The federal government encouraged new companies to enter the telephone business, and hundreds of new long-distance telephone companies soon appeared. As a result, long-distance capacity tripled, the price of a call fell by 50 percent, and telecommunications companies rushed to develop new products and services.[41]

The major area in regulatory policy where the Reagan administration broke ground of its own was in the loosening of antitrust rules and the deregulation of corporate mergers. Since the early 1950s, federal law and regulatory policy had been to limit strictly vertical and horizontal mergers—that is, to prevent one company from buying another in its own industry. As a result, during the 1960s and 1970s, many corporations grew by purchasing companies in other industries, becoming conglomerates consisting of many unrelated businesses. By the early 1980s, however, many conglomerates and other large corporations were in trouble. Conglomerates often were poorly run, as managers at the center had little knowledge of, or interest in, far away units. In many corporations, staffing had become bloated, and complacent managers were slow to adopt new technologies or respond to increasing foreign competition, while inflation allowed them to pass rising costs on to customers without addressing fundamental problems. Small wonder, noted *Business Week* in 1985, that since the mid-1970s, the average company's stock price was only two-thirds to three-quarters of the value of the underlying assets.[42]

Economists had long understood the opportunity that such a situation could present. The ownership of a corporation was like any other good and could be bought and sold in a marketplace—what economists called the market for corporate control. "The lower the stock price, relative to what it could be with more efficient management, the more attractive the takeover becomes to those who believe that they can manage the company more efficiently," wrote one scholar in 1965. "The potential return from the successful takeover and revitalization of a poorly run company can be enormous."[43]

The opportunity arrived in June 1982. That month, the Justice Department and Federal Trade Commission announced that they would take a more lenient view of mergers and allow greater concentration within markets. The previous year, moreover, a little-known investment banking firm called Drexel Burnham Lambert, led by a bond salesman named Michael Milken, began to make available large quantities of high-yield securities called junk bonds to finance corporate mergers and acquisitions. With the government staying out of the way, and Milken's bonds providing the financing, merger and acquisition activity exploded from about 1,500 deals worth $33 billion in 1980, to 3,500 deals worth $227 billion in 1988. A survey by the *Wall Street Journal* in mid-1985 of the eight hundred largest companies in the United States found that almost half had been involved in some kind of restructuring since January 1984, and by 1989 more than one hundred of the companies on the 1983 Fortune 500 list had been acquired, merged, or taken private.[44]

Takeover and merger activities fell into patterns. In a typical case, a corporation or investor would spot a company whose depressed stock price made its assets undervalued and, in a leveraged buyout financed by junk bonds, make a bid for the company at a price between its current market value and its estimated true value. In other cases, companies sold off divisions that were performing badly or were unrelated to the parent firm's main activity; the buyers often were investors or managers using debt to finance the deal. Most sales were completed quickly, although some turned into dramatic battles, covered on the front pages and evening news, as rival investors bid for a company or the firm tried to fend off buyers and remain independent. Once a deal was finished, the new owners often sold off parts of the company at prices closer to their true values and revamped the remaining operations. The latter usually included taking steps to cut costs and introduce new technologies and processes, as well as dismissing excess employees and managers. Success meant large profits for the investors—after Beatrice Foods was taken over in 1986, its divisions were sold off at a total profit of $1.8 billion—and tens of millions of dollars in fees for the lawyers and investment bankers who arranged the deals.[45]

The wave of buyouts and mergers created a controversy that raged throughout the Reagan years. Defenders of leveraged buyouts argued that the practice focused on identifying "poorly managed companies that have failed to adjust" to increasing competition, enabled stockholders to realize the true value of their assets, and pointed out that well-managed companies with strong stock prices had nothing to fear. Critics, such as the prominent financier Felix Rohatyn, charged that the buyouts benefited lawyers and bankers, but "often result in weaker companies" saddled with debt. Others, like Harvard government professor (and, later, Bill Clinton's secretary of labor) Robert Reich, likened the buyouts and related transactions, such as stock buybacks, to a con game and warned that instead of generating wealth, corporations were playing a "giant game of asset rearrangement that is largely unproductive."The critics also warned that, because the whole process was driven by the insatiable greed of Wall Street operators, a speculative bubble was bound to develop, followed by a market collapse.[46]

The critics turned out to be almost entirely wrong. Eventually, they could claim vindication on their prediction of a bubble—at the end of the decade, the buyout and junk bond markets overheated and crashed, Milken went to jail as part of a massive insider trading scandal, and Drexel went bankrupt. Merger activity then slumped until the mid-1990s. This, however, was of little consequence when compared to the benefits brought about by the mergers and buyouts. Takeovers and buyouts were a "powerful force for economic improvement," despite the pain of restructurings and firings, noted *Fortune* in 1987. Conglomerates shed many of their units and returned to their specialty areas, and *Business Week* pointed out that throughout the economy, takeovers or threats of takeovers forced companies to "become innovators in product development, marketing, and distribution—constantly discovering ways to do the job better and cheaper." Economists who have studied the buyouts of the Reagan era generally agree, as one put it, that "when the internal processes for change in large corporations [were] too slow, costly, and clumsy to bring about the required restructuring or change in managers efficiently," takeover markets quickly "forced managers to respond to new market conditions" and make their firms more efficient.[47]

There were many examples in the Reagan years of successful turn-arounds of large and small companies after a takeover or spinoff. In 1984, for example, Chevron took over chronically troubled Gulf Oil for $13.3 billion, the largest deal up to that time. Chevron moved quickly to cut some ten thousand jobs and sell Gulf assets, and by the summer of 1985 Gulf was making an increasing contribution to Chevron's overall earnings. Another case was that of Scott, a fertilizer and seed company sold in 1986 by its conglomerate owner, ITT, to a group of investors in a debt-financed buyout. Under ITT, Scott had been slow to pursue new customers, even as its inventories rose and overhead costs climbed, and its managers had few incentives to improve operations. The new owners moved quickly to slash inventories, renegotiate terms with Scott's suppliers, and use workers more flexibly; Scotts's managers were able to buy stock at a deep discount, which gave them a stake in the company they previously lacked, and motivated them to work more aggressively to increase sales and to improve production efficiencies. Within two years, Scott had paid off much of its takeover-related debt and was solidly profitable. A brief perusal of the business press of the 1980s will find many more such cases.[48]

Despite these successes, however, there was one deregulatory catastrophe during the Reagan years—the collapse of the savings and loan (S&L) industry. S&Ls, or thrifts, had long been a simple, dull business—under close regulatory supervision, they paid modest interest on deposits and loaned money for mortgages, also at modest rates. Starting in the late 1970s, however, inflation led customers to move their money out of S&Ls and into money market funds offered by deregulated brokerages. Congress partially deregulated S&Ls in 1980, allowing them to pay more interest, but their incomes still depended on the interest from old, long-term, low-interest mortgages, and Congress eased regulation again in 1982, allowing S&Ls to make loans for a wider range of properties and lowering the thrifts' capital requirements. S&Ls began lending money to much more speculative projects than before and, critically, the states and federal government at the same time scaled back their supervision and auditing of the thrifts. Following the passage of tax reform in 1986, which changed the rules for real estate depreciation, many of the loans went bad. Hundreds of S&Ls became insolvent, leaving taxpayers to pay hundreds of billions of dollars to clean up the mess.[49]

The S&L disaster notwithstanding, the long-term effects and benefits of Reagan's deregulation policies are difficult to overstate. Reagan made progress toward his strategic goal of rolling back the government's economic role by using the same tactics as he had with taxes and budgets—always focusing on long-range goals, retreating when necessary, and seizing opportunities as they arose. In this context, it is noteworthy that his greatest impact, freeing the market for corporate control, came in an obscure area where the administration was able to act without going through Congress. It is also noteworthy that, in this and other aspects of deregulation, the administration let events take their course rather than attempt to shape results. Because of this, companies either had to adapt to new circumstances or die. As messy and painful as the process could be, the results had great benefits for the American economy. Consequently, no administration since Reagan's has made an effort to reverse these policies, and takeovers and mergers have remained an accepted part of American economic life.

REAGANISM: FLOOD TIDE

Reagan's political fortunes hit bottom in the late summer and fall of 1982, but then began a remarkable recovery. The recession had been deep and seemed endless, and at the end of the summer Reagan's approval rating was about 48 percent. A majority of Americans believed he should not seek a second term, and in November the Democrats gained twenty-six seats in the House. By then, however, the first glimmers of recovery were becoming visible. In July, the Fed had begun to cut interest rates, and in mid-August the stock market—expecting more rate cuts—began to rise. Although it was not clear until later, the recession ended in November and the economy began an expansion that would last until July 1990. The raw statistics of the recovery remain impressive, as Reagan's supporters have always been quick to point out (see table 2 on p. 65). From the low point in 1982 through 1989, the GNP expanded by 30 percent. Inflation, meanwhile, fell from 10.3 percent in 1981 to 4.8 percent in 1989 (the fall was helped in no small part by a sharp decline in oil prices in 1985 and 1986), unemployment began declining in 1983, and the number of people employed rose from 100.4 million in 1981 to 117.3 million in 1989. Personal income, measured in constant dollars, rose from $2.6 trillion in 1980 to $3.4 trillion in 1989, an average annual increase of 2.9 percent during the period.[50]

The recovery brought controversies of its own, beginning with the question of who could take credit for the return of prosperity. Reagan, like any politician, was quick to stake his claim. Speaking on the radio in January 1984, he recited his critics' predictions of economic collapse, and then he noted that the recovery "has been one of the strongest since the 1960s," and that "America is moving forward, getting stronger, and confounding everyone who said it can't be done." Supply siders also claimed credit, viewing the recovery as vindication of their theories. Paul Craig Roberts, one of those who had denounced the betrayal of the supply side in 1982, wrote six years later, with no apparent sense of irony, that because of its supply-side foundations, the "Reagan economy was more successful than anyone thought possible." Independent and academic economists have found little evidence to support this claim, however, and have pointed out other explanations for the recovery. They have noted, for example, that Reagan's economic policies had many Keynesian parts, including tax cuts, deficit spending, and declining interest rates, and that part of the recovery's strength came from putting underutilized resources back to work. Critics also pointed out that the recovery was not as strong as the supply siders and Reagan himself had promised and that dangers lurked ahead. They noted that the average annual growth rate for GNP from 1980 to 1989, 2.9 percent, was only a hair above the rate of 2.8 percent for the period 1970 to 1979, personal income growth was slow, productivity growth and investment were weak, and many of the newly created jobs did not pay well. Furthermore, the United States ran huge trade deficits throughout the Reagan years, as the value of imports exceeded exports by hundreds of billions of dollars, and the country was transformed from being a net creditor to a debtor state. Some economists warned that these problems meant that the ultimate result of Reagan's policies would not be continued strength but, eventually, a severe economic crisis.[51]

The criticisms of Reagan's economic policies, like the closely related debates about budget deficits, had little real political impact. Even if growth rates were unexceptional, the inflation of the 1970s was gone. Unemployment remained high by historical standards but consistently moved downward after 1982. For most voters, these concrete realities were what mattered most, and discussions of inadequate investment or productivity increases were dull abstractions. The warnings of a future crisis, moreover, gradually lost credibility as the months and years went by and the collapse failed to materialize.

For Reagan himself, economic recovery brought clear political benefits. Most directly, as he started his reelection campaign in February 1984, Reagan's job approval rating reached 59 percent. The national mood, too, improved as the country started to put hard times behind it and Reagan's personal optimism, which may have seemed out of touch with reality in 1981 and 1982, now seemed vindicated. Academic researchers and journalists, for example, often credited his personal appeal as one of the reasons for the resurgence in popular confidence in government. Although confidence in government did not return to its pre-Vietnam, pre-Watergate levels, what some had called the "crisis of legitimacy" in the 1970s—the feeling that American constitutional and public institutions were no longer adequate for running a modern country—had clearly disappeared by mid-decade.[52]

Reagan also benefited from a patriotic revival that swept the country in the summer of 1984. It first became apparent on June 6, when Reagan stood above the beaches of Normandy and spoke to the veterans of the D-Day invasion. Deaver had carefully crafted the setting and timed the speech so that viewers of the morning television news shows in the United States would see Reagan addressing the aging veterans and thanking them for their bravery and sacrifices. Simultaneously, in preparation for the summer Olympics in Los Angeles, runners were relaying the Olympic torch across the United States. To the surprise of just about everyone, the relay became a patriotic rallying point as people turned out in even the most desolate areas and wee hours to see the torch and cheer for their country. The flame "bound together Americans in one exultant patriotic hurrah," reported the *Los Angeles Times* in early July, and a woman in Ohio told the *New York Times* that "when people see that torch, they relate it to patriotism. There's a hunger for that in the land." On July 28, Reagan opened the games, which

Campaigning in 1984. (Courtesy of the Ronald Reagan Library.)

then became a two-week patriotic festival as cheering crowds watched U.S. teams—with the Soviet bloc conveniently boycotting the games in retaliation for the U.S.-led boycott of the 1980 Moscow games—take three times as many medals as their closest competitor, West Germany.[53]

Not surprisingly, with this wind at his back Reagan cruised to an easy reelection. On November 6, he crushed his Democratic opponent, former Minnesota senator and vice president under Jimmy Carter, Walter Mondale, by taking forty-nine states and 525 electoral votes. In the popular vote, Reagan won with a record fifty-four million votes (a record total that stood until 2004) to Mondale's thirty-seven million, and the Republicans recovered sixteen seats in the House while holding the Senate.

Shortly after the election, Reagan made what proved to be a critical mistake. Reagan, as his critics never tired of pointing out, was an indifferent manager who often failed to pay adequate attention to high-level personnel matters. This weakness mattered little when he had strong, capable chiefs of staff, as Clark and Meese had been in California and Baker in Washington. Now, Baker, exhausted after four years as chief of staff, and Donald Regan, seeking a change after serving as secretary of the treasury for four years, decided to swap jobs. Reagan gave the matter little thought and agreed.

Regan was no Baker, however. The Texan came from a wealthy and prominent family, had been an experienced politician before signing on with Reagan, and—as in 1982—was unafraid to tell his boss when he was wrong and needed to change course. Regan, in contrast, came from a working-class background and had climbed the corporate ladder, working his way up from trainee to chairman of Merrill Lynch, and lacked Baker's polish. "He ruled Merrill Lynch with an iron hand and has a reputation for tyrannically chewing out subordinates," noted the *Washington Post* in February 1985. As chief of staff, Regan believed it was his job to execute his boss's orders without question and expected his subordinates to do the same. Regan also presented Reagan with fewer policy options, tailoring his choices to what he believed the president wanted to see. Baker, moreover, had been willing to share power with Meese and Deaver, but Meese now was leaving to become attorney general and Deaver was departing to become a lobbyist. As a result, Regan gathered into his hands much more power than Baker ever had, but without Baker's political sophistication. Others criticized him as a poor administrator, and a petty and vindictive man, and he eventually alienated much of official Washington. "Regan's relative inexperience and his brusque, commanding style have irritated key legislators, and have damaged White House relations with Congress," wrote journalist Bernard Weinraub in January 1986.[54]

In January 1985, however, Regan's problems lay in the future and the administration, prepared to concentrate on Ronald Reagan's priority for this second term, income tax reform. Income tax had become a national disgrace by the mid-1980s. Tax laws and regulations had been written haphazardly during the preceding decades, as groups and individuals had won tax breaks for themselves and successive administrations created tax incentives to support various social policies. Because of this, the tax base was narrowing as more people and corporations escaped paying income tax, the government was losing billions of dollars in revenues, taxes had become hideously complex, business decisionmaking often was governed by tax considerations rather than by what made economic sense, and popular anger was rising as more and more Americans concluded that the system was unfair. Reform seemed almost impossible, however, as efforts in the 1960s and 1970s all had been crushed by lobbyists and friendly members of Congress. Sen. Russell Long (D-LA), one of the major opponents of reform, had described the matter succinctly, if cynically: "Tax reform is a change in the tax law that I favor, or if it is the other man defining tax reform, it is a change in the tax law that he favors."[55]

Donald Regan deserves much of the credit for getting tax reform off the ground. Reform proposals during the 1980s, most notably a bill introduced in 1982 by Sen. Bill Bradley (D-NJ) and Rep. Richard Gephardt (D-MO) that would have radically overhauled the income tax and cut rates, had been going nowhere. Regan, however, had come to see the tax system as a "burden on the economy and an affront to economic and social justice," and began to push the issue with Reagan. The issue gradually began to attract an unlikely coalition of supporters. In Washington, liberals wanted to restore fairness and widen the tax base, while economists at the Treasury Department sought to reduce economic distortions. Outside Washington, corporate leaders were intrigued by the idea of eliminating preferences that helped one industry at the expense of another. Supply siders also adopted reform as part of their program. "If we are bold enough to press forward and achieve meaningful tax reform—reform that lowers rates and broadens the tax base—the economic benefits could be enormous," wrote one in *National Review*. Reagan, for his part, warmed to reform because it offered a chance to cut tax rates again, and in his 1984 State of the Union message, announced that he had instructed Regan to come up with a "plan for action to simplify the entire tax code, so all taxpayers, big and small, are treated more fairly."[56]

Regan delivered the plan in November 1984. Developed by Treasury specialists and incorporating ideas from Bradley-Gephardt, the proposal reduced the number of tax brackets for individuals from fourteen to three and cut the top individual tax rate to 35 percent. The plan also proposed eliminating many individual and business deductions and raising taxes on business by $150 billion to pay for the reductions for individuals. True to form, Regan had followed the president's orders to come up with a total overhaul—and, reflecting its writers, a model of applied economics—but Baker realized that the Treasury plan was too radical to survive the political process. The plan, Baker later recalled, "had been written by technicians with a tin ear for politics." Starting in January 1985, Baker oversaw a rewriting of the Treasury plan, which kept the core of the original proposal—three brackets and a top rate of 35 percent for individuals, cutting the corporate tax rate from 45 percent to 33 percent, and doing away with scores of preferences and deductions but not as many as in Regan's plan. Reagan endorsed the proposal and presented it to the country in late May.[57]

Tax reform dominated Washington politics for the next sixteen months. The struggle was dramatic and intense as business and interest groups of all types mobilized to save their tax breaks, and several times they came close to killing reform. As in 1981 and 1982, Baker led the administration's efforts, and used the same machinery—keeping close watch on daily developments, working out compromises, obtaining Reagan's approvals, and giving him names of lawmakers to call—to build support. In Congress, two unlikely heroes, Sen. Robert Packwood (R-OR) and Rep. Dan Rostenkowski (D-IL) saved the reform effort, although each had his own motives—Packwood wanted to overcome his reputation as a servant of special interests, and Rostenkowski wanted to ensure that the Democrats received as much credit for tax reform as the Republicans. Working with Baker and Reagan, Packwood and Rostenkowski finally brought a bill through Congress in September 1986, and Reagan signed it in a large ceremony on October 22. The Tax Reform Act of 1986 (TRA) collapsed the fourteen individual income tax brackets to two, 15 percent and 28 percent, dropped the top corporate tax rate from 48 percent to 34 percent, eliminated numerous loopholes and deductions, and raised the personal exemption enough to drop several million people from the tax rolls.

Economists were, overall, thrilled by TRA. While they realized that the compromises necessary to pass the reform meant that it was imperfect—taxes remained quite complex and Baker had protected preferences for the oil industry—the main drafter of the original Treasury plan concluded that it still was a major improvement in broadening the tax base and "taxing all economic income uniformly and consistently." Other economists believed it would reduce distortions in the economy, promote investment and work, and favor innovative, high-technology industries, although they still saw room for improvement by eliminating remaining deductions for state taxes and mortgage interest, and taxing fringe benefits.[58]

The 1986 tax reform never fulfilled these high hopes, but it still stands as a landmark political achievement. Surveying the research literature in 1997, economists Alan Auerbach and Joel Slemrod found that TRA actually had little impact on taxpayer and corporate behavior. By the twentieth anniversary of the legislation, it was clear to another analyst that TRA had been a "promise failed," if only because immediately after its passage, Congress returned to its old habits. "We wiped the blackboard fairly clean in 1986, but this only encouraged Congress to come up with a new generation of preferences . . . [and] reward favored constituencies by reducing their taxes," wrote James Baker in 2006. Nonetheless, TRA remains an example of the potential of American politics. Recognizing a need for change and determined to succeed, a disparate coalition was able to work together to make careful decisions on an issue of great complexity and, after months of patient work and building on the ideas of politically neutral experts in the federal bureaucracy, achieve many of their goals. It is also an unfortunate reality that in the bitter partisanship of post-Reagan America, this has not happened again.[59]

The early fall of 1986 must have been a wonderful time for Reagan, a period when all things seemed possible. Politicians and the media gave him full credit for seeing tax reform through. "No one doubts that the President deserves primary credit and responsibility for the new tax system," said the *New York Times* as he signed the bill. His approval ratings had been floating between 60 and 65 percent for most of the year, an extraordinary level for a president well into his second term. In mid-September, *Fortune*'s cover story claimed to tell "What Managers Can Learn From Manager Reagan," and noted that "you don't have to support Reagan to concede that he has had remarkable success . . . the Reagan Revolution has largely succeeded." Reagan even seemed to win when he lost. In the mid-term elections on November 4, the Republicans lost eight seats in the Senate, giving control of Congress to the Democrats, and gave up another five seats in the House. But mid-term Congressional losses are normal for the party holding the White House, and the Republicans had been defending an unusually large number of Senate seats because of their victory six years before. In this context, the Republicans' losses were small and the GOP could look to its addition of eight governorships in the election as evidence of its continuing strength. Democratic leaders, consultants, and pundits alike agreed that the Democrats had done as well as they had only because their candidates avoided attacking Reagan and, as Democratic pollsters Mark Penn and Douglas Schoen acknowledged, "demonstrate[d] that they accepted the basic outlines of the president's policies." Indeed, as Americans cast their votes on Election Day, it would have seemed inconceivable that Reagan's presidency was only days away from near collapse.[60]

CARETAKER

Fortune notwithstanding, Reagan's political successes had disguised his weaknesses as a manager. His management style was to "surround yourself with the best people you can find, delegate authority, and don't interfere as long as the policy you've decided upon is being carried out," he told the magazine's interviewers. As a result, while Reagan was deeply involved in those areas that he cared about the most, like tax reform, he largely ignored other areas and left the White House staff to make decisions about policies and personnel. As Reagan's early California experience showed, however, if he did not have a strong, competent chief of staff to oversee this system, he could soon run into serious problems. In Washington, moreover, the size and complexity of federal government operations, which were constantly scrutinized by a news media hungry for sensational stories, meant that a political scandal or crisis could start at any moment. A critical capability for the president's chief of staff and other high-level aides, therefore, was to be able to move quickly and deftly to contain breaking scandals and limit any damage to Reagan's political strength. When the Iran-Contra scandal began on Election Day 1986, Donald Regan showed that he was unable to do this, and the consequences of his failure still echo in American politics.[61]

The start of the Iran-Contra scandal devastated the administration. As revelations about the arms-for-hostages deals and the subsequent diversion of funds to the Nicaraguan rebels dripped out through November, the White House fell into chaos as Regan and his aides scrambled to find out exactly what had happened. (For a full account of the scandal, see the following essay by Michael Flamm.) In an effort to explain what had happened, Reagan first gave a television speech and then a press conference, but the two appearances only made it clear that he could not discuss the matter coherently. At the press conference, the *New York Times* noted in a classic understatement, Reagan showed a "lack of sureness about details" and contradicted what he had said in the speech. Reagan's popularity, the core of his power in Washington, nosedived. By the start of December, polls showed his job approval rating had fallen from 67 percent to 46 percent in just a month, that half of Americans believed he was lying about the scandal, and that more people believed that Jimmy Carter had done a better job on relations with Iran than Reagan had. "He has a long way to go to get his credibility back," one woman told the *Wall Street Journal*.[62]

Reagan clearly had the overall responsibility for the Iran-Contra fiasco. The disaster was the result of his decisions and, just as important, his failure to insist on strong management of the National Security Council. That said, Donald Regan also deserves much of the blame. At the start, he had not tried to dissuade Reagan from undertaking a policy that was illegal and clearly invited disaster. Once Reagan decided to go ahead, as the report of the Tower Commission, appointed by Reagan to investigate the affair, pointed out, Regan should have ensured that orderly decision-making processes were followed and that contingency plans were made in case the scheme became public. Because Regan did not do so, the Commission found, he bore "primary responsibility for the chaos that descended upon the White House" when the disclosure came. By the time the commission released its report on February 26, 1987, no one in Washington was willing to defend Regan. His imperious style had long since left him without friends. Regan "would never have got in this trouble if he hadn't gone

Receiving the Tower Commission Report, February 26, 1987. (Courtesy of the Ronald Reagan Library.)

around telling everyone that he ran everything and knew everything," an anonymous White House aide told the *New York Times* in December, and the press was filled with rumors and leaks about Regan's imminent demise throughout the winter. Finally, on February 27, Regan was unceremoniously fired. He learned about his dismissal from a CNN report, stormed out of the White House, and went home to write a bitter memoir.[63]

Reagan appointed Howard Baker, now retired from the Senate, to be his new chief of staff. Baker had been elected to the Senate in 1966, served on the Senate Watergate committee and, as majority leader from 1981 to 1985, helped move Reagan's programs through Congress. Not only was Baker an accomplished politician, known for his ability to broker compromises, but his managerial style was the same as James Baker's. Howard Baker, like James, worked as an honest broker for Reagan, presenting him with well-developed, comprehensive policy options rather than Regan's narrow choices. Baker was a moderate Republican, however, not a Reagan conservative, and the right was divided about his appointment. William F. Buckley Jr. called Baker's appointment "very good news," and predicted that he would work to achieve Reagan's policy goals. Conservative activist and fund-raiser Richard Viguerie, however, said that despite Baker's support during Reagan's first term, conservatives felt "abandoned and betrayed" by the appointment. In an editorial reminiscent of early 1982, the *Wall Street Journal* warned that if the administration did not stand firm on taxes, spending, and anti-Communism, it would be because Baker was in charge and manipulating the president.[64]

With Baker in charge of the White House, Reagan's position improved. On March 4, with his approval rating at 42 percent, Reagan spoke on national television to accept responsibility for Iran-Contra and apologize to the country. His poll ratings recovered to 50 percent approval in mid-1987 and to 60 percent by the fall of 1988, but he never again enjoyed the aura of success and popular trust that he had before the scandal. Another effect of the scandal was that it had turned the winter of 1986–1987 into a wasted period. The administration had not had a priority program to follow TRA and, once Iran-Contra began, was unable to develop one. Now politically weakened and facing a Democratic Congress, Reagan was in no position to develop ambitious plans. Consequently, Howard Baker was chief of staff for a caretaker president, seeking to protect the gains of the past rather than take on any major new issues.[65]

Reagan's one attempt to break out of his caretaker status came in the summer and fall of 1987, when he nominated Judge Robert Bork to be an associate justice of the Supreme Court. Judicial appointments were especially important to conservatives, who viewed liberal control of the courts as having made possible the social changes of the 1960s and 1970s that they most wanted to roll back, such as the banning of school prayer and legalization of abortion. Understanding this and also wanting to ensure that he appointed judges who shared his conservatism, Reagan paid close attention to judicial appointments. Starting when he became president, the administration revamped the procedures for appointing judges, moving the process to the White House from its traditional home in the Justice Department, and carefully reviewing the ideological backgrounds of candidates for judgeships. Reagan, with opportunities created by an expansion of the federal courts, appointed more than 360 judges during his two terms, and established a firm conservative base in the judiciary.

Despite this progress, capturing the Supreme Court remained the most important goal for conservatives. Until 1987, in the view of many conservatives, Reagan's record on Supreme Court appointments was mixed. In 1981, to fulfill a campaign pledge to select the first woman for the Court, he appointed Sandra Day O'Connor, a moderate Republican. Conservatives grew dismayed by O'Connor, who turned out not to have strong conservative views and was reluctant to overturn precedents. In 1986, when Chief Justice Warren Burger retired, Reagan nominated Justice William Rehnquist to take his place, and chose Antonin Scalia to fill in behind

William Rehnquist sworn in as Chief Justice, with Antonin Scalia at far left, September 26, 1986. (Courtesy of the Ronald Reagan Library.)

Rehnquist. Rehnquist drew heavy fire from liberals and thirty-three senators voted against his confirmation, but he deflected attention from the far more conservative Scalia, who was confirmed unanimously. Now, in the summer of 1987, when moderate Justice Lewis Powell announced his retirement, the Court was finely balanced, with four conservative justices.

Bork represented conservatives' greatest hope for the Court. Bork had been a distinguished legal scholar and served as solicitor general (he had carried out Richard Nixon's order to fire Watergate special prosecutor Archibald Cox in October 1973) before Reagan appointed him to the federal bench in 1982. He firmly believed that the Constitution had to be interpreted according to the intent of the Founders and rejected the idea that new rights could be discovered. "Bork's ideology is only the conviction that judges must obey the Constitution rather than rewriting it," noted one article in *National Review*. Consequently, Bork believed that many of the Court's decisions in such matters as civil rights and abortion had resulted from the use of litigation to escape the political process and, therefore, were constitutionally invalid. Not only would his confirmation give the Court a conservative majority but, given that he was born in 1927, Bork could be expected to serve as the intellectual and ideological leader of the Court for at least a decade.[66]

Liberals, desperate after having lost so many battles to Reagan and realizing the consequences if Bork were confirmed, prepared for an epic battle. The fight began on July 7, the day that Reagan announced the nomination and on which Sen. Edward Kennedy (D-MA) rose in the Senate to declare that "Robert Bork's America is a land in which women would be forced into back alley abortions, blacks would sit at segregated lunch counters, rogue police could break down citizens' doors." Liberal groups undertook a campaign to purchase print and television advertising, and write letters, op-eds, and articles opposing Bork. Much of their rhetoric descended to near-hysteria and character assassination. "His legal writings are full of scornful attacks on past constitutional decisions," declared Anthony Lewis in the *New York Times*, while liberal constitutional scholar Ronald Dworkin warned readers of the *New York Review of Books* that Bork was a "constitutional radical" who argued an "antilegal" philosophy. Conservatives fought back with fund-raising and determined political efforts of their own, but their counterattack, ironically, was impeded from the start by the White House. Baker was unenthusiastic about Bork and did not craft or execute a coherent strategy to support the nomination, thereby leaving the initiative to Bork's opponents.[67]

As much as Reagan had moved American politics to the right, the Bork nomination showed the limits of popular backing for conservative change. As the debate roared on, public support for Bork steadily declined, and by mid-October a majority of Americans opposed his confirmation. Many of Reagan's usual allies in the Senate understood the implications, especially when it came to questions regarding Bork's doubts about the Court's civil rights decisions. Southern Democratic senators who had won their seats in 1986 on the strength of black votes opposed Bork, as did other conservative Democrats who did not want to reopen old civil rights battles—"we've already fought those fights, and we're happy with the outcome," said Sen. Lloyd Bentsen (D-TX)—and even some Republican senators who normally supported Reagan opposed the nomination. On October 23, the Senate rejected Bork, by a vote of 58–42 (six Republicans voted against Bork and only two Democrats, from Oklahoma and South Carolina, voted for him). Later in the fall, the Senate confirmed Anthony Kennedy, who was almost as conservative as Bork but lacked his intellectual prestige and prickly personality, to take Powell's seat.[68]

The Bork nomination turned out to be an important moment in recent American political history. Before Bork, it was rare for a nominee to a high government position to come under a sustained personal attack, let alone one as intense and, as Dworkin admitted afterward, as unfair and inaccurate as the one Bork suffered. A new verb, "to Bork," entered the Washington lexicon, meaning to unleash an all-out personal attack on a nominee. Conservatives concluded that the Bork episode showed that liberals were so determined to cling to power that they would respect no boundaries. "The entire Left came together . . . in its ugly demagogic way," to destroy Bork, declared *National Review*, and conservatives swore revenge. "I've never been so angry before," raged Sen. Jake Garn (R-UT). "I've voted for liberal judges before. That will never happen again." Indeed, since the Bork episode, pressure groups of all political persuasions have worked to uncover and publicize any views or behavior they see as unacceptable in nominees and have made borking a routine tactic, as the cases of Clarence Thomas (nominated to the Supreme Court by the first President Bush) and Lani Guinier (nominated by Bill Clinton to head the Justice Department's Civil Rights Division) demonstrate. This, in turn, has distorted the nomination process by rewarding media sensationalism and creating incentives for nominees to shade the truth during their confirmation hearings; judicial nominees now routinely deny that they hold views on controversial topics, such as abortion. The result has been to undermine the quality of appointees and the legitimacy of governing institutions.[69]

EVERYDAY LIFE

The most intensely debated question of the Reagan presidency, and of the era of conservative ascendancy that followed, has been whether his economic policies benefited ordinary Americans. Before 1981, critics of supply-side proposals had predicted that they would benefit only a minority and, during the Reagan years, many economists and commentators picked up on the data showing that overall economic growth was unimpressive and argued that prosperity was passing by large segments of the population. Their criticisms focused especially on income inequality, which grew sharply during the Reagan years. Reagan's critics argued that his tax cuts helped transfer tens of billions of dollars from lower- and middle-income households to those at the top, a point that was bolstered by Census Bureau reports showing that the top fifth of households, and especially the top 5 percent, had greatly increased their shares of national income from 1980 to 1988, while the shares of households in the lower quintiles actually fell (see table 3 on p. 65). Reagan's critics further claimed that his economic policies had not prevented the replacement of well-paid industrial jobs with lower-paid, part-time service work, and the stagnation of middle-class incomes and living standards. Harvard University economist Benjamin Friedman summarized these views when he wrote that the "Reagan recovery has not been all that great on average, and many Americans have missed it altogether." Twenty years later, historians still made the same point. "Prosperous but hardly affluent Americans," wrote Sean Wilentz in 2008, "thought they were enjoying prosperity" while they actually were falling into debt and ignoring the nation's growing economic problems.[70]

Many of these statements about the economy and the relative positions of Americans were true. At the same time, however, many of the criticisms of Reagan's policies missed important details about how the economy was changing. A careful look at the economic data from the Reagan years, in fact, shows that the situation was more complex and nuanced than the critics realized. The large body of economic and social research developed since the 1980s shows that for most Americans the Reagan years were a time of growing opportunities and living standards, and it helps explain why, even as they were told at the time that their lives were becoming harder, they supported Reagan.

A useful way to start understanding the impact of Reagan-era economic change on ordinary people is to begin by remembering the impact of deregulation, corporate restructuring, and increased competition on the companies that employed them. In this environment, companies knew they

had to adopt new methods or processes that might make them more efficient. This was especially true for information technologies. Smart corporate managers by the mid-1980s understood clearly that computers and new
communications technologies had the potential to change industry structures and give individual companies significant competitive advantages.
Similarly, they knew from observing foreign competitors that they could
organize workers and assembly processes more efficiently. The result was a
wave of experimentation, as companies installed computers—the number
of personal computers in the workplace rose from 1.2 million in 1981 to
20.3 million in 1988—and looked for ways to use them, whether it was to
take over routine tasks such as filing and sorting in offices, running ma-
chines in factories, or collecting and sharing data instantly. Similarly, firms
sought new ways to deploy their employees. When they found the right
ways to reorganize work, companies found that they could make stunning
gains. A General Electric circuit breaker plant, for example, increased its
productivity by 20 percent in one year and cut its manufacturing costs by
30 percent after expanding the use of computers in design and ordering,
and reorganizing production teams on the factory floor. In another case,
Harley-Davidson was able to cut by more than half the time it needed to
design a new motorcycle and reduce plant employment by 25 percent.
Economists' research makes it clear that these examples were typical of the
impact of technology and restructuring throughout the economy.[71]

Changes in the workplace had much to do with the growth of income
inequality during the 1980s. Rising inequality was not a new phenomenon
during the 1980s. After a long decline during the postwar era, inequality
had started to grow after 1968 and economists have concluded that the reason for the start of the increase was the growth of the service sector of the
economy relative to manufacturing. Service jobs generally required workers with greater skills and education, and the demand for such employees
raised their wages relative to those of less skilled and educated production
workers. This gap in wages, termed the "skill premium" by economists,
grew slowly in the 1970s, but then started to increase at a much faster rate
starting around 1981. In the late 1970s, for example, college graduates
earned 38 percent more than workers with only a high school diploma; by
1989, the difference was 58 percent. The differences among younger workers were even more striking, with the wage differential rising from 28 percent at the start of the 1980s to 69 percent at the end.[72]

The adoption of new technologies and reorganization of work were
responsible for much of the acceleration of the skill premium and inequality during the Reagan years. To start with, companies needed skilled and

educated workers to operate the computers and other new technologies they adopted in their efforts to stay competitive. As firms installed their new information systems they soon found that they could collect and organize vast amounts of data that hitherto they had not been able to capture. Companies needed more educated employees to manipulate and analyze this information and, as it turned out, these workers found new uses for the data. This, in turn, created more jobs requiring high levels of skill. "Highly-educated workers have a comparative advantage with respect to learning and implementing new technologies," one study noted in 1987. "Sectors or industries characterized by high rates of innovation . . . will tend to create the most opportunities (demand) for highly-educated workers."Not surprisingly, the rising demand for such workers outstripped the supply and led to rapid increases in their wages during the 1980s, while the wages of low-skill workers or those with only high school diplomas fell. "The U.S. economy has a strong capacity for making productive use of workers with large investments in schooling," was how one economist dryly described this insatiable demand.[73]

American workers generally were well positioned to benefit from the rising demand for skill. Since World War II, the workforce had steadily become better educated and this trend continued through the Reagan years. High school graduation rates rose, and college enrollments increased from 12 million to 13.4 million. Significantly, 45 percent of adults in their twenties, the workers just starting their careers, had one or more years of college in 1988, up from 32 percent in 1980. Educated workers flowed into jobs that offered bright futures and fast-growing earnings. Of the eighteen million jobs created in the United States from 1980 to 1988, some six million were in the professional, managerial, and technical categories, which included well-paid positions for engineers, scientists, and management consultants, as well as for the people who supervised their work. Another seven million jobs were created in sales, which included such potentially lucrative areas as real estate and securities, as well as sales management. Within these categories, some specialties did extraordinarily well—the number of people working in computer-related fields almost tripled, for example, and the economy added 1.8 million jobs in finance. Students clearly understood these developments and shifted their fields of study to take advantage of them. The number of bachelor's degrees awarded in the social sciences dropped during the 1980s, but the number of computer science degrees awarded nearly tripled, and engineering and management degrees rose by one-third. It was little wonder, then, that a poll in August 1984 found that a majority of Americans—and 70 percent of those under thirty—believed they were better off than in 1980.[74]

Another result of the changing economy was a decrease in sexual and racial discrimination. In the more competitive environment of the 1980s, employers could ill afford not to hire and take advantage of skilled and experienced workers simply because of their gender or ethnic origin. Women probably gained the most, as it was far easier for them to fill jobs involving technology and well-developed cognitive skills than it had been to undertake physically demanding industrial work. Women also were in a fortunate position because, as a result of the greater movement of women into the workforce in the 1970s, a large pool of experienced female workers was ready to begin moving into more senior positions. In addition, starting in the 1970s, young women had begun moving out of traditionally female professions, such as teaching, and into fields such as engineering, and thus were in demand during the Reagan years. By the end of the 1980s, younger women, and particularly younger women with college degrees, were earning 80 percent of what male workers earned, a dramatic shrinkage of the male-female wage gap. Immigrants, too, benefited from an economy that rewarded skill and education. Some 7.3 million people immigrated to the United States between 1981 and 1990, many of them from Latin America and Asia, and with widely varying levels of education and English. The immigrants were diverse and, in general, those with few skills or poor English wound up in lower-paying work, but those who came with an education or who went to school after arriving in the United States experienced rapid wage growth and, in some cases, soon were making as much or more than native-born Americans.[75]

Not everyone prospered during the Reagan years, however, and for many workers lacking the skills demanded by the changing economy, the 1980s were disastrous. Workers in declining industries probably suffered the most. About two million industrial jobs disappeared during the decade, many of them lost during the recession, while others vanished later in the decade as computers took over office tasks, and assembly lines, like Harley-Davidson's, were automated or reorganized. The number of workers in the steel industry fell by half, for example, while the mining sector lost one-third of its jobs, and the unemployment rate for production workers remained well above the national rate throughout the decade. Because displaced workers, as they were categorized, tended to have lower education levels, they often took years to find new jobs and, once they found work, earned much less than before. Later in the decade, as corporate restructuring spread, job displacement hit managers and white-collar workers. Their skills and education enabled them to find new work faster than displaced industrial workers had, although they also often earned less than before. Similarly, women with low skill and education levels lost ground, and the poor did not share in the prosperity because they did not have the skills employers sought.[76]

Unionized workers also were big losers in the Reagan years, as their numbers fell from 20 percent of the workforce in 1980 to only 16 percent a decade later. The arrival in Washington of an administration that was unsympathetic to organized labor—Reagan's decision to fire the PATCO strikers often is seen as an important signal to employers that they could take a hard line with unions—may have been one reason for the decline. More important, however, was the disappearance of industrial jobs at the same time that deregulation and the appearance of new, nonunion, firms in industries that had formerly been entirely unionized placed pressure on the high wages of union members. In industries such as trucking and airlines, the *Wall Street Journal* reported in 1984, "deregulation has suddenly unleashed a horde of new, nonunion competitors with low wage rates, few cumbersome work rules and modest overhead." Across the economy, unions had to agree to wage cuts or "two-tier" wage scales that paid new workers less. Boeing, for example, struck a deal that allowed it to pay new, unskilled workers 40 percent less than those already employed in its plants. In another reflection of the unions' weakening position, the number of strikes dropped sharply; the spread of information technology further increased the difficulty of shutting down a company. "We can't strike Equitable [Life Assurance]," complained an organizer in Syracuse, New York. "With this technology, they could flick a switch and the work could be in Kansas City."[77]

All of these trends were to be found in the diverse experiences of African Americans. Blacks had made tremendous economic progress since 1960, as first the end of legalized discrimination and then the growth in demand for black workers created by affirmative action, led to large wage gains and created a substantial black middle class. But, overall, black economic progress appeared to stop in the Reagan years—in 1980, black men earned an average of 70 percent of what white men earned, a figure that was essentially unchanged in 1988. This statistic, however, disguised important differences among segments of the black population. Black industrial workers suffered large drops in income relative to whites, largely because they were hit hard by job losses in the Midwest. Black male college graduates did much better than less-educated blacks, but still lost ground relative to white men with degrees. This surprising development seems to have occurred because educated black men still tended to be found disproportionately in jobs such as teaching, rather than in the professional and managerial jobs that benefited the most from the growing skill bias. (Older, educated black men, whose skills and experience were in demand, saw their incomes rise.) Black women, however, did better than black men—they tended to work in the same jobs as white women and, therefore, gained from the overall movement of women into higher-paid work. Taken as a whole, these data suggest that blacks in the 1980s, rather than suffering from large-scale racial discrimination in the workplace, now had to cope with the same problems as other groups.[78]

In addition to questions about the quality of jobs, a large part of the Reagan-era economic debates centered on the issue of middle-class incomes and living standards. Citing data that showed real incomes were stagnating or dropping, poverty rates were rising, and the proportion of households in the middle class was falling, critics filled the popular press with warnings that American standards of living soon would decline, if they had not already begun to do so. "There is overwhelming evidence [the standard of living is] already slipping for many people and may drop even more," reported *Business Week* in April 1987. The dire results, others predicted, would go well beyond material issues. Social critic Barbara Ehrenreich declared on Labor Day weekend 1986 that the United States was dividing into a country of rich and poor, with few in the middle, and that "our identity and future as a nation may be endangered." Political journalist Thomas Edsall predicted a society with a "mocking disparity between the good life available to the few and the life that the many settle for—resignation, guilt, social hopelessness."[79]

None of this happened, of course, which raises intriguing questions about how so many people misinterpreted the situation. Part of the reason was a selective reading of the data. It was true, for example, that the proportion of households in the middle-income ranges fell during the Reagan years. But it was equally true, and more important, that the proportion in the lower income brackets also decreased, while the proportion in the upper income levels rose. On average, therefore, the middle shrank because people of all races generally were moving up the income ladder rather than down (see table 4 on p. 65). The critics were not always at fault, however, for it turned out that much of the data that informed their observations and predictions was wrong. Looking back in the 1990s, economists realized that the government statistical models used to measure GDP growth, incomes, and inflation had not been adjusted rapidly enough to capture the effects of the wave of new technologies and innovation that had begun in the early 1980s. The annual measurement errors likely were small, but were compounded every year, and eventually made official statistics more and more inaccurate. Indeed, as one economist put it, the "statistics seem out of touch with reality."[80]

Simply looking around at the time would have shown that life was improving for most Americans during the Reagan years. Americans lived more comfortably than ever before. The average new home built in 1988 was about 15 percent larger than a home built in 1980, which often translated into an extra bedroom or bathroom. Three-quarters of new houses had central air conditioning, and people quickly filled their homes with appliances—microwaves, video cassette recorders (VCRs), and computers—that until the 1980s had been luxuries or had not even been on the market. More and more, people hired housecleaning services and ate out—the number of restaurants in the United States increased by one-third from 1980 to 1988. People also had more leisure time and shopped more. Retail sales rose by one-third in real terms during this period, the number of malls and shopping centers increased from twenty-two thousand to thirty-six thousand, and the stores were filled with new goods, like compact disc players and cell phones, that quickly became commonplace. Travel also increased. Americans took about 20 percent more vacations in 1988 than at the start of the decade, and the number of people visiting foreign countries increased by more than 60 percent from 1980 to 1988. People seemed to be able to pay for all this with reasonable ease—credit card spending and debt both doubled from 1980 to 1988, but the credit card default rate actually fell. All in all, this was hardly the portrait of a nation sliding into mass impoverishment.[81]

For many Americans, in addition, the Reagan years were a time of growing personal wealth. The 1981 tax bill had changed the rules for contributions to Individual Retirement Accounts (IRAs), allowing all workers as of January 1, 1982, to contribute up to $2,000 per year (plus another $250 for a nonworking spouse) to the tax-deferred accounts. Sensing an opportunity, people rushed to open accounts and began depositing some $30 billion to $40 billion per year. Simultaneously, in the summer of 1982, just as the recovery was starting, the stock market began to rise and then boom, gaining more than 250 percent before the crash of October 1987. During that period, IRA money flowed into stocks, and individual investors watched the value of their holdings rise until, by the end of 1988, IRAs held almost $400 billion. Similarly, people also poured hundreds of billions

Speaking to the country for the tax bill, July 27, 1981. (Courtesy of the Ronald Reagan Library.)

of dollars of non–IRA savings into the stock market through mutual funds and purchases of individual companies' shares. The volume of stock trading roughly quadrupled during the Reagan years, and the value of mutual fund deposits quintupled. Despite the 1987 crash, investors generally held on to most of the money they made during the Reagan years.

In retrospect, it is clear that the Reagan years were the beginning of an extended period of prosperity and change in the ways in which Americans worked and lived. Driven by increasing competition, work demanded more technological skills and generously rewarded those who had them, even as jobs became less secure. The Reagan administration, consistent with its philosophies, did not interfere with these changes but instead stood by as the changing economy showed that it could bring concrete improvements to ordinary people's lives. This, in turn, helped solidify popular support for Reagan's economic position as well as for conservative policies in general. The effects of this lasted long after Reagan left office. The installation of computers in the workplace and experiments with new organizations in the 1980s did much to help build the foundations of the prosperity of the 1990s, when these innovations paid off in greater productivity and even more rapid advances in technology and living standards. It is noteworthy, too, that as with tax rates and deregulation, the presidents who followed

Reagan let these developments continue without significant interference. Thus, in ways that affect almost every American on a daily basis, Reagan set the country on a long-lasting path.

OPPOSITION

If the growing strength of conservatism amid economic and technological change was the dominant trend of the 1980s, it should not obscure the fact that many Americans remained deeply opposed to Reagan and his policies. Some of the opposition was obvious, coming from Democrats opposed to Reagan on principle or from those who were left out of the prosperity of the 1980s. But opposition to Reaganism also grew out of a variety of issues, some large, some small, and some still prominent in American politics. A look at some of the major concerns of his opponents sheds light not only on the question of why not all Americans supported Reagan but also why, given that his opponents sometimes represented large constituencies, they were unable to form a consistent, effective counter to Reagan's policies.

African Americans were virtually unanimous in their opposition to Reagan. Blacks had been wary of Reagan even before he took office because of his criticisms of government programs that benefited minorities, as well as in response to campaign rhetoric that sometimes won praise from extremist groups, such as the Ku Klux Klan. (In 1980, Reagan launched his campaign near Philadelphia, Mississippi, the site of the notorious murder of three civil rights workers in 1964, and made a statement in support of states' rights.) Once Reagan was president, poor blacks found themselves hard hit as the administration moved to cut the budgets for food stamps, public service jobs, job-training programs, housing subsidies, and other social welfare programs. Soon after, working-class blacks realized that they were being hit disproportionately by the recession and changes in the labor market. The Census Bureau reported, for example, that the poverty rate for America's twenty-eight million blacks had fallen steadily during the 1970s, to a low of 30.6 percent in 1978, before rising to almost 36 percent in 1983. Similarly, according to a 1986 report by the Center on Budget and Policy Priorities, the increase in the proportion of the black population that had fallen into poverty was twice the proportion of whites who had become poor since 1980.[82]

Beyond economics, black Americans disliked Reagan because of his opposition to affirmative action and what they saw as his lax enforcement of civil rights laws. Affirmative action had done much to improve the standing of blacks during the 1970s, but conservative intellectuals criticized it as a needless intrusion into the marketplace—economist Milton Friedman argued, for example, that any firm foolish enough to discriminate on the basis of race in its hiring would soon find itself at a competitive disadvantage—and also because its quota systems categorized Americans by group and race rather than treated all citizens as the same. To the surprise of many conservatives, however, the system turned out to have a good deal of support among corporations, which saw it as protecting them from discrimination suits. Americans in general moreover, while not enamored of affirmative action, were sympathetic to its goal of helping the disadvantaged and therefore did not support its abolition. Thus, as in so many other areas, Reagan declined to get into a major battle and instead made no effort to dismantle affirmative action, despite the fears of blacks.[83]

Reagan did, however, change Justice Department policy on civil rights. Under Assistant Attorney General William Bradford Reynolds, the Civil Rights Division shifted to a policy of protecting individual rights, seeking relief for individuals who suffered specific acts of discrimination but not supporting groups that had been victims in the past, and supporting minority recruitment for hiring but not the use of quotas. Not surprisingly, blacks and their liberal allies saw these as backward steps for civil rights. In 1988, for example, New York City police commissioner Benjamin Ward declared that civil rights progress had ended at the "time of the election of President Reagan," and black academics and popular media wrote of an increase in racism. Reagan also sometimes made symbolic missteps that reinforced black dislike of him. The most notable of these cases was when he argued against the establishment of a federal holiday for the birthday of Martin Luther King Jr., suggesting that "there's no way we could afford all the holidays" that other groups might then want to honor their icons. Reagan eventually reversed his stand and approved the new holiday, but the damage to his image among blacks remained. It was no surprise that Reagan received only 9 percent of the black vote in 1984.[84]

Political analysts during the 1980s also viewed women as a potentially large pool of anti-Reagan votes. Women had narrowly supported Reagan over Carter in 1980, giving him 47 percent of their votes, compared to 45 percent for Carter, but public opinion researchers soon realized that women's policy views and priorities were at odds with Reagan's. Women, pollsters found, generally were most concerned with policies relating to social welfare, health, education, and programs to help the disadvantaged, as well as with such obvious issues as abortion rights and equality between the sexes; unlike men, moreover, women tended to view Reagan's foreign policies as overly aggressive and risky. Many women and organized women's groups saw Reagan's budget cuts, including funding reductions for child care, food and nutrition programs, family planning services, and job training, as intolerable assaults on their main areas of interest. Reagan's proposed budget, according to a statement issued by forty-one women's groups in March 1981, was "bound to impact disproportionately and harshly on women," and especially poor women with children. By early 1982, polls showed Reagan's support among women dropping sharply, with a two-to-one margin agreeing that he should change his economic programs. "Women have become the have-nots in society," declared National Organization for Women president Eleanor Smeal. "Their economic interests are not being served by the Reagan administration."[85]

Women did not become overwhelmingly opposed to Reagan, however. His approval ratings among women always lagged those of men—the so-called gender gap—but as the economy recovered after 1982, women began to view him more favorably. In February 1984, the Gallup Poll found that 53 percent of women approved of Reagan (compared with 61 percent of men), and other polls found that even women who disapproved of Reagan's policies liked and respected him on a personal level. These ratings held about steady through the 1984 election, even though Democratic nominee Walter Mondale chose a woman, Rep. Geraldine Ferraro (D-NY), as his running mate, and in November Reagan gained 57 percent of women's votes. It is worth noting, however, that Reagan seems to have derived a unique benefit from his personal appeal; the gender gap has grown since he left office, to the disadvantage of Republicans and conservatives.[86]

The AIDS epidemic was another policy area that had the potential to become a focus for opposition to Reagan. The disease appeared in the United States in 1981 and, by the time Reagan left office, some seventy-eight thousand Americans had contracted AIDS, of whom about fifty thousand died. Fear spread, especially in the middle of the decade, that AIDS would spread beyond its main victims, gay men and intravenous drug users, and begin ravaging the general population, and polls showed that the people viewed AIDS as second only to cancer as a health concern. Even as pressure built on Reagan to formulate a policy to halt the epidemic, however, he did not act. At first, he was slow to realize the importance of AIDS as a public health issue. Then, as concerns about AIDS grew, Reagan came under pressure from conservatives—some on the right believed that AIDS was nature's retribution for the unnatural practices of homosexuals, while others worried that frank talk about prevention and the use of condoms would encourage promiscuity among the young—which kept him from speaking out on the issue and formulating a coherent policy. It was not until after the death from AIDS of his friend, actor Rock Hudson, that Reagan realized the seriousness of the situation and began taking steps to come up with a national AIDS strategy. Starting in 1986, the federal government rapidly expanded funding for AIDS research, but critics largely viewed Reagan's actions as tardy and half-hearted.[87]

Although at first glance the opposition to Reagan from blacks, women, and other groups who saw their interests as hurt by his policies would seem to have had the potential to form the core of an effective anti-Reagan movement, it was actually a weak alliance. The people who cared the most about affirmative action and women's and gay rights already were Democrats and, once prosperity returned after 1982, it was extremely difficult for them to attract voters who were otherwise satisfied with Reagan. In addition, for some members of these groups, such as women who were prospering in the workplace, the reasons to support Reagan outnumbered the reasons to oppose him. To compound the difficulties, Southern white men were deserting the Democratic Party in droves and throwing their support to Reagan. It would have taken enormous numbers of minority, women, and other voters alienated by Reagan—more than were available to become Democrats—to overcome these trends.

One man, however, did try to form an anti-Reagan coalition. In 1983 the Rev. Jesse Jackson, long a leader in the civil rights movement, led a successful voter registration drive among blacks in the South, which led to talk of him as a presidential candidate. Jackson declared his candidacy that November and spoke of building a "Rainbow Coalition" of the poor, dispossessed, and those of all races left behind by Reagan's policies. Running on a platform of cutting the defense budget, raising spending on public works, eliminating tax breaks for the wealthy, and making full use of his extraordinary talent as a speaker, Jackson won 3.5 million primary votes and 384 delegates, which brought him third place in the 1984 Democratic nomination race. His candidacy, however, exposed fissures that hurt the Democrats and opposition to Reagan. In particular, the *Washington Post* revealed in February 1984 that Jackson had casually referred to Jews as "Hymies," and New York as "Hymietown," which infuriated Jewish Democrats and exacerbated long-simmering black-Jewish tensions within the party. Jackson ran again in 1988 and took about 30 percent of the Democratic primary votes, but this time was snubbed by the party's leadership, which was trying to appeal to centrists and other voters who might be peeled away from the Republicans. Jackson's efforts against Reagan, therefore, had little immediate effect. Looking back, however, it is clear that Jackson was a pioneer. Even as he ran his campaigns on a shoestring, Jackson had shown that a black candidate could be competitive at the national level and blazed the trail that Barack Obama would follow twenty years later.[88]

One final group merits discussion, not because its members opposed Reagan, but because they remained loyal supporters despite numerous disappointments. This was the Christian right. Christian conservatives worked tirelessly in 1980 and after to support not only Reagan, but candidates who supported "traditional" values and tried to advance legislation that would roll back Court decisions on abortion and school prayer as well as other developments that, they believed, had undermined American morality. They claimed much of the credit for Reagan's victory and expected him to back their agenda in return.[89]

Despite their efforts, the Christian conservatives turned out to have little influence and failed to achieve their goals. Indeed, when Reagan left office abortion remained legal, prayer had not returned to the schools, homosexuality was more accepted than ever, and the pornography industry—thanks to the spread of VCRs and cheap video technology—was flourishing. Several factors explain their failure. Perhaps most important, the strength of the Christian conservative movement was vastly overstated by both its supporters and its opponents; instead of thirty million or more, its true strength may have been as low as five million to ten million. Theologically conservative Christians, in addition, were not always politically conservative, and some objected to religious leaders becoming involved in politics and thus did not support activist leaders such as Falwell. The Christian right also was fighting an uphill battle, as Americans in general had become much more tolerant in the decades leading up to the 1980s as well as during the Reagan years. While such social issues as abortion and gay rights had generated enormous controversies when they first became subjects of national debate, by the 1980s a rough live-and-let-live consensus was developing around them—large numbers of Americans still disapproved of such behaviors, but they were not willing to interfere in other peoples' lives. Thus, as the Bork debate demonstrated, there was little public appetite for large-scale battles on these issues. Reagan, as usual, understood this quite clearly. He consistently gave verbal support to Christian conservatives, but at the same time he stuck to his general strategy of avoiding divisive fights, worked to make it clear that he was not beholden to the religious right and its policy preferences, and never undertook any serious efforts on behalf of the social conservatives' priorities. For their part, Christian conservative leaders like Falwell eventually realized that Reagan was doing little to repay their support, but instead found themselves tied closely to him and had no other politician they could turn to for support.[90]

DEMOCRATS

The Reagan years were a miserable time for the Democrats. Throughout his presidency, they struggled to understand why Reagan was so successful and to find ways to counter him. They failed at almost every point. Indeed, the plight of the Democrats during the 1980s was largely the result of an intellectual failure. Liberal intellectuals, whose role it was to supply ideas that Democratic politicians could turn into effective campaign themes and policy proposals, misunderstood the changes going on around them and thus supplied terrible advice. Democratic politicians, wedded to old ways and not realizing that Reagan had changed the ground rules of politics, could not develop effective strategies to defeat him. The result was that liberalism became inward-looking, pessimistic, and increasingly out of touch with the daily realities of American life, while the Democrats suffered devastating defeats in the elections of 1984 and 1988.

Many liberals spent the early Reagan years in a state of disbelief. As bad as it was, in their view, that he had won the 1980 election, it was impossible for them to conceive that Reagan's economic policies could succeed. "The Reagan program in these conditions is likely to be wildly inflationary," wrote economic historian Emma Rothschild in the *New York Review of Books* a few days after Reagan took office. "There may be far worse to come," she concluded. Such views were understandable in 1981 and 1982, when Reagan's prospects were uncertain and the recession seemed endless. It is more difficult to see why liberals persisted in such dismissive judgments long afterward. "Our economy will not expand much beyond its present bounds . . . a high level of unemployment may be with us for the rest of this century," wrote sociologist Andrew Hacker in June 1983, as growth returned and job creation started up again. Similarly, liberal commentators saw the new jobs as unimpressive. Robert Kuttner, then an editor at the *New Republic*, wrote in 1983 that "few economists expect the booming high-technology field to be an important source of new jobs." For liberals, the implications of these analyses were clear. Like Tip O'Neill, they believed they only had to wait for Reagan's policies to fail, and the people would return to supporting liberalism and the Democrats.[91]

For the Democratic politicians who had to face Reagan in Washington, however, just waiting him out was only part of the task. In addition,
they needed practical advice that would help them attract voters and pre-
pare to govern again. In response, two main policy schools developed during Reagan's first term, the best known of which was called neoliberalism.
Championed by political journalist Charles Peters and his magazine, the
Washington Monthly, neoliberalism sought to update liberal views to appeal
to the new generation of voters who were well educated, working with
new technologies in growing industries, and too young to have had their
views shaped by the experiences of the 1960s. Neoliberalism, Peters declared, believed in the traditional liberal values of "liberty and justice and
a fair chance for all, and in mercy for the afflicted and help for the down
and out," but opposed reflexive support for organized labor, big government programs, and regulations that discouraged competition. Instead, said
Peters, "our hero is the risk-taking entrepreneur who creates new jobs and
better products." Peters further criticized what he viewed as liberals' self-
defeating snobbery toward religious, patriotic, and family values, and the
socially conservative people to whom these were important. On the political side, neoliberalism's most important adherents were senators Paul
Tsongas (D–MA)—"liberals must talk in terms that mean something to a
new generation," wrote Tsongas—and Gary Hart (D–CO). Although neoliberal ideas found their way into the Democratic mainstream during Bill
Clinton's presidency, in the 1980s the majority of liberals saw them as too
close to Reaganism and, therefore, as unacceptably conservative. "Neoliberalism is reaction," wrote political columnist Richard Reeves in 1984.
Historian Arthur M. Schlesinger Jr. who had done much to define
Truman- and Kennedy-era liberalism, called it a "hoax," and its skepticism
of government a "bow to fashion."[92]

The other major strand of liberal thought was industrial policy, whose
leading advocates were financier Felix Rohatyn and Harvard's Robert
Reich. Proponents of industrial policy viewed the troubles of heavy industry and the loss of industrial jobs as signs of overall economic decline, and
they built on the argument that corporate restructuring only rearranged assets and enriched traders without improving company performance. Looking at what they believed were successful Japanese and European programs
in which government and business worked together to keep industries
competitive in world markets, they argued for creating an arrangement
through which, as Rohatyn put it, "Business, labor, and government
[would] cooperate to save the economy." Rohatyn proposed setting up a
board with representatives of the three groups and, working with a gov-

ernment bank, provided with $5 billion in capital and authority to borrow another $50 billion, assist industries by providing credits, tax subsidies, and help with international trade problems. Industrial policy quickly caught on with Democratic politicians, who were attracted not only by its promises of economic renewal but, no doubt, also by the prospect of delivering billions of dollars in favors to unions and other favored constituencies.[93]

Industrial policy rested on weak foundations, however. Professional economists—industrial policy advocates generally were not economists—and journalists well-schooled in economics pointed out that the core assumptions about American industrial decline and the superiority of the Japanese and European models were myths based on flawed interpretations of the data. "Anyone presenting Europe as a model of successful economic adjustment ought to have his head examined," wrote Robert Samuelson in 1983. Skeptics also asked pointed questions about how industrial policy could be implemented without politics distorting the decisions and making matters worse. In one extraordinary case, however, industrial policy was put before the voters. In 1983, working with the government of Rhode Island, a young policy consultant named Ira Magaziner developed an industrial policy for the Ocean State that called for spending $250 million to create research centers in new, high-technology industries and also to revive the state's troubled older industries. Magaziner claimed that his plan would create sixty thousand jobs, though how he came up with this projection remained unexplained, and Brown University economists labeled the scheme "crackpot economics." In addition, no one could quite determine how a state well known for its corruption could be trusted with so much money. In a referendum on June 12, 1984, the plan was defeated by a 4–1 margin, and liberal discussions of industrial policy quickly ended (although Magaziner went on to help create the Clinton administration's health care plan in 1993).[94]

The Democrats' lack of new ideas contributed to the magnitude of Walter Mondale's defeat in 1984. Mondale had prepared carefully for his run, building a national organization and securing traditional liberal endorsements from labor, women's groups, and scores of prominent Democrats. Gary Hart mounted an unexpectedly strong challenge in the primaries and, although Mondale finally defeated Hart in the late spring, the former vice president by then had spent months criticizing Hart's neoliberal ideas and making himself look like the candidate of the traditional Democratic interest groups rather than the representative of any compelling force that could take on Reagan. Just as bad, Mondale had been attracted to industrial policy as a campaign issue, but the Rhode Island referendum took that away from him. Consequently, Mondale was left with little to offer voters. In his speech accepting the nomination he made a suicidal promise to raise taxes to close the deficits, and he then spent much of the campaign trying to paint Reagan as a right-wing extremist. While it is unlikely that anyone could have beaten Reagan in 1984, the Democrats' ideological vacuum undoubtedly made Mondale's situation worse than it would have been otherwise and made the scale of his defeat all the more embarrassing.[95]

The Mondale disaster left liberal intellectuals virtually speechless. The debates among traditional liberals, neoliberals, and industrial policy advocates during Reagan's first term had been lively, if ultimately futile, but after 1984 liberals of all stripes descended into a gloomy silence. Reich, Rohatyn, and others who had been major voices in the arguments from 1980 to 1984 now wrote less, and newspapers covering Democratic politics noted that party debates were unusually muted and civil because, even as intellectuals put forth policy papers, they shied away from advancing any controversial ideas. Their proposals, the *New Republic* editorialized in October 1986, "take the easy way out, calling for an end to defense waste and better tax collection—positions favored by everyone and taken seriously by no one." In this vacuum, with little to excite them, the Democrats' intellectual leaders fell into pessimistic ruts. Rohatyn, having seen his dream of industrial policy fail, published bitter denunciations of takeovers and the corruption of the financial industry, and then he began warning that the United States was in a fatal economic decline. Referring to the country's trade deficits and foreign debts, Rohatyn wrote in June 1987 that "for the first time in our history, we depend on foreign capital to finance day-to-day operations of our government . . . we are being colonized." "We now conform to the classic model of a failing economic power," he asserted eight months later. The idea of national decline caught on among liberal intellectuals and led them to write a number of books on the topic. The best known of these was historian Paul Kennedy's *The Rise and Fall of Great Powers* (1987), which forecast the gradual decline of the United States into the ranks of second-rate states. Whatever the validity of these analyses, and to date they arguably have turned out to have none at all, they were simply too pessimistic for Democratic politicians to use with an electorate that responded best to positive, optimistic rhetoric.[96]

The consequences of the Democrats' lack of usable ideas were painfully evident during the 1988 presidential campaign, when Michael Dukakis was the party's nominee. Dukakis, then midway through his third term as governor of Massachusetts, was a reformist liberal from the well-to-do Boston suburb of Brookline. A humorless, cerebral, and rigidly self-righteous man, he managed during his first term as governor (1975 to 1979) to alienate both his fellow Democrats and the business community, and then lost in the primary when he ran for reelection. Dukakis made a comeback in 1982—his successor was even more inept—and returned to office just as the recovery of the 1980s turned Massachusetts, with its concentration of technology industries, financial institutions, and universities, into one of the most prosperous states in the country. Dukakis claimed credit for the "Massachusetts Miracle" and, even before he was reelected in a landslide in 1986, boosters and friendly journalists were talking about him as a potential president. But those who knew him best saw from the start that he would be a poor candidate. One Massachusetts activist noted in 1987 that "Dukakis doesn't believe in anything," and the *Boston Globe* noted acidly that he still was arrogant and reserved, a "hands-on manager who immerses himself in the policy details of government but whose ability to step back and speak thematically of his vision for the future is in question."[97]

Dukakis presented himself as a technocrat who would use his management skills to solve the country's problems, just as he claimed to have done in Massachusetts. When he announced he was running, Dukakis declared that he had "the strength to run this country, the experience to manage our government and the values to lead our people." Dukakis tried to appeal to centrist voters by repeating the assertions that, under Reagan, middle-class incomes and living standards had stagnated during the Reagan years, and making a vague claim that he could fix matters. "Unquestionably, some segments of the electorate are doing well, but to say that it extends to the middle class and working class is a delusion," was how one senior Dukakis campaign official summarized the argument in September 1988. "We're saying [things] can be better." This was a hard point to make, however, given that the middle class and substantial segments of the working class were doing quite well in the late 1980s. To make matters more difficult, throughout his campaign Dukakis carefully avoided identifying himself as a liberal, though he was, or advancing any large ideas or proposals. "This election is not about ideology," he told the Democratic convention, "it's about competence." This made it difficult for voters inclined to support Democrats to find a reason to vote for him. "We've gone from visionaries to functionaries," groused one liberal Democrat. The absence of ideas in his campaign even affected Dukakis's television advertising, which was confusing, passionless, badly produced, and often far behind campaign events— points that were particularly troubling for a candidate running on a claim to be a skilled manager.[98]

The Republican candidate was Vice President George H. W. Bush. Conservatives had long distrusted Bush, remembering his roots in the pre-Reagan moderate Republican establishment and his opposition to the supply side, but he worked hard during Reagan's two terms to secure their support by promising to carry on Reagan's policies. "George Bush represents the Republican Party's best hope for keeping the Reagan coalition together," declared Rep. Robert Dornan, a conservative leader from California, in 1987. "The fact is that George Bush has always been a conservative and it is about time that conservatives recognized him as such." Continuing prosperity and Reagan's popularity gave Bush an advantage, but he took no chances and unleashed a nasty campaign against Dukakis. Throughout the late summer and fall of 1988, Bush painted Dukakis as a caricature of liberalism. The vice president constantly reminded his audiences that Dukakis had vetoed a bill requiring Massachusetts teachers to lead students in the Pledge of Allegiance, suggesting that the governor was unpatriotic, and ridiculed Dukakis's membership in the American Civil Liberties Union, painting him as out of touch with the values of the majority of the population. Most notoriously, the Bush campaign appealed to racial fears by repeatedly describing the case of Willie Horton, a black prisoner in Massachusetts serving time for murder who had raped a woman in Maryland while he was on a furlough.[99]

Dukakis was easy prey for Bush. Although the governor had enjoyed a substantial lead in the polls following the Democratic convention in July, Dukakis had no experience in national politics, and nothing in his Massachusetts background had prepared him for such a sustained, well-organized attack. Dukakis's lead was gone by Labor Day, and he became paralyzed and indecisive. Only at the end of October, as his situation grew desperate and his supporters marveled at his ineptitude as a campaigner, did Dukakis declare himself to be a liberal, but one of the FDR-Truman-Kennedy variety. Not only did this highlight his own lack of current ideas—Kennedy, after all, had been dead for twenty-five years—but it made Dukakis look foolish. "Mr. Dukakis's proud declaration of liberal identity comes after months in which he tried to run a determinedly nonideological campaign," the *New York Times* noted dryly. "From one end of the country to another, he touted his managerial expertise and . . . when pressed on his political philosophy, Mr. Dukakis's standard answer was that labels were meaningless." The results were predictable. On November 8, Bush took 53 percent of the popular vote and forty states with 426 electoral votes.[100]

Bush's victory showed how much Reagan had changed the electoral landscape. While Bush's share of the vote came nowhere near Reagan's

1984 landslide, he won a greater share of the popular vote than Reagan had in 1980. The breakdown of the vote, furthermore, shows how the economic and social changes of the 1980s had greatly increased the appeal of the Republican Party and Reagan's brand of conservatism. For the first time since the 1930s, the number of voters identifying themselves as Republicans about matched the number of Democrats. Bush, in addition, won a larger proportion of younger voters than Reagan had in 1980, and he matched or exceeded Reagan's showing eight years before among middle-income voters, professionals, educated workers, and blue-collar workers. In geographic terms, he matched Reagan's 1980 proportion of western votes and ran well ahead of Reagan's 1980 performance in the South. Given that these were the fastest growing areas of the country and that Bush had won crushing victories across the former Confederate states (74 percent of the popular vote in Georgia, for example, and 63 percent in Florida), the future for the Democrats looked especially bleak. Even though the Democrats made slight gains in Congressional elections, picking up two seats in the House while the Senate remained unchanged, it was a taste of how the Republicans would come to dominate the South in the 1990s and early 2000s and use that base to gain control of Congress, making life miserable for President Bill Clinton.[101]

LEGACY

That Ronald Reagan moved the center of American politics to the right is beyond dispute. The reasons for his success remain the subject of debate, however, with various authors attributing it to cultural factors, economics, slick political manipulation, or the absence of an effective Democratic opposition. But the simplest explanation probably is the best: Reagan came into office promising that his policies would deliver prosperity without inflation and, for the most part, he succeeded. This, combined with his decision not to challenge large parts of the established political and social order, brought Reagan the support of voters, enabled a Republican to succeed him, and gave conservative policies a credible track record on which a successor generation could build. The successors, headed first by Rep. Newt Gingrich (R-GA) and then by George W. Bush, held the line against Democrats during the 1990s and returned to power in 2001.

Reagan also changed the framework for political and policy debates. He established low taxes, suspicion of large government programs, and deregulation as the norms for national economic policy. Despite the widespread disapproval of large budget deficits, Reagan not only established them as a common phenomenon, but also proved that they did not have much political impact and so could be tolerated by presidents and Congress alike, if they chose. Politicians learned that going against these tides was perilous. In 1990, the Democrats maneuvered President George H. W. Bush into accepting a budget deal that included modestly higher taxes. Bush soon found his conservative support drifting away, and the tax increase was a major reason for his defeat in 1992. The victor in the election, Bill Clinton, in turn came to grief when he challenged Reagan's legacy on social programs by trying to establish a national health care system in 1994. Conservatism's most basic critique of federal social programs, that their functions almost always were better carried out by the private sector, had gained enough strength from the prosperity of the 1980s that Clinton's proposals ran into a storm of opposition and died in the Democratic-controlled Congress, even though they had been a centerpiece of the Democrats' campaign two years before. This failure, in turn, was a large reason that the Republicans, led by Gingrich, were able to take over Congress in the 1994 elections and leave Clinton on the political defensive for much of the remainder of his presidency.

Clinton's presidency demonstrated the durability of Reagan's legacy in other ways, too. Generally a neoliberal, Clinton was sympathetic to deregulation and encouraging technological change and often found himself (although sometimes reluctantly) continuing many of Reagan's policies. Most notably, he made no effort to reverse deregulation or reduce merger activity and, in fact, embraced the extension of deregulation. Clinton approved, for example, the deregulation of telecommunications and banking, and his administration did nothing to stop takeovers and mergers, such as Boeing-McDonnell Douglas and Exxon-Mobil, that dwarfed the deals of the 1980s. Clinton made a much greater commitment to free trade than had been the case under Reagan. Early in his term, he fought hard for Congressional approval of the North American Free Trade Agreement (NAFTA), and through the remainder of his presidency he worked hard for other trade liberalization agreements and to reduce barriers to trade.

Because of this, Clinton sometimes found himself in the strange position of benefiting from many of the Reagan administration policies that Democrats disliked most. By the second half of the 1990s, Reagan-style deregulated, technology-based, merger-friendly capitalism had come to be portrayed by politicians of both parties and the popular media as the answer to all economic problems, and was celebrated in terms that exceeded even Reagan's praise for free enterprise. One commentator in the *Wall Street Journal* summarized this view when he wrote in 1999 that because of the changes Reagan set in motion, "There is a new, technology-based economy roaring toward the year 2000 and . . . Americans are its primary driving force." Thrilled both by the returns they brought to ordinary Americans and the tax revenues they generated for the Treasury, Clinton was content to allow the technology and stock market booms to continue unimpeded, even though they continued to drive growth in income inequality and raised the same fears as in the late 1980s that a dangerous bubble was developing in the financial markets. Similarly, the greatest success in social policy during the 1990s, welfare reform, was based on conservative ideas dating to the Reagan years and even earlier. The Republican Congress forced Clinton to accept this in 1996, taking advantage of his election-year need to show voters that he had kept his neoliberal promise from four years earlier to fix the nation's welfare system. Finally, when the boom turned the budget deficits into surpluses during Clinton's second term, he found little support for spending on new social programs, and debates, instead, revolved around whether to use the revenues to retire debt, lower taxes, or to fund social security.[102]

Unfortunately, Reagan's successors did not learn some of the important lessons of the 1980s. This was especially the case with deregulation, where Congress and successive administrations continued to forget that even after deregulation, the remaining rules for an industry still needed to be modernized and enforced, and financial excesses curbed. Enforcement and oversight were lax in the financial industry in the late 1990s, when the technology boom and apparently ever-rising stock market combined with enthusiasm for free markets to make it politically impossible to strengthen oversight of the markets by the Securities and Exchange Commission. The results became evident early in the new century, when the financial industry was discovered to have been rife with improper accounting, questionable investment banking practices, and insider trading. Many of the highest-flying companies of the 1990s, like Cisco, were revealed to have massaged their accounting to pump up earnings figures while others, like Enron and MCI, turned out to have been engaged in gigantic frauds. Several large companies went under and, as the stock market bubble collapsed, individual Americans saw the value of their holdings shrink by trillions of dollars. The lessons remained unlearned, however, and the experience was repeated on a greater and more disastrous scale in the housing bubble and subsequent financial crisis of 2008.

As this is written, in December 2008, Barack Obama is preparing to enter the White House and commentators of all political stripes are suggesting that the long era of conservative power has come to an end. They point to economic troubles, the disgracefully high level of inequality, the un-popular war in Iraq, incompetence in government, and recurrent scandals among Republicans as evidence that conservatism is exhausted as a govern-ing philosophy. Even the *Wall Street Journal* concluded in July 2008 that these problems had created a "major challenge to the movement toward deregula-tion that has defined American governance" since the start of the Reagan era. Furthermore, in this analysis, Barack Obama's election heralds the start of a new era of liberal dominance and activist government. Perhaps so. But just as Reagan and his conservative successors left in place many of the core institutions created by their liberal predecessors, so those who follow George W. Bush will find it difficult to undo the work of almost thirty years of Reagan-style conservatism. Many of the policy proposals put forward today would raise taxes only relatively slightly, restore regulation only on the mar-gins, and maintain the main features of welfare reform; there are no serious suggestions—except in the area of health care—to go back to the levels of taxes, regulation, and social welfare that existed before1981. Thus, even as politicians claim they will bring change, much of what Reagan built will continue to stand, and guide, American politics.[103]

My thanks to Robert Collins, Mike Flamm, and James Patterson for their helpful comments and criticism of earlier drafts.

Table 1.   Federal Budget Receipts, Outlays, and Deficits, 1980–1988 (Billion \$)

Year	Receipts	Outlays	Deficit
1980	517.1	590.9	73.8
1981	599.3	678.2	78.9
1982	617.8	745.7	127.9
1983	600.6	808.3	207.7
1984	666.5	851.8	185.3
1985	734.1	946.3	212.2
1986	769.1	990.3	221.2
1987	854.1	1,003.8	149.7
1988	909.0	1,064.0	155.1
1989	990.7	1,142.6	152.0

(Figures may not add up because of rounding.)
Source: Statistical Abstract of the United States, 1992.

Table 2.   GNP Growth, Inflation, Employment, and Unemployment, 1981–1988

Year	GNP Growth (%)	Inflation (CPI, %)	Persons Employed (millions)	Unemployment (%)
1980	−0.2	13.5	99.3	7.0
1981	1.9	10.3	100.4	7.5
1982	−2.5	6.2	99.5	9.5
1983	3.6	3.2	100.8	9.5
1984	6.8	4.3	105.0	7.4
1985	3.4	3.6	107.2	7.1
1986	2.7	1.9	109.6	6.9
1987	3.4	3.6	112.4	6.1
1988	4.5	4.1	115.0	5.4
1989	2.5	4.8	117.3	5.2

Source: Statistical Abstract of the United States, 1988 and 1991.

Table 3.   Share of Aggregate Income Received by Each Fifth of Households, 1980–1988

	Percent Distribution of Aggregate Income					
Year	First Fifth	Second Fifth	Third Fifth	Fourth Fifth	Top Fifth	Top 5%
1980	4.1	10.2	16.8	24.8	44.2	16.5
1981	4.0	10.1	16.7	24.8	44.4	16.5
1982	3.9	10.0	16.5	24.6	45.0	17.0
1983	3.9	9.9	16.4	24.7	45.1	16.9
1984	4.0	9.9	16.3	24.6	45.2	17.1
1985	3.9	9.8	16.2	24.4	45.7	17.6
1986	3.8	9.7	16.2	24.3	46.1	18.1
1987	3.8	9.6	16.1	24.3	46.2	18.2
1988	3.8	9.6	16.0	24.2	46.3	18.3

Source: U.S. Bureau of the Census, *Trends in Income by Selected Characteristics: 1947 to 1988, Series P60-167* (Washington, DC, 1992).

Table 4.   Money Income of Households, 1980 and 1988, by Race (Constant 1988 dollars)

	Year	Percentage of Households in Each Income Bracket			
		0–9,999	10,000–24,999	25,000–50,000	50,000 and up
All Households	1980	18.3	31.1	35.0	15.8
	1988	17.0	28.9	33.3	20.8
White	1980	16.3	30.6	36.3	16.9
	1988	15.8	28.8	34.6	21.0
Black	1980	34.8	35.1	23.8	6.3
	1988	33.8	32.5	23.9	9.9

(Totals do not add up because of rounding.)
Source: Statistical Abstract of the United States, 1991.

NOTES

1. Reagan quoted in John Patrick Diggins, *Ronald Reagan* (New York: Norton, 2007), 385.

2. For the influences that moved Reagan toward conservatism during the 1950s, see Thomas W. Evans, *The Education of Ronald Reagan* (New York: Columbia University Press, 2006).

3. Robert Dallek, *Ronald Reagan* (Cambridge, MA: Harvard University Press, 1984, reprint 1999), 58; Hugh Heclo, "Ronald Reagan and the American Public Philosophy," in W. Elliot Brownlee and Hugh Davis Graham, eds., *The Reagan Presidency* (Lawrence: University Press of Kansas, 2003); and Diggins, *Ronald Reagan*, 51, 53.

4. For Reagan's campaign for governor, see Matthew Dallek, *The Right Moment* (New York: Free Press, 2000).

5. Jules Duscha, "Not Great, Not Brilliant, But a Good Show," *New York Times Magazine*, December 10, 1967, 29. The best history of Reagan's governorship is Lou Cannon, *Governor Reagan* (New York: Public Affairs, 2003).

6. "Reagan Nears End of Tenure With Positive Rating, Poll Finds," *Los Angeles Times*, August 27, 1974; Charles Hobbs, "How Ronald Reagan Governed California," *National Review*, January 17, 1975, 29, 42.

7. Richard Reeves, *President Reagan* (New York: Simon & Schuster), 456, 38; "Reagan Assessed as Being the Batman of Politics," *New York Times*, July 23, 1967; Jules Tygiel, *Ronald Reagan* (New York: Pearson, 2006), 167.

8. Duscha, "Good Show," 30; "Reagan Future: Which Office to Aim For?" *Los Angeles Times*, August 13, 1974; "Reagan Urges His Party to Save Itself By Declaring Its Conservative Beliefs," *New York Times*, December 16, 1976; "Weakened by Defeat, Party Is Likely to Move Further to the Right," *Wall Street Journal*, November 4, 1976; William F. Buckley Jr., "The Case Against Reagan," *National Review*, February 16,1979, 256.

9. On Reagan's professionalism and the tendency of others to underestimate him, see Cannon, *Governor Reagan*, 159–61.

10. The classic dismissal of conservatives as troubled people is Richard Hofstadter, "The Pseudo-Conservative Revolt—1954," reprinted in Richard Hofstadter, *The Paranoid Style in American Politics* (Chicago: University of Chicago Press, 1979).

11. For liberal troubles during Carter's presidency, see Burton Kaufman, *The Presidency of James Earl Carter* (Lawrence: University Press of Kansas, 1993). For a review of Carter's economic policies, see Herbert Stein, *Presidential Economics*, 3rd ed. (Washington, DC: AEI Press, 1994), chap. 6.

12. For the history of regulation and deregulation, see Thomas McGraw, *Prophets of Regulation* (Cambridge, MA: Harvard University Press, 1984); Martha Derthick and Paul Quirk, *The Politics of Deregulation* (Washington, DC: Brookings Institution, 1985); and Richard Vietor, *Contrived Competition* (Cambridge, MA: Harvard University Press, 1994).

13. "Little Impact Seen in Coast Tax Slash," *New York Times*, February 11, 1979; "Prop. 13: Change, but not Disaster," *Los Angeles Times*, June 3, 1979; "California Finding Proposition 13 Less Potent Than Was Predicted," *New York Times*, June 5, 1979; "Tax-Cut Plan Gives GOP a New Issue," *Wall Street Journal*, September 19, 1978.

14. For brief histories of the growth of the conservative movement in the 1970s, see E. J. Dionne, *Why Americans Hate Politics* (New York: Simon & Schuster, 1991); and John Micklethwait and Adrian Wooldridge, *The Right Nation* (New York: Penguin, 2004).

15. For the major ideas of the supply side and its development, see R. A. Mundell, "A Reconsideration of the Twentieth Century," *American Economic Review* 90 (June 2000): 327–40; Jude Wanniski, "It's Time to Cut Taxes," *Wall Street Journal*, December 11, 1974; Jude Wanniski, "The Mundell-Laffer Hypothesis—A New View of the World Economy," *Public Interest* (Spring 1975): 31–52; Jude Wanniski, "Taxes, Revenues, and the 'Laffer Curve,'" *Public Interest* (Winter 1978): 3–16; Paul Craig Roberts, "Supply-Side Economics," *Wall Street Journal*, February 28, 1980; "A Walk on the Supply Side," *Newsweek*, June 2, 1980, 65–66. For the unleashing of technology and the faith aspect of the supply side, see George Gilder, *Wealth and Poverty* (New York: Basic Books, 1981), chap. 21.

16. "An Interview with Ronald Reagan," *Wall Street Journal*, May 6, 1980.

17. Paul Craig Roberts, "The Economic Case for Kemp-Roth," *Wall Street Journal*, August 1, 1978; Michael Kinsley, "Alms for the Rich," *New Republic*, August 19, 1978, 19; Walter Heller, "The Kemp-Roth-Laffer Free Lunch," *Wall Street Journal*, July 12, 1978; Herbert Stein, "The Never-Never Land of Pain-Free Solutions," *Fortune*, December 31, 1979, 74; Thomas Supel, "Supply-Side Tax Cuts: Will They Reduce Inflation?" *Federal Reserve Bank of Minneapolis Quarterly Review* (Fall 1980): 1.

18. "President, Accepting Nomination, Assails GOP Program as 'Fantasy,'" *New York Times*, August 15, 1980; "Closing Statements," *New York Times*, October 29, 1980; "Displeasure with Carter Turned Many to Reagan," *New York Times*, November 9, 1980. For an analysis of the election results, see Andrew Busch, *Reagan's Victory* (Lawrence: University Press of Kansas, 2005), chap. 4.

19. Haynes Johnson, *Sleepwalking Through History* (New York: Doubleday, 1991; reprint, New York: Anchor, 1992), 14; Garry Wills, *Reagan's America* (New York: Doubleday, 1987; reprint, New York: Penguin, 1988), 447.

20. James A. Baker III, *Work Hard, Study . . . And Keep out of Politics* (New York: Putnam, 2006), 125, 171. For an evaluation of the transition period, see John Burke, "A Tale of Two Transitions: 1980 and 1988," *Congress & The Presidency* 28 (Spring 2001): 1–18.

21. Wallace Walker and Michael Reopel, "Strategies for Governance: Transition and Domestic Policymaking in the Reagan Administration," *Presidential Studies Quarterly* 16 (Fall 1986): 740; Baker, *Work Hard*, 174–75. For evaluations of the Baker-Meese-Deaver triumvirate, see Hedrick Smith, "The Presidential Troika," *New York Times Magazine*, April 19, 1981, 15ff; "The Big 3," *Washington Post*, May

24, 1981; and David Cohen, "From the Fabulous Baker Boys to the Master of Disaster: The White House Chief of Staff in the Reagan and G. H. W. Bush Administrations," *Presidential Studies Quarterly* 32 (September 2002): 463–83. For more on LSG, see Ken Collier, "Behind the Bully Pulpit: The Reagan Administration and Congress," *Presidential Studies Quarterly* 26 (Summer 1996): 805–15.

22. Mark Hertsgaard, *On Bended Knee* (New York: Farrar Straus Giroux, 1988), 23, 33; Larry Speakes, *Speaking Out* (New York: Scribner's, 1988), 220. For the Saturday radio addresses, see Robert Rowland and John Jones, "'Until Next Week': The Saturday Radio Addresses of Ronald Reagan," *Presidential Studies Quarterly* 32 (March 2002): 84–110.

23. Hertsgaard, *On Bended Knee*, 33; John Herbers, "The President and the Press Corps," *New York Times Magazine*, May 9, 1982, 45. For additional complaints of manipulation, see Tom Hamburger, "How the White House Cons the Press," *National Journal* (January 1982); 22–25; and Sidney Blumenthal, "Reagan the Unassailable," *New Republic*, September 12, 1983, 11–16.

24. Reagan, *Inaugural Address*, January 20, 1981; Reagan, *Address Before a Joint Session of the Congress on the Program for Economic Recovery*, February 18, 1981; and Reagan, *White House Report on the Program for Economic Recovery*, February 18, 1981. These and all of Reagan's presidential statements and speeches are available at the Reagan Presidential Library's website for Reagan's public papers, www.reagan.utexas.edu/archives/speeches/publicpapers.html.

25. Speakes, *Speaking Out*, 220. For an assessment of White House strategy and Reagan's personal efforts to pass his legislation, see M. Stephan Weatherford and Lorraine McDonnell, "Ronald Reagan as Legislative Advocate: Passing the Reagan Revolution's Budgets in 1981 and 1982," *Congress & the Presidency* 32 (Spring 2005): 1–29.

26. Reagan, *Address Before a Joint Session of the Congress on the Program for Economic Recovery*, April 28, 1981; Reagan, *Address to the Nation on Federal Tax Reduction Legislation*, July 27, 1981. "Rise in U.S. Optimism on Economy Bolsters Reagan Support, Poll Hints," *New York Times*, April 30, 1981; "Poll Indicates Turn Toward Optimism on Nation's Future," *New York Times*, July 1, 1981; "Public Approves of President Far More than of His Policies," *Washington Post*, June 4, 1981.

27. "Some Democrats Accuse O'Neill of a Lack of Strong Leadership," *New York Times*, April 30, 1981; John Farrell, *Tip O'Neill* (Boston: Little Brown, 2001), 546, 558; "After Two Decades, the 'Boll Weevils' Are Back, Whistling Dixie," *Washington Post*, April 26, 1981.

28. "Ship of State to Starboard," *National Review*, August 21, 1981, 938; "The President Attains Mastery at the Capitol," *New York Times*, July 30, 1981; E. J. Dionne, "Reagan Wins May Be Far-Reaching," *Washington Post*, August 13, 1981.

29. David Stockman, *The Triumph of Politics* (New York: Harper & Row, 1986), 271; "The President Fights for Credibility," *Wall Street Journal*, August 31, 1981.

30. "Five 'Gypsy Moths' Urge $20 Billion Pentagon Cut," *Washington Post*, September 4, 1981; "'Gypsy Moth' Group Plans Its Strategy," *New York Times*, October 11, 1981; "Some Tax Bill Backers Now Urge Retreat," *Washington Post*, September

22, 1981; "Supply Side: Is the Bubble Bursting?" *Washington Post*, November 9, 1981; William Greider, "The Education of David Stockman," *Atlantic*, December 1981, 38, 44; "Stockman's Views Touch Off Furor," *New York Times*, November 12, 1981; "President Promises to Hold Line on Taxes," *Washington Post*, December 28, 1981; Reagan, *The President's News Conference*, December 17, 1981.

31. Stockman, *Triumph of Politics*, 353; "Reign of Panic," *Wall Street Journal*, October 23, 1981; "Forces of Reaction," *Wall Street Journal*, December 14, 1981; Baker, *Work Hard*, 187.

32. "Reagan's Brain Drain," *Wall Street Journal*, March 25, 1982; Jack Kemp, "Talking Back to the Skeptics," *National Review*, June 11, 1982, 690. For a supply-side criticism of Stockman, see Paul Craig Roberts, "The Stockman Recession: A Reaganite's Account," *Fortune*, February 22, 1982. For the structures of Reagan-era tax increases, see Martin Feldstein, "American Economic Policy in the 1980s: A Personal View," and James Poterba, "Federal Budget Policy in the 1980s," both in Martin Feldstein, ed., *American Economic Policy in the 1980s* (Chicago: University of Chicago Press, 1994), 1–79.

33. Leslie Gelb, "The Mind of the President," *New York Times Magazine*, October 6, 1985, 23. On Reagan's political tactics, see also Martin Anderson, *Revolution* (Stanford, CA: Hoover Press, 1988), chap. 23. For Reagan's use of polls and caution in going against public opinion, see Shoon Kathleen Murray, "Private Polls and Presidential Policymaking: Reagan as a Facilitator of Change," *Public Opinion Quarterly* 70 (Winter 2006): 477–98.

34. "Most in Poll Oppose Public Worker Strikes," *New York Times*, August 16, 1981; "Harris Poll Finds Most Oppose the Air Strike," *New York Times*, August 21, 1981. For a narrative of the PATCO strike, see Herbert Northrup, "The Rise and Demise of PATCO," *Industrial and Labor Relations Review* 37 (January 1984): 167–84.

35. O'Neill quoted in Cannon, *President Reagan*, 253. For details of Stockman's proposal, see Stockman, *Triumph of Politics*, 181–93. For the Greenspan compromise, see Alan Greenspan, *The Age of Turbulence* (New York: Penguin, 2007), 94–96.

36. For examples of the complexities of deficit measurement and budget issues, see Robert Eisner and Paul Pieper, "A New View of the Federal Debt and Budget Deficits," *American Economic Review* 79 (March 1984): 11–29; and Alice Rivlin, "Reform of the Budget Process," *American Economic Review* 74 (May 1984): 133–37. On the uncertainty of the effects of the deficits, see Allan Meltzer, "Economic Policies and Actions in the Reagan Administration," *Journal of Post Keynesian Economics* 10 (Summer 1988): 537. For public and politicians' attitudes toward the deficits and alternatives for deficit reduction, see Paul Peterson, "The New Politics of Deficits," *Political Science Quarterly* 100 (Winter 1985–1986): 575–601; Andre Modigliani and Franco Modigliani, "The Growth of the Federal Deficit and the Role of Public Attitudes," *Public Opinion Quarterly* 51 (Winter 1987): 459–80; and Steven Schier, "Deficits Without End: Fiscal Thinking and Budget Failure in Congress," *Political Science Quarterly* 107 (Autumn 1992): 411–33.

37. Reagan, *Address Before a Joint Session of the Congress on the Program for Economic Recovery*, February 18, 1981; "The Burden of Economic Regulation," in *Economic Report of the President, 1983* (Washington, DC: GPO, 1983), 96.

38. "Environmental Agency: Deep and Persisting Woes," *New York Times*, March 6, 1983; "New EPA Chief Seeks More Funds," *New York Times*, December 6, 1983.

39. "Car Import Limit Eases U.S.-Japan Trade Rift," *Wall Street Journal*, May 4, 1981; "Reagan Vows to Seek Voluntary Steel Import Curbs," *Wall Street Journal*, September 18, 1984; "U.S. Steelmakers Buoyed by Reagan Plan to Seek Voluntary Restraints on Imports," *Wall Street Journal*, September 20, 1984. For the economic effects of the auto and steel quotas, see Robert Crandall, "The Effects of U.S. Trade Protection for Autos and Steel," *Brookings Papers on Economic Activity* (1987): 271–88; Stefani Lenway, Randall Morck, and Bernard Young, "Rent Seeking, Protectionism and Innovation in the American Steel Industry," *Economic Journal* 106 (March 1996): 410–21; Steven Berry, James Levinsohn, and Ariel Pakes, "Voluntary Export Restraints on Automobiles: Evaluating a Trade Policy," *American Economic Review* 89 (June 1999): 400–430.

40. "Fidelity Group Unit Speeds Banks' Entry into Discount Stock Brokerage Business," *Wall Street Journal*, June 18, 1982; "Cash Management Accounts Proliferating as Banks, Brokers Vie for People's Money," *Wall Street Journal*, November 15, 1982; Thomas Moore, "U.S. Airline Deregulation: Its Effects on Passengers, Capital, and Labor," *Journal of Law & Economics* 29 (April 1986): 1–28; Severin Borenstein, "The Evolution of U.S. Airline Competition," *Journal of Economic Perspectives*, 6 (Spring 1992): 45–73.

41. William Taylor and Leter Taylor, "Postdivestiture Long-Distance Competition in the United States," *American Economic Review*, 83 (May 1983): 185–90.

42. "The Raiders," *Business Week*, March 4, 1985, 83. For the problems of conglomerates and other corporations, see Arthur Louis, "America's New Economy: How to Manage in It," *Fortune*, June 23, 1986, 21–26; Andrei Shleifer and Robert Vishny, "Takeovers in the '60s and the '80s: Evidence and Implications," *Strategic Management Journal* 12 (1991): 51–59; and Alfred Chandler, "The Competitive Performance of U.S. Industrial Enterprises Since the Second World War," *Business History Review* 68 (Spring 1994): 1–72.

43. Henry Manne, "Mergers and the Market for Corporate Control," *Journal of Political Economy* 73 (April 1965): 113.

44. "U.S. Eases Merger Guidelines, Allowing Somewhat More Concentrated Markets," *Wall Street Journal*, June 15, 1982; "Surge in Restructuring Is Profoundly Altering Much of U.S. Industry," *Wall Street Journal*, August 12, 1985; John Newport, "A New Era of Rapid Rise and Ruin," *Fortune*, April 24, 1989, 77. For details of the workings of the junk bond and takeover markets, see Connie Bruck, *The Predators' Ball* (New York: Simon & Schuster, 1988); and James Stewart, *Den of Thieves* (New York: Simon & Schuster, 1991).

45. George Baker, "Beatrice: A Study in the Creation and Destruction of Value," *Journal of Finance* 47 (July 1992): 1108.

46. "The Raiders," *Business Week*, March 4, 1985, 82, 89; Felix Rohatyn, "On a Buyout Binge and a Takeover Tear," *Wall Street Journal*, May 18, 1984; "Surge in Company Takeovers Causes Widespread Concern," *New York Times*, July 3, 1984; "Corporate America Buys Itself Back," *New York Times*, August 17, 1986; Robert Kuttner, "The Truth About Corporate Raiders," *New Republic*, January 20, 1986, 16.

47. Myron Magnet, "Restructuring Really Works," *Fortune*, March 2, 1987, 38–46; "America's Leanest and Meanest," *Business Week*, October 5, 1987, 78. For studies of the effects of takeovers, see Clifford Winston, "Economic Deregulation: Days of Reckoning for Microeconomists," *Journal of Economic Literature* 31 (September 1993): 1284. Michael Jensen, "Takeovers: Their Causes and Consequences," *Journal of Economic Perspectives* 2 (Winter 1988): 27, 34; Andrei Shleifer and Robert Vishny, "Value Maximization and the Acquisition Process," *Journal of Economic Perspectives* 2 (Winter 1988): 17.

48. "Gulf's Managers Find Merger into Chevron Forces Many Changes," *Wall Street Journal*, December 5, 1984; "Surge in Restructuring Is Profoundly Altering Much of U.S. Industry;" "Leveraged Buyouts Make Some Companies Tougher Customers," *Wall Street Journal*, September 15, 1988; Magnet, "Restructuring Really Works."

The literature on corporate restructuring and takeovers in the Reagan years is vast. For overviews, see Sanjai Bhagat, Andrei Shleifer, and Robert Vishny, "Hostile Takeovers in the 1980s: The Return to Corporate Specialization," *Brookings Papers on Microeconomics* (1990): 1–84; and Bengt Holmstrom and Steven Kaplan, "Corporate Governance and Merger Activity in the United States: Making Sense of the 1980s and 1990s," *Journal of Economic Perspectives* 15 (Spring 2001): 121–44. For examples of corporate restructuring, see "Gulf's Managers Find Merger into Chevron Forces Many Changes," *Wall Street Journal*, December 5, 1984; "Leveraged Buyouts Make Some Companies Tougher Customers," *Wall Street Journal*, September 15, 1988; and Myron Magnet, "What Merger Mania Did to Syracuse," *Fortune*, February 3, 1986, 94–99.

49. For the S&L debacle, see R. Dan Brumbaugh and Andrew Carron, "Thrift Industry Crisis: Causes and Solutions," *Brookings Papers on Economic Activity* (1987): 349–88; and Lawrence White, "A Cautionary Tale of Deregulation Gone Awry: The S&L Debacle," *Southern Economic Journal* 59 (January 1993): 496–514.

50. "Reagan Should Not Seek Second Term, Majority Believes," *Washington Post*, September 17, 1982. Business cycle dates as reported by the National Bureau of Economic Research.

51. Reagan, *Radio Address to the Nation on the Economic Recovery Program*, January 21, 1984; Paul Craig Roberts, "'Supply-Side' Economics—Theory and Results," *Public Interest* (Fall 1988): 26; Wallace Peterson and Paul Estenson, "The Recovery: Supply-Side or Keynesian?" *Journal of Post Keynesian Economics* 7 (Summer 1985): 447–62; Meltzer, "Economic Policies and Actions," 534; Lawrence Chimerine and Richard Young, "Economic Surprises and Messages of the 1980's," *American*

Economic Review 76 (May 1986): 32; Michael Boskin, "Tax Policy and Economic Growth: Lessons from the 1980s," *Journal of Economic Perspectives* 2 (Fall 1988): 93. For a warning on the coming crisis, see Benjamin Friedman, *Day of Reckoning* (New York: Random House, 1988).

52. "Majority in Poll Prefers Complete Marine Pullout," *Washington Post*, February 17, 1984; "Torch Ignites Patriotic Response Across U.S.," *Los Angeles Times* July 2, 1984; "More Than Olympic Flame Crosses America," *New York Times*, June 10, 1984. For the recovery of confidence, see Jack Citrin and Donald Green, "Presidential Leadership and the Resurgence of Trust in Government," *British Journal of Political Science* 16 (October 1986): 431–53; and Seymour Martin Lipset and William Schneider, "The Confidence Gap During the Reagan Years, 1981–1987," *Political Science Quarterly* 102 (Spring 1987): 1–23.

53. "More Than Olympic Flame Crosses America," *New York Times*, June 10, 1984; "Torch Ignites Patriotic Response Across U.S.," *Los Angeles Times*, July 2, 1984; "Patriotism: A Movable Feast," *Los Angeles Times,* July 4, 1984.

54. Bernard Weinraub, "How Donald Regan Runs the White House," *New York Times Magazine*, January 5, 1986, 12; "Regan," *Washington Post*, February 13, 1985; Cohen, "Fabulous Baker Boys," 473; "The Stormy Siege of Don Regan," *Washington Post*, December 5, 1986.

55. Long quoted in Jeffrey Birnbaum and Alan Murray, *Showdown at Gucci Gulch* (New York: Random House, 1987; reprint, Vintage, 1988), 15. For background on the income tax system in the 1980s and the poor outlook for reform, see James Wetzler, "Tax Reform a la the Bradley-Gephardt Bill," *National Tax Journal* 37 (September 1984): 265–70; Joseph Pechman, "Tax Reform: Theory and Practice," *Journal of Economic Perspectives* 1 (Summer 1987): 11–28; and David Beam, Timothy Conlan, and Margaret Wrightson, "Solving the Riddle of Tax Reform: Party Competition and the Politics of Ideas," *Political Science Quarterly* 105 (Summer 1990): 193–95.

56. Donald Regan, *For the Record* (New York: Harcourt Brace Jovanovich, 1988), 195; John McLaughlin, "The Politics of Tax Reform," *National Review*, January 11, 1985, 23; Bruce Bartlett, "Read It and Weep," *National Review*, April 20, 1984, 38; Reagan, *Address Before a Joint Session of the Congress on the State of the Union*, January 25, 1984.

57. Baker, *Work Hard*, 217.

58. Charles McLure, "The 1986 Act: Tax Reform's Finest Hour or Death Throes of the Income Tax?" *National Tax Journal* 41 (September 1988): 303; Pechman, "Tax Reform: Theory and Practice,"17–19, 21; Edward Yorio, "Equity, Efficiency, and the Tax Reform Act of 1986," *Fordham Law Review* 55 (March 1987): 440; Joseph Pechman, "The Future of the Income Tax," *American Economic Review* 80 (March 1990): 1–20.

59. Alan Auerbach and Joel Slemrod, "The Economic Effects of the Tax Reform Act of 1986," *Journal of Economic Literature* 35 (June 1997): 589–632; Michael

Graetz, "Tax Reform Unraveling," *Journal of Economic Perspectives* 21 (Winter 2007), 72; Baker, *Work Hard*, 233.

60. "The Tax Reform of 1986: Political Implications," *New York Times*, October 23, 1986; "Reagan Rating High, Despite Problems," *San Francisco Chronicle*, September 4, 1986; Ann Dowd, "What Managers Can Learn From Manager Reagan," *Fortune*, September 15, 1986, 33; Mark Penn and Douglas Schoen, "Reagan's Revolution Hasn't Ended," *New York Times*, November 9, 1986.

61. Dowd, "What Managers Can Learn," 33.

62. "Confusion Over Iran," *New York Times*, November 20, 1986; "46% Approve Reagan's Work, Down 21 Points," *New York Times*, December 2, 1986; "New Poll Shows 47% Hold View Reagan is Lying," *New York Times*, December 10, 1986; "Americans' Confidence in Reagan is Punctured by Iran-Nicaragua Arms Scandal, Poll Shows," *Wall Street Journal*, December 5, 1986.

63. *Report of the President's Special Review Board*, February 26, 1987, IV–1; "High-Level Efforts to Replace Regan Are Reported," *New York Times*, December 11, 1986.

64. William F. Buckley Jr., "Baker's Mission," *National Review*, April 10, 1987, 61; "New Staff Chief Baker to Wield Power in a Conciliatory Way," *Wall Street Journal*, March 2, 1987; "The Baker Regency?" *Wall Street Journal*, March 2, 1987. For evaluations of Baker's performance as chief of staff, see Cohen, "From the Fabulous Baker Boys."

65. "Poll Shows Reagan Approval Rating at 4-Year Low," *New York Times*, March 3, 1987; "Majority in New Poll Still Find Reagan Lied on Iran-Contra Issue," *New York Times*, July 18, 1987; "Poll Shows Voter Optimism Is Helping Bush in the Campaign," *New York Times*, October 13, 1988.

66. Richard Vigilante, "Who's Afraid of Robert Bork," *National Review*, August 28, 1987, 25; Jonathan O'Neill, "Shaping Modern Constitutional Theory: Bickel and Bork Confront the Warren Court," *Review of Politics* 65 (Summer 2003): 333.

67. Kennedy quoted in Ethan Bronner, *Battle For Justice* (New York: W. W. Norton, 1989), 99; Anthony Lewis, "Bork and History," *New York Times*, September 10, 1987; Ronald Dworkin, "The Bork Nomination," *New York Review of Books*, August 13, 1987, reprinted in *Cardozo Law Review* 9 (October 1987): 101; "How Reagan's Forces Botched the Campaign for Approval of Bork," *Wall Street Journal*, October 7, 1987.

68. "Majority Opposes Bork, Poll Shows," *Washington Post*, October 16, 1987; Bentsen quoted in Bronner, *Battle*, 291

69. "The Bork Disaster," *National Review*, November 6, 1987, 16; "10 Senators Join Bork Opposition," *Washington Post*, October 8, 1987. On the effects of the Bork episode on the Supreme Court, see Stephen Carter, "The Confirmation Mess," *Harvard Law Review* 101 (April 1988): 1185–1201.

70. Friedman, *Day of Reckoning*, 162; Sean Wilentz, *The Age of Reagan* (New York: HarperCollins, 2008), 203, 206. For basic data on income inequality, see U.S.

Census Bureau, *Trends in Income by Selected Characteristics, 1947–1988* (Washington, DC: U.S. Government Printing Office, 1990); and U.S. Census Bureau, "A Brief Look at Postwar U.S. Income Inequality," (Washington, DC: U.S. Census Bureau, 1996). See also Thomas Edsall, "The Reagan Legacy," in Edsall and Sidney Blumenthal, eds., *The Reagan Legacy* (New York: Pantheon, 1988).

71. Brian Dumaine, "How Managers Can Succeed Through Speed," *Fortune*, February 13, 1989, 56; "Working Better and Faster With Fewer People," *Wall Street Journal*, May 15, 1987. See also Michael Porter and Victor Millar, "How Information Gives You Competitive Advantage," *Harvard Business Review* (July–August 1985): 149–62.

72. Kevin Murphy and Finis Welch, "The Structure of Wages," *Quarterly Journal of Economics* 107 (February 1992): 286. There is a vast literature on the rising demand since the 1960s for workers with greater cognitive skills. For a good introduction, see David Autor, Frank Levy, and Richard Murnane, "The Skill Content of Recent Technological Change: An Empirical Exploration," *Quarterly Journal of Economics* 118 (November 2003): 1279–333.

73. Ann Bartel and Frank Lichtenberg, "The Comparative Advantage of Educated Workers in Implementing New Technology," *Review of Economics and Statistics* 69 (February 1987): 1, 3; Marvin Kosters, "Schooling, Work Experience, and Wage Trends," *American Economic Review* 80 (May 1990): 311; Bharat Trehan, "Real Wages in the 1980s," *Federal Reserve Bank of San Francisco Weekly Letter*, November 22, 1991. See also Claudia Goldin and Lawrence Katz, "The Race Between Education and Technology: The Evolution of U.S. Educational Wage Differentials, 1890 to 2005," National Bureau of Economic Research Working Paper 12984, March 2007.

74. "Most in Poll Say They're Better Off Than in 1980," *New York Times*, August 17, 1984. For summaries of the job market in the 1980s, see Lois Plunkert, "The 1980s: A Decade of Job Growth and Industry Shifts," *Monthly Labor Review*, September 1990, 3–16; Maury Gittleman, "Earnings in the 1980s: An Occupational Perspective," *Monthly Labor Review*, July 1994, 16–27; and Neal Rosenthal, "The Nature of Occupational Employment Growth: 1983–93," *Monthly Labor Review*, June 1995, 45–54.

75. For the overall decline in discrimination, see Michael Hout, "More Universalism, Less Structural Mobility: The American Occupational Structure in the 1980s," *American Journal of Sociology* 93 (May 1988): 1358–1400. For reviews of women's progress during the Reagan years, see June O'Neill and Solomon Polachek, "Why the Gender Gap in Wages Narrowed in the 1980s," *Journal of Labor Economics* 11 (January 1993): 205–28; Eric Eide, "College Major Choice and Changes in the Gender Gap," *Contemporary Economic Policy* 12 (April 1994): 55–64; and Francine Blau, "Trends in the Well-Being of American Women, 1970–1995," *Journal of Economic Literature* 36 (March 1998): 112–65. On immigrants, see Joseph Meisenheimer, "How Do Immigrants Fare in the U.S. Labor Market?" *Monthly Labor Review*, December 1992, 3–19; Edward Funkhouser and Stephen Trejo, "The

Labor Market Skills of Recent Male Immigrants: Evidence From the Current Population Survey," *Industrial and Labor Relations Review* 48 (July 1995): 792–811; and Robert Schoeni, "New Evidence on the Economic Progress of Foreign-Born Men in the 1970s and 1980s," *Journal of Human Resources* 32 (Fall 1997): 683–717.

76. For overviews of job displacement, see Henry Farber, "The Incidence and Costs of Job Loss: 1982–91," *Brookings Papers: Microeconomics* (1993): 73–132; Richard Caves and Matthew Krepps, "Fat: The Displacement of Nonproduction Workers from U.S. Manufacturing Industries," *Brookings Papers: Microeconomics* (1993): 227–88; and Bruce Fallick, "A Review of the Recent Empirical Literature on Displaced Workers," *Industrial and Labor Relations Review* 50 (October 1996): 5–16. On poverty, see Rebecca Blank, "Why Were Poverty Rates so High in the 1980s?" National Bureau of Economic Research Working Paper 3878, October 1991.

77. "Even Profitable Firms Press Workers to Take Permanent Pay Cuts," *Wall Street Journal*, March 6, 1984; "Computers in the Office Change Labor Relations," *New York Times*, May 22, 1984. For overviews of unions' problems during the Reagan years and the impact of deregulation on organized labor, see Audrey Freedman, "How the 1980s Have Changed Industrial Relations," *Monthly Labor Review*, May 1988, 35–38; Linda Bell, "Union Concessions in the 1980s," *Federal Reserve Bank of New York Quarterly Review* (Summer 1989): 44–58; and James Peoples, "Deregulation and the Labor Market," *Journal of Economic Perspectives* 12 (Summer 1998): 111–30.

78. James Smith and Finis Welch, "Race and Poverty: A Forty-Year Record," *American Economic Review* 77 (May 1987): 152–58; June O'Neill, "The Role of Human Capital in Earnings Differences Between Black and White Men," *Journal of Economic Perspectives* 4 (Fall 1990): 25–45; Joseph Meisenheimer, "Black College Graduates in the Labor Market, 1979 and 1989," *Monthly Labor Review* (November 1990): 13–21; John Bound, "What Went Wrong: The Erosion of Relative Earnings and Employment Among Young Black Men in the 1980s," *Quarterly Review of Economics* 107 (February 1992): 201–32; and Francine Blau and Andrea Beller, "Black-White Earnings Over the 1970s and 1980s: Gender Differences in Trends," *Review of Economics and Statistics* 74 (May 1992): 276–86.

79. "Warning: The Standard of Living is Slipping," *Business Week*, April 20, 1987, 46; Barbara Ehrenreich, "Is the Middle Class Doomed?" *New York Times Magazine*, September 7, 1986, 50; Thomas Edsall, "The Return of Inequality," *Atlantic*, June 1988, 88.

80. Erik Brynjolfsson and Loren Hitt, "Beyond Computation: Information Technology, Organizational Transformation and Business Practice," *Journal of Economic Perspectives* 14 (Fall 2000): 42. On the middle class, see Michael Horrigan and Steven Haugen, "The Declining Middle-Class Thesis: A Sensitivity Analysis," *Monthly Labor Review*, May 1988, 3–13; and Mary Daly, "The 'Shrinking' Middle Class?" *Federal Reserve Bank of San Francisco Economic Letter*, March 7, 1997. For the inaccuracies of economic statistics in the Reagan years, see Daniel Slesnick, "The

Standard of Living in the United States," *Review of Income and Wealth* 37 (December 1991): 363–86; Michael Boskin, Ellen Dulberger, Robert Gordon, Zvi Griliches, and Dale Jorgenson, "Consumer Prices, the Consumer Price Index, and the Cost of Living," *Journal of Economic Perspectives* 12 (Winter 1998): 3–26; and Robert Fogel, "Catching Up with the Economy," *American Economic Review* 89 (March 1999): 1–21.

81. Data on housing, spending, vacations, and credit card debt may be found in *Statistical Abstract of the United States, 1990*. See also Kenneth Labich, "The Innovators," *Fortune*, June 6, 1988, 50–64; Eva Jacobs and Stephanie Shipp, "How Family Spending Has Changed in the U.S.," *Monthly Labor Review*, March 1990, 20–27; Maureen Gray, "Consumer Spending on Durables and Services in the 1980s," *Monthly Labor Review*, May 1992, 18–26; and Rose Rubin and Kenneth Koelin, "Elderly and Nonelderly Expenditures on Necessities in the 1980s," *Monthly Labor Review*, September 1996, 24–30; Mark Aguiar and Erik Hurst, "Measuring Trends in Leisure: The Allocation of Time Over Five Decades," *Quarterly Journal of Economics* 122 (August 2007): 989–1006.

82. "Reagan Wins Endorsement of a Major Klan Group," *New York Times*, July 31, 1980; "Race Issue in Campaign: A Chain Reaction," *New York Times*, September 27, 1980; U.S. Census Bureau, *Poverty in the United States, 1985* (Washington, DC: U.S. Census Bureau, 1987), 2; Center on Budget and Policy Priorities, "Falling Behind: A Report on How Blacks Have Fared Under Reagan," *Journal of Black Studies* 17 (December 1986): 153.

83. "Quotas in Hiring are Anathema to President Despite Minority Gains," *Wall Street Journal*, October 24, 1985; Daniel Seligman, "Affirmative Action is Here to Stay," *Fortune*, April 19, 1982, 162; Anne Fisher, "Businessmen Like to Hire by the Numbers," *Fortune*, September 6, 1985, 28. For public opinion on affirmative action, see Charlotte Steeh and Maria Krysan, "Affirmative Action and the Public, 1970–1995," *Public Opinion Quarterly* 60 (1996): 128–58.

84. William Bradford Reynolds, "The Reagan Administration and Civil Rights: Winning the War Against Discrimination," *University of Illinois Law Review* (1986): 1020; "Ward Blames Reagan for Poor Racial Climate," *New York Times*, January 20, 1988; "Wave of Conservatism Makes Life Tougher for America's Blacks," *Ebony*, January 1982, 31; Walter Leavy, "What's Behind the Resurgence of Racism in America?" *Ebony*, April 1987, 132; "Reagan Sympathetic, but Cautious on a King Holiday," *New York Times*, May 11, 1982; "President to Support King Holiday," *Washington Post*, August 6, 1983.

85. "Feminist Groups Attack Reagan Budget Cutbacks," *New York Times*, March 27, 1981; "Women Shifting Sharply Away From Reagan, Republican Party," *Washington Post*, March 29, 1982. For women's political priorities, see Robert Shapiro and Harpreet Mahajan, "Gender Differences in Policy Preferences: A Summary of Trends from the 1960s to the 1980s," *Public Opinion Quarterly* 50 (Spring 1986): 42–61; and Barbara Norrander, "The Evolution of the Gender Gap," *Public Opinion Quarterly* 63 (Winter 1999): 566–76.

86. "Poll Says Job Rating of Reagan is Moving Up," *New York Times*, February 23, 1984; "Many Who See Failure in His Policies Don't Blame Their Affable President," *New York Times*, March 2, 1984. On the post-Reagan gender gap, see Janet Box-Steffensmeier, Suzanna De Boef, and Tse-Min Lin, "The Dynamics of the Partisan Gender Gap," *American Political Science Review* 98 (August 2004): 515–28.

87. For a summary of Reagan and AIDS, see Lou Cannon, *President Reagan* (New York: Simon & Schuster, 1991), 814–19. For the fear of AIDS, see "Poll Finds Many AIDS Fears that the Experts Say Are Groundless," *New York Times*, September 12, 1985; and "AIDS Overtakes Disease of Heart as No. 2 Worry," *New York Times*, March 25, 1987. For Reagan's slow reaction, see Fred Barnes, "The Politics of AIDS," *New Republic*, November 4, 1985, 11–14; and Tina Perez and George Dionisopoulos, "Presidential Silence, C. Everett Koop, and the *Surgeon General's Report on AIDS*," *Communications Studies* 46 (Spring/Summer 1995): 18–33.

88. "Peace With American Jews Eludes Jackson," *Washington Post*, February 13, 1984; "Jackson and the Jews," *New Republic*, March 19, 1984, 9–10; "Rainbow's End," *New Republic* (April 30, 1984): 7; "Jewish Leaders Criticize Jackson; The Democrats Are Also Warned," *New York Times*, July 11, 1984. For Jackson's 1984 candidacy, see also Adolph Reed, *The Jesse Jackson Phenomenon* (New Haven, CT: Yale University Press, 1986); and Lucius Barker and Ronald Walters, eds., *Jesse Jackson's 1984 Presidential Campaign* (Urbana: University of Illinois Press, 1989).

89. For anger on social issues turning people toward conservatism during the 1970s, see Jonathan Rieder, *Canarsie* (Cambridge, MA: Harvard University Press, 1985); J. Anthony Lukas, *Common Ground* (New York: Alfred A. Knopf, 1985); Ronald Formisano, *Boston Against Busing* (Chapel Hill: University of North Carolina Press, 1991); Samuel Freedman, *The Inheritance* (New York: Simon & Schuster, 1996); and Lisa McGirr, *Suburban Warriors* (Princeton, NJ: Princeton University Press, 2001). For a history of the rise of the religious right and its activities during the Reagan years, see Matthew Moen, *The Christian Right and Congress* (Tuscaloosa: University of Alabama Press, 1989). For Reagan's relations with the religious right, see David Marley, "Ronald Reagan and the Splintering of the Christian Right," *Journal of Church and State* 48 (Autumn 2006): 851–68.

90. For estimates of the strength of the Christian right, see Michael Lienesch, "Right-Wing Religion: Christian Conservatism as a Political Movement," *Political Science Quarterly* 97 (Fall 1982): 403–25; Jeffrey Brudney and Gary Copeland, "Evangelicals as a Political Force: Reagan and the 1980 Religious Vote," *Social Science Quarterly* 65 (December 1984): 1072–79. For growing tolerance on social issues, see Tom Smith, "The Sexual Revolution," *Public Opinion Quarterly* 54 (Autumn 1990): 415–35; Michelle Dillon, "Argumentative Complexity of Abortion Discourse," *Public Opinion Quarterly* (Autumn 1993): 305–14; Alan Yang, "Trends: Attitudes Toward Homosexuality," *Public Opinion Quarterly* 61 (Autumn 1997): 477–507; and Leonie Huddy, Francis Neely, and Marily Lafay, "Trends: Support for the Women's Movement," *Public Opinion Quarterly* 64 (Autumn 2003): 309–50. For the Christian right's frustration with Reagan, see Marley, "Splintering," 866–68.

91. Emma Rothschild, "Reagan and the Real America," *New York Review of Books*, February 5, 1981, 12, 18; Andrew Hacker, "Where Have the Jobs Gone?" *New York Review of Books*, June 30, 1983, 27; Robert Kuttner, "The Declining Middle," *Atlantic*, July 1983, 64.

92. Charles Peters, "A Neoliberal's Manifest," *Washington Monthly*, May 1983, 9, 10; Paul Tsongas, "Update Liberalism or It's a 60s Relic," *New York Times*, June 30, 1980; Richard Reeves, "Old Wine in New Skins," *New York Times Book Review*, July 29, 1984, 12; Arthur M. Schlesinger Jr., "Requiem for Neoliberalism," *New Republic*, June 6, 1983, 29.

93. Felix Rohatyn, "Time for a Change," *New York Review of Books*, August 18, 1983, 47, 49. See also Robert Reich, "Playing Tag with Japan," *New York Review of Books*, June 24, 1982; Felix Rohatyn, "Alternatives to Reaganomics," *New York Times Magazine*, December 5, 1982; "The Democrats' New Guru," *Newsweek*, February 28, 1983, 61; and Sidney Blumenthal, "Drafting a Democratic Industrial Plan," *New York Times Magazine*, August 28, 1983.

94. Robert Samuelson, "The Policy Peddlers," *Harper's*, June 1983, 62; "Industrial Referendum Pits Elite Against Skeptics in Rhode Island," *Washington Post*, June 8, 1984; "A 'New Idea' Fizzles on Launch," *Washington Post*, July 15, 1984. See also Robert Z. Lawrence, "Is Trade Deindustrializing America? A Medium-Term Perspective," *Brookings Papers on Economic Activity* (1983): 129–57, and R. D. Norton, "Industrial Policy and American Renewal," *Journal of Economic Literature* 24 (March 1986): 1–40.

95. Blumenthal, "Drafting," 57.

96. "Where's the Moral Fire?" *New Republic*, October 20, 1986, 10; Felix Rohatyn, "On the Brink," *New York Review of Books*, June 11, 1987, 3; Felix Rohatyn, "Restoring American Independence," *New York Review of Books*, February 18, 1988, 8.

97. "Taking the Measure of Michael Dukakis," *Boston Globe*, March 17, 1987. For Dukakis's rise and campaign themes, see "Dukakis Gaining National Admirers," *Boston Globe* February 16, 1986; Fred Barnes, "Dukakis Rising," *New Republic*, April 14, 1986, 13–16; and Fox Butterfield, "Dukakis," *New York Times Magazine*, May 8, 1988, 22ff.

98. "Dukakis' Statement to the Public," *Boston Globe*, March 17, 1987; "'Misery Index' Sets up Challenge for Dukakis," *Washington Post*, September 19, 1988; "Transcript of the Speech by Dukakis Accepting the Democrats' Nomination," *New York Times*, July 22, 1988; "The Democrats Recast Party to Recapture Lost Suburban Vote," *Wall Street Journal*, July 19, 1988; "Campaign Ads: Emotional vs. Cerebral," *Washington Post*, September 27, 1988; "Dukakis Ads: Blurred Signs, Uncertain Path," *New York Times*, October 19, 1988.

99. Robert Dornan, "Stop Beating Around the Bush," *National Review*, November 6, 1987, 32, 33.

100. David Nyhan, "How Dukakis is Self-Destructing," *Boston Globe*, October 16, 1988; "Dukakis Asserts He Is a 'Liberal,' But in Old Tradition of His Party," *New York Times*, October 31, 1988.

101. For statistics comparing the votes in 1980, 1983, 1984, see "Voters Delay Republican Hopes of Dominance in Post-Reagan Era," *New York Times*, November 10, 1988. For a review of trends in the 1988 election, see Everett Carll Ladd, "The 1988 Elections: Continuation of the Post-New Deal System," *Political Science Quarterly* 104 (Spring 1989): 1–18.

102. George Melloan, "Yes, America Has a 'New Economy': Technology," *Wall Street Journal*, September 21, 1999.

103. "Amid Turmoil, U.S. Turns Away From Decades of Deregulation," *Wall Street Journal*, July 25, 2008. For summaries of the case for the end of the conservative era, see Sean Wilentz, "Sunset in America," *New Republic*, May 7, 2008, 24–26; and E. J. Dionne, "Capitalism's Reality Check," *Washington Post*, July 11, 2008.

1

EXCERPTS FROM "INAUGURAL ADDRESS" (JANUARY 20, 1981)

Senator Hatfield, Mr. Chief Justice, Mr. President, Vice President Bush, Vice President Mondale, Senator Baker, Speaker O'Neill, Reverend Moomaw, and my fellow citizens:

To a few of us here today this is a solemn and most momentous occasion, and yet in the history of our nation it is a commonplace occurrence. The orderly transfer of authority as called for in the Constitution routinely takes place, as it has for almost two centuries, and few of us stop to think how unique we really are. In the eyes of many in the world, this every-4-year ceremony we accept as normal is nothing less than a miracle. . . .

The business of our nation goes forward. These United States are confronted with an economic affliction of great proportions. We suffer from the longest and one of the worst sustained inflations in our national history. It distorts our economic decisions, penalizes thrift, and crushes the struggling young and the fixed-income elderly alike. It threatens to shatter the lives of millions of our people.

Idle industries have cast workers into unemployment, human misery, and personal indignity. Those who do work are denied a fair return for their labor by a tax system which penalizes successful achievement and keeps us from maintaining full productivity.

But great as our tax burden is, it has not kept pace with public spending. For decades we have piled deficit upon deficit, mortgaging our future and our children's future for the temporary convenience of the present. To continue this long trend is to guarantee tremendous social, cultural, political, and economic upheavals. . . .

The economic ills we suffer have come upon us over several decades. They will not go away in days, weeks, or months, but they will go away. They will go away because we as Americans have the capacity now, as we've had in the past, to do whatever needs to be done to preserve this last and greatest bastion of freedom.

In this present crisis, government is not the solution to our problem; government is the problem. From time to time we've been tempted to believe that society has become too complex to be managed by self-rule, that government by an elite group is superior to government for, by, and of the people. Well, if no one among us is capable of governing himself, then who among us has the capacity to govern someone else? All of us together, in and out of government, must bear the burden. The solutions we seek must be equitable, with no one group singled out to pay a higher price.

We hear much of special interest groups. Well, our concern must be for a special interest group that has been too long neglected. It knows no sectional boundaries or ethnic and racial divisions, and it crosses political party lines. It is made up of men and women who raise our food, patrol our streets, man our mines and factories, teach our children, keep our homes, and heal us when we're sick—professionals, industrialists, shopkeepers, clerks, cabbies, and truck drivers. They are, in short, "We the people," this breed called Americans. . . .

So, as we begin, let us take inventory. We are a nation that has a government—not the other way around. And this makes us special among the nations of the Earth. Our government has no power except that granted it by the people. It is time to check and reverse the growth of government, which shows signs of having grown beyond the consent of the governed.

It is my intention to curb the size and influence of the Federal establishment and to demand recognition of the distinction between the powers granted to the Federal Government and those reserved to the States or to the people. All of us need to be reminded that the Federal Government did not create the States; the States created the Federal Government.

Now, so there will be no misunderstanding, it's not my intention to do away with government. It is rather to make it work—work with us, not over us; to stand by our side, not ride on our back. Government can and must provide opportunity, not smother it; foster productivity, not stifle it. . . .

It is no coincidence that our present troubles parallel and are proportionate to the intervention and intrusion in our lives that result from unnecessary and excessive growth of government. It is time for us to realize that we're too great a nation to limit ourselves to small dreams. We're not, as some would have us believe, doomed to an inevitable decline. I do not believe in a fate that will fall on us no matter what we do. I do believe in a fate that will fall on us if we do nothing. So, with all the creative energy at our command, let us begin an era of national renewal. Let us renew our determination, our courage, and our strength. And let us renew our faith and our hope.

We have every right to dream heroic dreams. Those who say that we're in a time when there are not heroes, they just don't know where to look. You can see heroes every day going in and out of factory gates. Others, a handful in number, produce enough food to feed all of us and then the world beyond. You meet heroes across a counter, and they're on both sides of that counter. There are entrepreneurs with faith in themselves and faith in an idea who create new jobs, new wealth and opportunity. They're individuals and families whose taxes support the government and whose voluntary gifts support church, charity, culture, art, and education. Their patriotism is quiet, but deep. Their values sustain our national life. . . .

Can we solve the problems confronting us? Well, the answer is an unequivocal and emphatic "yes." To paraphrase Winston Churchill, I did not take the oath I've just taken with the intention of presiding over the dissolution of the world's strongest economy.

The Public Papers of President Ronald W. Reagan, Reagan Presidential Library, www .reagan.utexas.edu/archives/speeches/1981/12081a.htm (accessed December 17, 2008).

2

EXCERPTS FROM "ECONOMIC REPORT OF THE PRESIDENT" (1985)

Competition plays a particularly important role in the market for control of publicly traded corporations. . . .

These corporations are generally owned by stockholders who delegate substantial decisionmaking authority to a group of hired managers. Managers make the corporation's investment, pricing, production, and research and development decisions, and are primarily responsible for the corporation's success or failure. Typically, managers own a relatively small percentage of the firm's shares . . .

The delegation of authority from stockholders to management is not, however, without risk to stockholders and the economy at large. In particular, the delegation creates a possibility that management will operate the corporation in management's best interests, and not in the best interests of the corporation's stockholders. Such divergences of interest can result because stockholders are concerned primarily with maximizing the value of their shares, while managers' incentives are often more complex and can involve assurances of continued employment by an independent, publicly traded corporation.

These divergent incentives can give rise to an agency problem within the corporation—a situation in which managers are poor agents for their stockholders because they do not act in the stockholders' best interests . . .

In particular, a management team may believe that it is maximizing the value of the corporation when, in fact, it is not. Under these circumstances, management will not change corporate strategy on its own accord. Moreover, unless stockholders independently conclude that corporate performance can be improved by changing management teams, and unless some stockholders mount an expensive proxy contest to oust incumbent management, a change in corporate strategy is unlikely to occur. The labor market for management services can thereby allow a corporation to continue to be controlled by an entrenched management that does not maximize the value of the corporation's shares.

Under these circumstances, the external market for corporate control provides an important set of checks and balances. In this market, bidders directly approach stockholders and offer to purchase the corporation's shares at a premium above market price. These bidders often install new management in the event their bid succeeds. In some cases the bid is made directly by a new management team that believes it can improve the target corporation's performance. . . .

Contests for corporate control are part of a larger merger and acquisition process that plays an important role in the economy's adjustment to changing market circumstances. . . .

. . . Mergers and acquisitions are responses to new opportunities created by deregulation. Deregulation in the banking, finance, insurance, transportation, brokerage, and investment industries has opened new opportunities for distribution economies, as well as economies of scope that can be achieved by mergers and acquisitions. . . .

A significant percentage of recent merger and acquisition activity thus appears to be related to competitive pressures to adapt to new market conditions. Accordingly, any policy that would influence merger and acquisition activity must recognize the valuable role these transactions play in allowing industries to adapt to changing circumstances and the costs that can be imposed by inhibiting such responses. . . .

The evidence is overwhelming that successful takeovers substantially increase the wealth of stockholders in target companies. Although estimates of the magnitude of the wealth increase vary, recent studies find average gains in the range of 16 to 34 percent of the targets' shares. . . .

The evidence is strong that takeovers generate aggregate net benefits to the economy. Although many potential sources of gain from these transactions can be identified, it is difficult to quantify the size of the gain that results from particular sources.

Production and distribution economies are one source of gain, particularly in transactions involving firms in related industries. An acquisition can also generate economies of scale and create opportunities for more efficient forms of distribution and contracting . . .

Substantial gains can also result when a takeover causes assets to be shifted to higher valued uses. A retail chain may, for example, possess real estate that is more valuable as office sites than retail outlets . . .

Improved management is another possible source of gain from mergers and acquisitions. Evidence suggests that the stock price of target firms tends to fall over long periods before a takeover attempt is announced. These firms may be disfavored by the market because they suffer from poor management. Takeovers of these firms can discipline managements and impose new corporate strategies in place of unsuccessful ones.

Economic Report of the President: 1985, chap. 6, fraser.stlouisfed.org/publications/ERP/ issue/1388/download/5873/ERP1985_Chapter6.pdf (accessed December 17, 2008).

3

EXCERPT FROM "WALTER MONDALE'S SPEECH ACCEPTING THE DEMOCRATIC NOMINATION" (JULY 19, 1984)

. . . Thank you very, very much. My fellow Democrats, my fellow Americans:
I accept your nomination.

. . . In 1980, Ronald Reagan beat the pants off us.

So tonight, I want to say something to those of you across the country who voted for Ronald Reagan—Republicans, independents, and yes, some Democrats:

I heard you. And our party heard you.

After we lost, we didn't tell the American people that they were wrong. Instead, we began asking you what our mistakes had been.

And for four years, I listened to all of the people of our country. I traveled everywhere. It seemed like I had visited very acre of America. . . .

We are wiser, stronger, and we are focused on the future. If Mr. Reagan wants to rerun the 1980 campaign, fine. Let them fight over the past. We're fighting for the American future—and that's why we're going to win this campaign.

One last word, one last word to those of you who voted for Mr. Reagan.

I know what you were saying. But I also know what you were NOT saying.

You did not vote for $200 billion deficits.

You did not vote for an arms race.

You did not vote to turn the heavens into a battleground.

You did not vote to savage Social Security and Medicare. . . .

Four years ago many of you voted for Mr. Reagan because he promised that you'd be better off. And today, the rich are better off. But working Americans are worse off, and the middle class is standing on a trap door. . . .

Here's the truth about the future: we are living on borrowed money and borrowed time. These deficits hike interest rates, clobber exports, stunt investment, kill jobs, undermine our growth, cheat our kids, and shrink our future.

Whoever is inaugurated in January, the American people will have to pay Mr. Reagan's bills. The budget will be squeezed. Taxes will go up. And anyone who says they won't is not telling the truth to the American people.

I mean business. By the end of my first term, I will reduce the Reagan deficit by two-thirds.

Let's tell the truth. That must be done, it must be done. Mr. Reagan will raise taxes, and so will I. He won't tell you. I just did.

There's another difference. When he raises taxes, it won't be done fairly. He will sock it to average-income families again, and he'll leave his rich friends alone. And I won't stand for it and neither will you and neither will the American people.

To the corporations and the freeloaders who play the loopholes and pay no taxes, my message is: Your free ride is over.

To the Congress, my message is: We must cut spending and pay as we go. If you don't hold the line, I will. That's what the veto is for.

Now that's my plan to cut the deficit. Mr. Reagan is keeping his plan secret until after the election. That's not leadership; that's salesmanship and I think the American people know the difference.

"Transcript of Mondale Address Accepting Party Nomination," *New York Times*, July 20, 1984.

4

"REMARKS ANNOUNCING THE NOMINATION OF ROBERT H. BORK TO BE AN ASSOCIATE JUSTICE OF THE SUPREME COURT OF THE UNITED STATES" (JULY 1, 1987)

Well, it's with great pleasure and deep respect for his extraordinary abilities that I today announce my intention to nominate United States Court of Appeals Judge Robert H. Bork to be an Associate Justice of the Supreme Court. Judge Bork is recognized as a premier constitutional authority. His outstanding intellect and unrivaled scholarly credentials are reflected in his thoughtful examination of the broad, fundamental legal issues of our times. When confirmed by the Senate as an appellate judge in 1982, the American Bar Association gave him its highest rating: "exceptionally well qualified." On the bench, he has been well prepared, evenhanded, and openminded [sic].

In taking this action today, I'm mindful of the importance of this nomination. The Supreme Court of the United States is the custodian of our Constitution. Justices of the Supreme Court must not only be jurists of the highest competence; they must be attentive to the specific rights guaranteed in our Constitution and proper role of the courts in our democratic system.

Judge Bork, widely regarded as the most prominent and intellectually powerful advocate of judicial restraint, shares my view that judges' personal preferences and values should not be part of their constitutional interpretations. The guiding principle of judicial restraint recognizes that under the Constitution it is the exclusive province of the legislatures to enact laws and the role of the courts to interpret them. We're fortunate to be able to draw upon such an impressive legal mind, an experienced judge and a man who already has devoted so much of his life to public service. He'll bring credit to the Court and his colleagues, as well as to his country and the Constitution.

Justice Lewis Powell, in announcing his retirement, said the courts should not be hampered by operating at less than full strength. And with this in mind, I urge the Senate to expedite its consideration of Judge Bork so the Court will have nine Justices when its October term begins. And I have every expectation that it will do so.

The Public Papers of President Ronald W. Reagan, Reagan Presidential Library, www .reagan.utexas.edu/archives/speeches/1987/070187c.htm (accessed December 17, 2008).

5

EXCERPTS FROM "NOMINATION OF ROBERT H. BORK TO BE AN ASSOCIATE JUSTICE OF THE SUPREME COURT, COMMITTEE ON THE JUDICIARY, UNITED STATES SENATE" (SEPTEMBER 15, 1987)

OPENING STATEMENT OF ROBERT H. BORK

. . . This is in large measure a discussion of judicial philosophy, and I want to make a few remarks at the outset on that subject of central interest.

That is, my understanding of how a judge should go about his or her work. That may also be described as my philosophy of the role of a judge in a constitutional democracy.

The judge's authority derives entirely from the fact that he is applying the law and not his personal values. That is why the American public accepts the decisions of its courts, accepts even decisions that nullify the laws a majority of the electorate or of their representatives voted for.

The judge, to deserve that trust and that authority, must be every bit as governed by law as is the Congress, the Presidency, the State Governors and legislatures, and the American people. No one, including a judge, can be above the law. Only in that way, will justice be done and the freedom of Americans assured.

How should a judge go about finding the law? The only legitimate way, in my opinion, is by attempting to discern what those who made the law intended. The intentions of the lawmakers govern, whether the lawmakers are the Congress of the United States enacting a statute or whether they are those who ratified our Constitution and its various amendments.

Where the words are precise and the facts simple, that is a relatively easy task. Where the words are general, as is the case with some of the most profound protections of our liberties—in the Bill of Rights and in the Civil War Amendments—the task is far more complex. It is to find the principle or value that was intended to be protected and to see that it is protected.

As I wrote in an opinion for our court, the judge's responsibility "is to discern how the framers' values, defined in the context of the world they knew, apply in the world we know."

If a judge abandons intention as his guide, there is no law available to him and he begins to legislate a social agenda for the American people. That goes well beyond his legitimate power . . .

. . . When a judge goes beyond this and reads entirely new values into the Constitution, values the framers and ratifiers did not put there, he deprives the people of their liberty. That liberty, which the Constitution clearly envisions, is the liberty of the people to set their own social agenda through the process of democracy. . . .

My philosophy of judging, Mr. Chairman, as you pointed out, is neither liberal nor conservative. It is simply a philosophy of judging which gives the Constitution a full and fair interpretation but, where the Constitution is silent, leaves the policy struggles to the Congress, the President, the legislatures and executives of the 50 States and the American people.

STATEMENT OF SENATOR EDWARD M. KENNEDY

Indeed, it has been said that the Supreme Court is the umpire of the federal system because it has the last word about justice in America. Above all, therefore, a Supreme Court nominee must possess the special quality that enables a justice to render justice. This is the attribute whose presence we describe by the words such as fairness, impartiality, open-mindedness, and judicial temperament, and whose absences we call prejudice or bias.

. . . Time and again, in his public record over more than a quarter of a century, Robert Bork has shown that he is hostile to the rule of law and the role of the courts in protecting individual liberty.

He has harshly opposed—and is publicly itching to overrule—many of the great decisions of the Supreme Court that seek to fulfill the promise of justice for all Americans.

He is instinctively biased against the claims of the average citizen and in favor of concentrations of power, whether that is governmental or private. . . .

It is easy to conclude from the public record of Mr. Bork's published views that he believes women and blacks are second-class citizens under the Constitution. He even believes that, in the relation to the executive, Members of Congress are second-class citizens, yet he is asking the Senate to confirm him. . . .

In Robert Bork's America, there is no room at the inn for blacks and no place in the Constitution for women, and in our America there should be no seat on the Supreme Court for Robert Bork.

Mr. Bork has been equally extreme in his opposition to the right to privacy. In an article in 1971, he said, in effect, that a husband and wife have no greater right to privacy under the Constitution than a smokestack has to pollute the air.

President Reagan has said that this controversy is pure politics, but that is not the case. I and others who oppose Mr. Bork have often supported nominees to the Supreme Court by Republican presidents, including many with whose philosophy we disagree. I voted for the confirmation of Chief Justice Burger and also Justices Blackmun, Power, Stevens, O'Connor, and Scalia. But Mr. Bork is a nominee of a different stripe. President Reagan has every right to take Mr. Bork's reactionary ideology into account in making the nomination, and the Senate has every right to take that ideology into account in acting on the nomination.

Senate Committee on the Judiciary, *Nomination of Robert H. Bork to Be Associate Justice of the Supreme Court of the United States*, 100th Congress, first sess., September 15, 1987.

6

EXCERPTS FROM "FAREWELL ADDRESS TO THE NATION" (JANUARY 11, 1989)

My fellow Americans:

This is the thirty-fourth time I'll speak to you from the Oval Office and the last. We've been together eight years now, and soon it'll be time for me to go. But before I do, I wanted to share some thoughts, some of which I've been saving for a long time. . . .

It's been quite a journey this decade, and we held together through some stormy seas. And at the end, together, we are reaching our destination.

The fact is, from Grenada to the Washington and Moscow summits, from the recession of '81 to '82, to the expansion that began in late '82 and continues to this day, we've made a difference. The way I see it, there were two great triumphs, two things that I'm proudest of. One is the economic recovery, in which the people of America created—and filled—nineteen million new jobs. The other is the recovery of our morale. America is respected again in the world and looked to for leadership.

Something that happened to me a few years ago reflects some of this. It was back in 1981, and I was attending my first big economic summit, which was held that year in Canada. The meeting place rotates among the member countries. The opening meeting was a formal dinner for the heads of government of the seven industrialized nations. Now, I sat there like the new kid in school and listened, and it was all Francois this and Helmut that. They dropped titles and spoke to one another on a first-name basis. Well, at one point I sort of leaned in and said, "My name's Ron." Well, in that same year, we began the actions we felt would ignite an economic comeback—cut taxes and regulation, started to cut spending. And soon the recovery began.

Two years later, another economic summit with pretty much the same cast. At the big opening meeting we all got together, and all of a sudden, just for a moment, I saw that everyone was just sitting there looking at me. And then one of them broke the silence. "Tell us about the American miracle," he said.

Well, back in 1980, when I was running for President, it was all so different. Some pundits said our programs would result in catastrophe. Our views on foreign affairs would cause war. Our plans for the economy would cause inflation to soar and bring about economic collapse. I even remember one highly respected economist saying, back in 1982, that "The engines of economic growth have shut down here, and they're likely to stay that way for years to come." Well, he and the other opinion leaders were wrong. The fact is, what they called "radical" was really "right." What they called "dangerous" was just "desperately needed."

And in all of that time I won a nickname, "The Great Communicator." But I never thought it was my style or the words I used that made a difference: it was the content. I wasn't a great communicator, but I communicated great things, and they didn't spring full bloom from my brow, they came from the heart of a great nation—from our experience, our wisdom, and our belief in the principles that have guided us for two centuries. They called it the Reagan revolution. Well, I'll accept that, but for me it always seemed more like the great rediscovery, a rediscovery of our values and our common sense.

Common sense told us that when you put a big tax on something, the people will produce less of it. So, we cut the people's tax rates, and the people produced more than ever before. The economy bloomed like a plant that had been cut back and could now grow quicker and stronger. Our economic program brought about the longest peacetime expansion in our history: real family income up, the poverty rate down, entrepreneurship booming, and an explosion in research and new technology. We're exporting more than ever because American industry became more competitive and at the same time, we summoned the national will to knock down protectionist walls abroad instead of erecting them at home. . . .

The lesson of all this was, of course, that because we're a great nation, our challenges seem complex. It will always be this way. But as long as we remember our first principles and believe in ourselves, the future will always be ours. And something else we learned: Once you begin a great movement, there's no telling where it will end. We meant to change a nation, and instead, we changed a world.

Countries across the globe are turning to free markets and free speech and turning away from the ideologies of the past. For them, the great rediscovery of the 1980s has been that, lo and behold, the moral way of government is the practical way of government: Democracy, the profoundly good, is also the profoundly productive.

When you've got to the point when you can celebrate the anniversaries of your thirty-ninth birthday you can sit back sometimes, review your life, and see it flowing before you. For me there was a fork in the river, and it was right in the middle of my life. I never meant to go into politics. It wasn't my intention when I was young. But I was raised to believe you had to pay your way for the blessings bestowed on you. I was happy with my career in the entertainment world, but I ultimately went into politics because I wanted to protect something precious.

Ours was the first revolution in the history of mankind that truly reversed the course of government, and with three little words: "We the People." "We the People" tell the government what to do; it doesn't tell us. "We the People" are the driver; the government is the car. And we decide where it should go, and by what route, and how fast. Almost all the world's constitutions are documents in which governments tell the people what their privileges are. Our Constitution is a document in which "We the People" tell the government what it is allowed to do. "We the People" are free. This belief has been the underlying basis for everything I've tried to do these past eight years.

But back in the 1960s, when I began, it seemed to me that we'd begun reversing the order of things—that through more and more rules and regulations and confiscatory taxes, the government was taking more of our money, more of our options, and more of our freedom. I went into politics in part to put up my hand and say, "Stop." I was a citizen politician, and it seemed the right thing for a citizen to do.

I think we have stopped a lot of what needed stopping. And I hope we have once again reminded people that man is not free unless government is limited. There's a clear cause and effect here that is as neat and predictable as a law of physics: As government expands, liberty contracts. . . .

And that's about all I have to say tonight, except for one thing. The past few days when I've been at that window upstairs, I've thought a bit of the "shining city upon a hill." The phrase comes from John Winthrop, who wrote it to describe the America he imagined. What he imagined was important because he was an early Pilgrim, an early freedom man. He journeyed here on what today we'd call a little wooden boat; and like the other Pilgrims, he was looking for a home that would be free. . . .

And how stands the city on this winter night? More prosperous, more secure, and happier than it was eight years ago. But more than that: After two hundred years, two centuries, she still stands strong and true on the granite ridge, and her glow has held steady no matter what storm. And she's still a beacon, still a magnet for all who must have freedom, for all the pilgrims from all the lost places who are hurtling through the darkness, toward home.

We've done our part. And as I walk off into the city streets, a final word to the men and women of the Reagan revolution, the men and women across America who for eight years did the work that brought America back. My friends: We did it. We weren't just marking time. We made a difference. We made the city stronger, we made the city freer, and we left her in good hands. All in all, not bad, not bad at all.

And so, goodbye, God bless you, and God bless the United States of America.

The Public Papers of President Ronald W. Reagan, Reagan Presidential Library, www .reagan.utexas.edu/archives/speeches/1989/011189i.htm (accessed December 17, 2008).

THE REAGAN PRESIDENCY AND FOREIGN POLICY: CONTROVERSIES AND LEGACIES

Michael W. Flamm

It was a moment of high drama and high stakes, witnessed by one hundred million viewers, the largest political audience in American history. In October 1980, one week before Election Day, the presidential candidates met face-to-face in Cleveland for the first and only time. Polls indicated that the race was too close to call. Both candidates knew the debate would prove critical. For the incumbent, Democrat Jimmy Carter, it was a last chance to persuade the American people that he deserved four more years in office despite an economy wracked by high inflation and unemployment. For the challenger, Republican Ronald Reagan, it was a final opportunity to persuade the voters that he was a rational and responsible leader, not an elderly extremist bent on nuclear confrontation with the Soviet Union.

During the campaign, Carter had repeatedly depicted Reagan as a conservative ideologue and warmonger who would launch "a massive nuclear arms race" that would represent a "serious threat to the safety and the security and the peace of our nation and of the world."[1] In the debate, the president pressed the same line of argument. But Reagan deflected it with a smile and a shrug. "There you go again," he implied in an amiable and genial manner honed by decades of practice in front of live audiences, radio microphones, and movie cameras. In a calm and confident manner, he also responded in his closing statement with a devastating series of rhetorical questions. The most famous was "Are you better off than you were four years ago?" But equally important were the questions that followed: "Is America as respected throughout the world as it was? Do you feel that our security is as safe? That we're as strong as we were four years ago?"[2]

For most voters, the answer to all of the above was no. The dark shadow cast by the Vietnam War continued to linger. The nation seemed adrift and vulnerable, buffeted by events beyond control. In 1979, four in particular reinforced the widespread unease that Americans were no longer the masters of their fate or the destiny of the world. In January, Islamic radicals inspired by the Ayatollah Khomeini forced into exile the shah of Iran, a repressive ruler but also a close friend of the United States and a crucial foe of Soviet expansionism in the oil-rich Persian Gulf. In July, a political coalition of liberals and leftists deposed the anti-Communist dictator Anastazio Somoza in Nicaragua, which soon fell under the control of the more radical Sandinista rebels. In November, less than two weeks after Carter had permitted the shah to come to New York for cancer treatment, student militants seized the American embassy in Tehran and took sixty-six American hostages, most of whom remained in captivity a year later. And in December the Soviets invaded Afghanistan in what a somber Carter called "the most serious threat to the peace since the Second World War."[3]

Americans debated the larger significance of these ominous and troubling international developments. Liberals tended to see them as confirmation that the country had entered an "age of limits," symbolized by the energy crises of the 1970s that had sapped economic strength. The emergence of rivals like Japan and Europe also contributed to economic anxiety. Nor could the United States arrogantly assume that it had the military power and moral stature to do what it wished when it wished, not in the ignominious aftermath of the Vietnam War. The days of acting alone had come to an end. Now the United States would have to accept and accommodate the needs and interests of other nations. In 1976, Carter appeared to endorse this view when he declared that it was time to make human rights, not national security, the litmus test of international relations.

Conservatives rejected this position, which they saw as unduly defeatist. On the contrary, the United States remained—for the moment at least—the indispensable nation, with the military might and moral right to act as it saw fit whenever vital interests were at stake. Ever confident, Reagan also believed that in the coming decades there was no way the Soviets could win the Cold War and no limit to what Americans could achieve if they demonstrated psychological resolve and political determination, if they made national security *the* national priority. In a 1982 address to the British Parliament, he called for a "crusade for freedom" and contended that "given strong leadership, time, and a little bit of hope, the forces of good ultimately rally and triumph over evil." (See "Excerpts from 'Address to Members of the British Parliament.'")

In retrospect, it is possible to exaggerate the differences between Carter and Reagan. Both were products of the Cold War, although the invasion of Afghanistan seemed to surprise Carter, who initially held a more accommodating view of the Soviets. Both men were ultimately determined to rebuild the nation's military strength, although Carter had entered office promising significant cutbacks in defense spending. Both were consumed by the need to free Americans held hostage by Islamic militants in the Middle East, which led each of them to pursue disastrous policies, whether it was Carter's abortive rescue attempt in April 1980 or Reagan's later involvement in the Iran-Contra scandal. Both leaders saw political issues in moral terms and had a religious sense of national purpose, although Carter tended to emphasize the internal sins of racism and materialism, whereas Reagan stressed the external threat of Communism. America was, he believed, a chosen nation blessed by God and bestowed with a sacred mission to spread the light of liberty to the corners of the earth.

But on Election Day in November 1980, voters saw a clear difference and made a clear choice. In the days after the debate, the race became a rout as Reagan won the popular vote by a large margin (51 percent to 41 percent) and the electoral vote by an overwhelming margin (489–49). The outcome was a resounding repudiation of Carter's leadership. Even his support among Democratic voters plummeted. Yet it was also a ringing response to Reagan's personality. His unrelenting optimism—his dismissal of doubt and faith in the future—resonated with most Americans more than his conservative principles. It was "no accident that Reagan rose to power at a moment when there was a rising wave of intellectual pessimism," wrote conservative columnist George Will years later. "The man and the moment had met."[4]

The election of Reagan marked a decisive turning point in American foreign relations. The rise of conservatives left liberals and moderates on the sidelines, unable to dictate national policy. Liberals, who since Vietnam had sought to restrict American power and reduce American commitments overseas, no longer had a firm institutional base because the Democratic Party was in disarray after the defection of millions of members to Reagan. Moderates, who had championed arms control and mutual accommodation with the Soviet Union, no longer dominated the Republican Party. The era of détente—when both parties in the 1970s supported a relaxation of tensions with Moscow—had ended. The conservative moment had arrived. Reagan was now prepared to challenge the conventional wisdom of both liberals and moderates. But whether he was ready or able to assume the mantle of leadership was a point of contention.

Liberals and many moderates viewed Reagan as unqualified and un-prepared to handle foreign affairs because his executive experience was limited to his two terms as governor of California from 1966 to 1974. Of equal concern was his apparent lack of interest in studying the complexities of international relations or mastering the details of arms control (he supposedly expressed surprise and dismay when informed that it was not possible to recall nuclear missiles once launched). As the oldest president ever elected, Reagan also seemed intellectually and physically unfit for office, especially after he was shot in an assassination attempt in March 1981. To detractors he had a disconcerting proclivity for naps (even during cabinet meetings), a disturbing penchant for anecdotes (often culled from questionable sources like *Reader's Digest*), and a distressing pattern of confusing fact and fiction (especially if he had said or seen it in a film). Critics frequently depicted the president as a likable lightweight or amiable airhead. During the 1980 campaign, the political cartoon *Doonesbury* featured a controversial series titled "In Search of Reagan's Brain." During the Iran-Contra scandal, the television program *Saturday Night Live* aired a satiric sketch in which comedian Phil Hartman parodied Reagan's image by portraying him as a leader who was decisive in private but acted befuddled in public because it best served his ulterior motives.

By contrast, conservatives and some moderates were confident that, regardless of appearances, Reagan was capable of meeting the challenges at hand. An experienced negotiator, he would bring to the bargaining table with the Soviet Union the practical lessons he had learned as a labor leader in Hollywood from the late 1940s to early 1960s—not to mention his tenure as California governor. For decades Reagan was also a regular reader of, and contributor to, serious conservative journals like *Human Events* and *National Review*. And from 1974 to 1980, when he was out of public office, he wrote more than a thousand radio addresses, most of which addressed foreign and defense policy. These demonstrated, according to Reagan's supporters, that he was ideologically consistent—not intellectually lazy—and physically capable of sustained study when motivated by the political moment and engaged by the briefing materials. Above all, Reagan instinctively grasped the need to develop and explain a few large ideas repeatedly until the public—or audience as he saw it—understood and accepted them.

In foreign affairs, Reagan had four overarching principles. The first was his assertive and abiding anti-Communism, which had deep personal, moral, and political roots. As an actor, he had faced verbal assaults and physical threats from radical activists in the film industry who sought to intimidate him. As a Christian, Reagan saw Communism as immoral because it denied the existence of the Almighty and the freedom of individuals to practice their faith. In the struggle against the Soviets, he also believed he was God's instrument, selected to serve God's will and execute God's plan.

As a capitalist, Reagan viewed Communism as impractical because it ignored the economic power of self-interest and inefficient because it could not meet the material desires of ordinary citizens. "Sometimes I think Adam and Eve must have been Russian," he often joked. "They didn't have a roof over their heads, nothing to wear, only one apple between them, and they called it paradise."[5] Capitalism, by contrast, unleashed the entrepreneurial energies of ambitious individuals, who reaped the rewards and spread the wealth. In the long run, therefore, Reagan was confident that capitalism was destined to triumph and Communism was doomed to defeat. It was, he informed a radio audience in May 1975, "a form of insanity—a temporary aberration which will one day disappear from the earth because it is contrary to human nature."[6] But in the short run, Soviet expansion and aggression—whether in Western Europe, Central Asia, or Latin America—posed a direct threat to national survival and international peace.

To meet the threat, Reagan articulated a second principle—peace through strength, not through a piece of paper (as he often liked to quip). In the 1970s, he claimed, the United States had fallen dangerously behind the Soviet Union in military might and defense spending. After a decade of neglect, a window of vulnerability had opened in which the Soviets might launch a surprise first strike that would cripple America's nuclear deterrent and leave it with the bitter choice of surrender or die. Whether in fact the Soviet Union had achieved strategic superiority—or even parity—was a matter of debate, especially among liberals, but not to conservatives like Reagan. In his view, the time had come to rebuild America's arsenal, to develop and deploy new bombers and missiles, tanks and planes, as soon as possible no matter the cost. It was imperative, he asserted, to send a message to friend and foe that the United States would spend whatever was necessary and never "accept second place in the arms race."[7]

The third principle Reagan espoused was strong opposition to arms talks with the Soviets unless they fundamentally altered their behavior or until the United States could negotiate from a position of superiority. Liberals may have believed that peaceful coexistence was possible and mutual disarmament was desirable, but conservatives were certain that the policy of détente, which had led to arms control agreements in the 1970s, was a mistake. According to Reagan, accommodation was appeasement—it had not worked with Fascism in the 1930s, as the Nazi invasion of Poland had shown, and it would not work with Communism in the 1980s, as the

Soviet invasion of Afghanistan demonstrated. Force was the only language the Communists understood. Reagan also harbored a deep distrust of Soviet leaders. Even if a real reformer appeared, which was doubtful, what assurances would the United States have that he had the authority to make—or, more important, keep—any agreements he negotiated? And what would happen when he was eliminated or removed from office?

The final principle Reagan advocated was the right and duty of the president, as commander in chief, to exercise American power when and where he deemed it proper and essential. He was determined to lift or loosen what he saw as unconstitutional restrictions placed on executive authority by the legislative branch after the Vietnam War, which he viewed as a "noble cause."[8] To restore the "imperiled presidency," Reagan also sought to dispel the lingering effects of the "Vietnam syndrome," which conservatives believed had weakened the resolve of the United States to use force and enabled the Soviet Union to make gains across the globe in the 1970s. By contrast, liberals opposed what they saw as an effort to revive the "imperial presidency." After all, it had led inexorably to the Vietnam quagmire, which in their view was a tragic mistake. More generally, liberals contended that the political legitimacy of military intervention depended upon multilateral support from international institutions such as the United Nations. Conservatives like Reagan, however, responded that unilateral action with or without international approval was often necessary and appropriate in the defense of freedom.

Freedom was the cornerstone of what became known as the "Reagan Doctrine," although the administration never formally adopted it.[9] "Freedom is not the sole prerogative of a chosen few; it is the universal right of all God's children," he declared in his 1985 State of the Union message. "Our mission is to nourish and defend freedom and democracy, and to communicate these ideals everywhere we can. . . . We must stand by all our democratic allies. And we must not break faith with those who are risking their lives—on every continent, from Afghanistan to Nicaragua—to defy Soviet-supported aggression and secure rights which have been ours from birth."[10] The words were a shot across the bow of the Brezhnev Doctrine, named after Soviet leader Leonid Brezhnev, who ruled the Kremlin from 1964 to 1982. In essence, it pledged that once a country fell under Communist control it would remain under Communist control. The Reagan Doctrine made it clear that the administration was determined to confront—not merely contain—the Soviet empire.

Implementing the Reagan Doctrine would, however, prove far more difficult than declaring it. Obstacles abounded, some external and some internal. Abroad, the United States faced strong opposition in Western Europe when it sought to deploy a new generation of cruise missiles to counter Soviet weapons. At home, the nuclear freeze movement staged mass rallies to protest the administration's policies, especially when Reagan announced plans in 1983 to develop the Strategic Defense Initiative (SDI), also known as "Star Wars." In the White House, major differences on policy matters divided the president's staff, which agreed on the end—the eventual defeat of Soviet Communism—but tended to differ on the means.

Secretary of Defense Caspar Weinberger, who had served with Reagan in California, adamantly opposed both diplomatic talks with the Soviet Union and military intervention unless there were clear objectives, a clear "exit strategy," and clear support from the president as well as the public. Secretary of State George Shultz, who joined the administration in 1982, was in favor of arms negotiation and saw little point in having a powerful military if the United States was never willing to deploy it. Both men were, however, in agreement that covert action was of limited use—in contrast to Central Intelligence Agency (CIA) director William Casey, who believed it could tilt the balance in the conflict with Communism. At the same time, the constant turnover in personnel, including six national security advisers in eight years, made continuity of policy a challenge and raised questions of who was in charge. Secretary of State Alexander Haig, whom Shultz replaced in 1982, wrote in his memoirs, "The White House was as mysterious as a ghost ship; you heard the creak of the rigging and the groan of the timbers and sometimes even glimpsed the crew on deck. But which of the crew had the helm?"[11]

The implication was unfair, for without a doubt the captain of the ship was Reagan, a man of firm conviction and broad vision. At times these qualities were a source of strength, as when he decided—against the advice of many advisers and most conservatives—to place his faith in Mikhail Gorbachev and pursue peace with the Soviet Union. At others they were a source of weakness, as when he directly or indirectly encouraged officials with the National Security Council to circumvent the law in an effort to free the hostages in Lebanon and aid the Contras in Nicaragua. But at no time was Reagan a prisoner of his staff, contrary to what many critics contended. Although he often delegated details to aides, particularly on matters not of personal interest, he was determined and diligent in his focus on those issues that meant the most to him.

In foreign affairs, some skeptics have depicted Reagan as the unwitting beneficiary of good fortune, as when Iran freed the embassy hostages on Inauguration Day in January 1981, perhaps because it wished to embarrass

Carter, perhaps because it feared what the new president might do. Other detractors have described him as the "Teflon president," who passively drifted from crisis to crisis, assuming credit and avoiding blame at every turn. But shortly after he left the White House, Reagan defended his record in terms he knew best. "I had an agenda I wanted to get done," he said with pride. "I had a script."[12] Truly he had, for better or worse. Yet at critical moments he also improvised, refusing to let the script dictate his performance in what an astute biographer has aptly called "the role of a lifetime."[13]

THE COLD WAR—FIRST TERM

From the start of his presidency, Reagan was determined to set an aggressive tone toward the Soviet Union. At his first press conference on January 29, 1981, nine days after the inauguration, he said the Communists viewed and treated détente as a "one-way street." The president added that "the only morality they recognize is what will further their cause, meaning they reserve unto themselves the right to commit any crime, to lie, to cheat . . . and we operate on a different set of standards."[14] Earlier that same day, the State Department sent a "sharp message" to the Soviet Union warning of "dire consequences" if it intervened militarily in Poland, where the Communist government faced mass protests organized by a trade union. Led by a shipyard electrician named Lech Walesa, Solidarity had mobilized millions of workers and represented the most powerful challenge to Soviet domination in Eastern Europe since the uprising in Czechoslovakia in 1968. To lend support, the administration directed the Central Intelligence Agency (CIA) to funnel money and supplies—including photocopiers for underground newspapers—to Solidarity covertly via the Catholic Church and trade unions in Western Europe. The White House also imposed economic sanctions after the Polish government declared martial law, and it offered moral encouragement via Radio Free Europe and the Voice of America. The president's actions were widely appreciated in Poland. When a French magazine surveyed Polish tourists about who was the "last hope" for their country, Reagan received more votes than Walesa and trailed only Polish-born Pope John Paul II and the Virgin Mary.[15]

Soon after the first presidential press conference, confrontation briefly gave way to conciliation. In April 1981, Reagan fulfilled a campaign promise and lifted the grain embargo President Carter had imposed on the Soviet Union in response to the invasion of Afghanistan. Despite strong opposition from the State Department, Reagan also wrote a personal, handwritten letter to Soviet leader Leonid Brezhnev. "Is it possible that we have permitted ideology, political and economic philosophies, and governmental policies to keep us from considering the very real, everyday problems of peoples?" he asked. He then noted that when the United States had unquestioned atomic and economic dominance at the end of World War II, it had sought to repair and rebuild the war-torn world, not seek dominion over it. "It is in this spirit," he concluded, "in the spirit of helping the people of both our nations, that I have lifted the grain embargo."[16] The letter had little effect. But it was an unfiltered window into Reagan's mindset and suggests that he was more open in his approach toward the Soviet Union than many liberals or conservatives might like to concede, although his appeal would not bear fruit for years.

In the meantime, the White House initiated a major expansion of the conventional arsenal and a complete modernization of the nuclear arsenal, which rested on a strategic triad of land-based missiles, submarine-launched missiles, and air-launched missiles from manned bombers. Carter had already increased the defense budget, but Reagan took it to new heights, although as a percentage of the Gross National Product (GNP) it remained substantially below what Dwight Eisenhower had spent in the 1950s, when the Cold War was in full force, and what John Kennedy and Lyndon Johnson had spent in the 1960s, when the United States was embroiled in the Vietnam War. The massive buildup of the 1980s, unprecedented for peacetime, nevertheless resulted in more ships and Trident submarines for the navy, more missiles and B-1 bombers for the air force, and more soldiers and Abrams tanks for the army. It also strengthened Reagan's reputation as a tough anti-Communist, which in turn gave the conservative Republican the political cover to negotiate with Moscow that a liberal Democrat would never have had.

The defense buildup meant, moreover, a boost in American confidence and a blow to Soviet confidence as well as the Soviet economy. The latter consideration was critical. From the outset Reagan saw military spending as a win-win proposition—it would strengthen the United States and weaken the Soviet Union, which could not afford to match American expenditures. The Soviets, he told a reporter in October 1981, "cannot vastly increase their military productivity because they've already got their people on a starvation diet." More cuts in consumer goods might lead to public unrest. Here Reagan was repeating conservative wisdom from the 1960s. As *National Review* associate editor and CIA consultant James Burnham had predicted four decades earlier, the superiority of capitalism to socialism made an arms race "probably the most effective form of political-economic warfare we can conduct against our enemy."[17] In due course the Soviet system would buckle under the strain, leading to economic crisis and political discontent. Thus an arms race was not an unnecessary evil, as most liberals believed. On the contrary, it was a positive good that in time would contribute to the collapse of Communism.

But when would it? The consensus across the political spectrum was that the Soviet Union was not on the verge of failure. Most liberals agreed because they wished to promote the idea of peaceful coexistence. Most conservatives agreed because they wished to promote the need for a strong defense. "To be sure, the Soviet system is beset by serious weaknesses," Secretary of State George Shultz advised Reagan. "But it would be a mistake to assume that the Soviet capacity for competition with us will diminish at any time during your presidency."[18] In a similar vein, the liberal scholar Arthur Schlesinger Jr. warned, "Those in the United States who think the Soviet Union is on the verge of economic collapse, ready with one small push to go over the brink, are . . . only kidding themselves."[19] If so, then perhaps it was Reagan who had the last laugh.

The intent of the White House was to wage economic warfare against the Soviet Union with oil as the weapon of choice. In October 1981, the administration courted controversy when it announced that it would sell planes equipped with Airborne Warning and Control Systems (AWACS) to Saudi Arabia as part of the largest foreign arms deal in history to date. Critics portrayed the sale as threatening to Israel and destabilizing to the Middle East. But Reagan saw it as an opportunity to improve relations with Saudi Arabia, which subsequently increased the production of oil. As a result, the price of a barrel dropped sharply by the mid-1980s. In the United States, inflation fell and the GNP rose. But the decline in oil prices cost the Soviet Union, an energy exporter, billions of dollars a year in hard currency, which forced it to cancel the purchase of millions of tons of American grain and slow the production of consumer goods. To maintain economic pressure, the White House also banned technology transfers to the Soviet Union and delayed Kremlin plans to build a natural gas pipeline to Western Europe. The "small push" Schlesinger had suggested had become a hard shove.

In November 1981, Reagan went on the offensive at the bargaining table. In a speech to the National Press Club, he expressed his dismay at the Soviet military buildup and disappointment with the Strategic Arms Limitation Talks (SALT) of the 1970s. In their place, he suggested that the United States and the Soviet Union begin Strategic Arms Reduction Talks (START). As an opening proposal, he announced that his administration would cancel the planned deployment of intermediate-range Pershing II and Tomahawk nuclear missiles in Western Europe if Moscow would remove the intermediate-range SS-20 nuclear missiles already targeted on West Germany, Britain, and France. If accepted, the "zero-zero option" would have immediately eliminated all intermediate-range nuclear forces (INF) in Europe—an appealing vision that reassured America's allies in Bonn, London, and Paris, who feared both nuclear war and nuclear blackmail if the Soviet Union's INF advantage was not redressed.

But the offer was one-sided in favor of the United States. It required that the Soviets remove existing missiles while the Americans had only to promise not to deploy new ones. It made no mention of British and French nuclear weapons, and it left untouched sea-launched and air-launched missiles, two sides of the American nuclear triad, while it concentrated on land-based missiles, the foundation of Soviet nuclear defenses. In sum, the offer was a nonstarter, a nonnegotiable proposal that Moscow was bound to reject. This dismayed liberals and reassured conservatives, who worried that a weakened American nuclear shield would lead to an emboldened Soviet Red Army, whose numerically superior conventional forces (soldiers, tanks, and artillery) caused grave concern. But Reagan remained undaunted. "Wherever there is oppression, we must strive for the peace and security of individuals as well as states," he declared on behalf of the human rights of political prisoners in the Soviet bloc. He added, "There is no reason why people in any part of the world should have to live in permanent fear of war or its specter."[20]

By 1982 the specter of nuclear war had mobilized a mass transatlantic movement dedicated to achieving a nuclear freeze—a mutual and verifiable halt by the United States and the Soviet Union on the testing, production, and deployment of all nuclear weapons. It was a simple alternative to the complex reality of the arms race. Conservatives condemned the nuclear freeze as simplistic and dangerous, a threat to national and international security because it would leave the military forces of the United States at a permanent disadvantage. But liberals portrayed it as a moral imperative. As the economist John Kenneth Galbraith stated, "It's the question, after all, of whether we, our children, and our grandchildren live."[21] Soon the idea had won the support of dozens of municipal, county, and state governments as well as 128 members of the House, 17 members of the Senate, and 238 Catholic bishops. In June, the movement held a huge rally in Central Park, where a crowd estimated at seven hundred thousand (the largest political demonstration in American history) rallied in support of the freeze. Two years later, Governor Mario Cuomo of New York elicited wild cheers at the

Democratic Convention when he proclaimed "the utter insanity of nuclear proliferation and the need for a nuclear freeze, if only to affirm the simple truth that peace is better than war because life is better than death." (See "Excerpts from 'Addresses . . . the Democratic National Convention.'")

As the nuclear freeze rally in New York took place in June 1982, Reagan was in Europe meeting with foreign leaders who had to contend with domestic opposition as well. In Rome, he met with the pope, who agreed to let the CIA use secret Vatican bank accounts to channel money to the Solidarity Movement. In London, the president met with British Prime Minister Margaret Thatcher, a personal friend and political ally. Then he gave an important address to Parliament in which he alluded to the "revolutionary crisis" faced by the Soviet Union at home and in Poland. At the same time, Reagan acknowledged the threat of nuclear war and the appeal of the freeze movement. "Must civilization perish in a hail of fiery atoms?" he asked. "Must freedom wither in a quiet, deadening accommodation with totalitarian evil?" His answer was a resounding no. On the contrary, he predicted that "the march of freedom and democracy . . . will leave Marxism-Leninism on the ash-heap of history as it has left other tyrannies which stifle the freedom and muzzle the self-expression of the people." (See "Excerpts from 'Address to Members of the British Parliament.'")

To promote the march of freedom, the White House in January 1983 issued National Security Decision Directive (NSDD) 75, which renounced the concept of peaceful coexistence with the Soviet Union and stated that henceforth American policy would consist of three main elements. The first was "internal pressure" to weaken Soviet society by promoting human rights and economic warfare. The second was reciprocal negotiations intended to ease or eliminate "outstanding disagreements." In a memo to the president, Shultz called for "an intensified dialogue with Moscow to test whether an improvement in the U.S.-Soviet relationship is possible." The secretary of state, an unflappable and pragmatic man who ultimately encouraged arms negotiations with the Soviet Union, was not optimistic. But in the case of failure, at least "the onus will rest clearly on Moscow; if it leads to actual improvement, all the better."[22] Few inside or outside the White House expected that it would.

The third element of NSDD 75 was "external resistance" to Soviet imperialism. The CIA was already secretly supporting the mujahideen in Afghanistan, a cause that—unlike aid to the Contras in Nicaragua—enjoyed broad bipartisan support in Washington. But in Kabul the mission was in trouble because the Red Army outgunned the Islamic guerrillas, "who don't stand the slightest chance of winning" according to a *Washington Post* columnist. He added, pessimistically, that "Afghanistan is not the Soviet version of Vietnam."[23] But in 1985 the White House doubled aid to the mujahideen, who now received long-range sniper rifles, wire-guided anti-tank missiles, and, most critical of all, shoulder-fired surface-to-air Stinger missiles. These weapons—especially the Stingers, which destroyed hundreds of Soviet helicopter gunships—turned the tide of battle. By the time the last of the Soviet soldiers had withdrawn in 1989, almost twenty thousand had died, more than one hundred thousand had suffered severe wounds, and hundreds of thousands of bitter and alienated veterans were back at home, adrift in civilian society. In the end, the war in Afghanistan was a wound from which the Soviet empire could not recover. But in the longer term it would also have unforeseen and unintended consequences for the United States, as shocked Americans would discover on September 11, 2001.

Two months after NSDD 75 appeared, Reagan directly challenged the political wisdom of the freeze movement and the moral legitimacy of the Soviet Union. In a March 1983 speech to evangelical Christians, he criticized the nuclear freeze as a "dangerous fraud" akin to "simple-minded appeasement" or "wishful thinking." Peace through strength was the only path to security. "I would agree to a freeze if only we could freeze the Soviets' global desires," he stated. Then, in the most famous phrase from the address, the president called the Soviet Union "the focus of evil in the modern world" and an "evil empire," although it was on the road to extinction. "I believe that Communism is another sad, bizarre chapter in human history whose last pages even now are being written," he concluded. "I believe this because the source of our strength in the quest for human freedom is not material, but spiritual." (See "Excerpts from 'Address to the Annual Convention of the National Association of Evangelicals.'") Liberals were outraged by the speech, particularly the overt appeals to prayer and faith. Among the adjectives used to denounce it were primitive and dangerous. It was, asserted historian Henry Steele Commager bluntly, "the worst presidential speech in American history, and I've read them all."[24]

Reagan was undeterred. Later in March 1983 he offered a stunning announcement that caught even Shultz, Secretary of Defense Caspar Weinberger, and the Joint Chiefs of Staff largely by surprise: The United States intended to abandon the traditional policy of nuclear deterrence based on the established doctrine of mutual assured destruction (MAD). To replace the balance of terror, which had so far averted nuclear war, the White House planned to construct a space-based system of rockets, satellites, and lasers that would destroy incoming missiles before they could detonate on American soil. The president termed the proposed nuclear shield the Strategic Defense Initiative

(SDI). Critics immediately and derisively labeled it "Star Wars"—a reference to the immensely popular 1977 science fiction film featuring a mythic confrontation between good (Luke Skywalker) and evil (Darth Vader). But Reagan welcomed the opportunity to end reliance on MAD once and for all. "It was like having two westerners standing in a saloon aiming their guns at each other's head—permanently," he wrote in his memoir. "There had to be a better way."[25]

In the search for a better way, SDI appealed on many levels to Reagan, who unlike most conservatives saw a nuclear exchange as fundamentally unwinnable. The defense shield reflected his optimism that the superior technology of the United States could turn swords into plowshares. In a personal appeal that he wrote himself, Reagan implored American scientists "to turn their great talents now to the cause of mankind and world peace, to give us the means of rendering these nuclear weapons impotent and obsolete."[26] SDI also reflected his fear and faith as an evangelical Christian that nuclear war might signal the coming of Armageddon, when Christ and his followers would confront an evil empire led by the anti-Christ in a final battle for the soul of humanity. And it reflected his love of science fiction and Hollywood films. As an actor in *Murder in the Air* (1940), Reagan had played Secret Service agent Brass Bancroft, who had to protect a secret weapon called the "Inertia Projector" that disabled enemy planes. As a fan of *Torn Curtain* (1966), he supposedly recalled with pleasure a line uttered by scientist Paul Newman, who promised that "we will produce a defensive weapon that will make all nuclear weapons obsolete, and thereby abolish the terror of nuclear warfare."[27]

The basis of Reagan's commitment to SDI remains cloudy. Legend has it that as governor of California in 1967 he visited Lawrence Livermore Laboratory, where Edward Teller, the famous physicist and controversial creator of the hydrogen bomb, impressed upon him the scientific possibilities of missile defense. Legend also has it that in 1979 Reagan toured the North American Aerospace Defense Command (NORAD) in Colorado and was shocked to learn that the air force had no defense against even a single incoming Soviet missile. But since the mid-1970s conservatives had contended that the Soviets were in violation of the Anti-Ballistic Missile (ABM) treaty of 1972, which reinforced MAD by prohibiting both nations from developing either land-based or space-based nuclear defenses. In 1980 the Republican platform had explicitly rejected the doctrine of MAD and demanded "research and development of an effective anti-ballistic missile system, such as is already at hand in the Soviet Union."[28]

Critics both inside and outside the administration had deep doubts about SDI. While Weinberger was a believer, Shultz was a skeptic who worried that it violated the ABM treaty and jeopardized arms negotiations with the Soviet Union, which reacted with predictable alarm and anger. "Was it science fiction, a trick to make the Soviet Union more forthcoming," wondered General Secretary Mikhail Gorbachev later, "or merely a crude attempt to lull us in order to carry out the mad enterprise—the creation of a shield which would allow a first strike without fear of retaliation?"[29] Meanwhile, liberals contended that SDI would extend the arms race into outer space and was technically unfeasible—most scientists agreed that no system would ever achieve close to a 100 percent success rate, making it essentially useless since one or two undestroyed missiles could kill tens of millions, and as of 2009 it remains effectively untested and unproven. Detractors also claimed that SDI was financially and politically irresponsible, more likely to squander billions of dollars and destabilize relations with the Soviet Union than promote world peace, even though Reagan had pledged to share the technology once it was developed. In a March 1983 editorial titled "Nuclear Facts, Science Fictions," the *New York Times* described SDI as "a pipe dream, a projection of fantasy into policy."[30]

But Reagan's determination to follow his dream was unshakable, in part because it was a way to cut the "Gordian knot" of nuclear weapons, in part because he feared the consequences if the Soviets pursued the possibility on their own, which he and other conservatives believed they were already doing. "I wonder why some of our own carping critics who claim SDI is an impractical wasted effort don't ask themselves, if it's no good how come the Russians are so upset about it?" he wrote to a retired Marine Corps general. He also refused to think of SDI as a way to undercut the freeze movement or bankrupt the Soviet Union. Nor would he use it as leverage in negotiations with the Kremlin, which supportive advisers like Robert McFarlane of the National Security Council (NSC) had assumed was his intention from the start. In personal letters to a close friend, Reagan stressed that SDI was not a "bargaining chip" and that he had "never entertained a thought that it was."[31] But regardless of what he intended, SDI ultimately became a psychological, technological, and financial challenge that the Soviets could not face or flee.

Despite or perhaps because of Reagan's promotion of SDI, a nuclear confrontation with the Soviet Union seemed like a realistic—and terrifying—possibility in the fall of 1983. In September, the Soviets shot down a South Korean airliner with 269 civilians aboard, including 61 Americans. At first the Reagan administration claimed it was an act of murderous aggression; later the White House realized it was shocking evidence of extreme incompetence. "If anything," Reagan wrote later, the incident "demonstrated how close the world had come to the precipice. If . . . the Soviet pilots simply mistook the airliner for a military plane, what kind of imagination did it take to think of a Soviet military man with his finger close to a nuclear push button making an even more tragic mistake?"[32]

In October 1983, the president viewed an advance screening of *The Day After*, an ABC television film that dramatized the aftermath of a nuclear attack on Lawrence, Kansas. "It is powerfully done . . . and left me greatly depressed," commented Reagan in his diary. "My own reaction was one of our having to do all we can to have a deterrent and to see there is never a nuclear war."[33] When aired in November, *The Day After* attracted an audience of one hundred million—and the next day a poll in the *Washington Post* showed that 83 percent of those surveyed supported a nuclear freeze. Meanwhile, North Atlantic Treaty Organization (NATO) forces simulated a nuclear scenario in a large-scale military exercise codenamed "Able Archer 83." But many Soviets feared that it was a clever cover for an actual assault. In December, CIA director William Casey warned the president that Moscow perceived a serious threat of war.

Others were equally troubled. In January 1984, the editors of the *Bulletin of Atomic Scientists* moved the setting of the Doomsday Clock to three minutes from midnight (it had stood at seven minutes prior to Reagan's election in November 1980). In the White House, political advisers worried about the potential impact of American-Soviet tensions on the president's reelection. Nancy Reagan began to express apprehension about her husband's historical legacy. The stage was set for a dramatic twist in the plot that almost no one expected, with the possible exception of Reagan himself, who had always left open the door to negotiations and now had the support of pragmatists like Shultz. A turning point in the Cold War had arrived, although most were slow to recognize it.

Reagan signaled the new direction in a televised speech to the American people in January 1984. He first emphasized that the United States was in a strong position: "Our defenses are being rebuilt, our alliances are solid, and our commitment to defend our values has never been more clear." Then the president stressed that his top priority was to reduce the risk of war through "a policy of credible deterrence, peaceful competition, and constructive cooperation." Finally, he introduced two couples—Jim and Sally, Ivan and Anya—who if somehow brought together would soon discover that their common concerns outweighed their ideological differences. "Above all, they would have proven that people don't make wars," Reagan said. "People want to raise their children in a world without fear and without war." (See "Excerpts from 'Address to the Nation and Other Countries on United

States–Soviet Relations.'") The conciliatory tone was in sharp contrast to the confrontational mood of September 1983, when the president had written to a retired admiral that "I have never believed in any negotiations with the Soviets that we could appeal to them as we would to people like ourselves."[34]

The change attracted little attention at first. The Soviets took little notice and Democrats gave it little credit. At the Democratic Convention in June 1984, Massachusetts Senator Edward Kennedy was scathing in his criticism of Reagan's election-year conversion from arms-control adversary to advocate. "The voters will not forget Ronald Reagan's real and perilous views on the nuclear issue," said Kennedy. "He intends to spend billions on 'Star Wars' in outer space, and that is why we must send him back to Hollywood, which is where both 'Star Wars' and Ronald Reagan really belong." Whereas the Republican president would accelerate "an arms race that could end the human race," the Democratic nominee, former Vice President Walter Mondale, would agree to a nuclear freeze. (See "Excerpts from Addresses . . . the Democratic National Convention.") But the words were in vain—in November Reagan won in a landslide.

After the election, Reagan received a stroke of good fortune. In November 1982, Brezhnev died after eighteen years as Soviet leader. He was replaced by Yuri Andropov, who died in February 1984 of kidney failure. His successor was Konstantin Chernenko, another geriatric who barely lasted a year. Reagan would later remark, only half in jest, that he would have begun to negotiate sooner with the Soviets if only their leaders had not kept dying on him. The death of Chernenko led to the appointment of Mikhail Gorbachev as general secretary of the Communist Party in March 1985 amid an economic crisis exacerbated by American pressure. A relatively young and vigorous official from a collective farm family, he eventually came to believe that radical reform was essential if the Soviet Union were to survive. Unlike many of his predecessors, he also read and traveled widely. As deputy general secretary, he met in London with Thatcher, who found him refreshingly different from past Soviet leaders. "I like Mr. Gorbachev," she said. "We can do business together."[35] Thatcher relayed her assessment to Reagan, who heeded her advice. At last he had found a partner for peace, although it would take him two years to realize it.

THE MIDDLE EAST AND THE GRENADA INVASION

Ronald Reagan experienced on October 23, 1983, what he would later describe as "the saddest day of my presidency, perhaps the saddest day of my life."[36] In the early hours of a Sunday morning, a radical Shiite suicide bomber crashed a delivery truck packed with high explosives into the main barracks of the American compound at the Beirut airport. The sentries on duty could not respond in time because, under the rules of engagement then in place, their weapons were not locked and loaded. In the rubble and debris, 241 servicemen died, most of them Marines who were asleep. The bombing in Lebanon was—and remains—the deadliest single attack on American military personnel stationed overseas since the Battle of Iwo Jima during World War II. It was also the highest death toll for a single day since the Tet Offensive during the Vietnam War.

In the White House, the dismay and despair were palpable. As Colin Powell, who at the time was Secretary of Defense Caspar Weinberger's military aide, recalled, "Each of my calls was like a physical blow to the secretary. Eighty bodies pulled out. A hundred. A hundred and fifty."[37] Neither man would ever forget the experience, which reinforced their resolve not to place American troops in harm's way when the objectives of the mission—in this case to act as peacekeepers in a nation wracked by civil war and foreign interference—were ambiguous at best. For his part, the tragedy in Lebanon left Reagan "in a state of grief, made almost speechless by the magnitude of the loss."[38] The shock waves from the Beirut bombing, which intelligence sources linked to Hezbollah ("Party of God"), a terrorist organization with close ties to Iran, would reverberate for the remainder of his presidency.

It was in the Middle East that the limitations of the Reagan Doctrine would emerge most starkly. The overarching goal of the United States was to forge a "strategic consensus" between the Arabs and the Israelis to prevent the Soviet Union from gaining influence in the region. The underlying reality was that a variety of factors made the formation of an effective anti-Communist alliance unlikely under any circumstances. The rise of Islamic fundamentalism pitted moderates against extremists and threatened to destabilize pro-American regimes in Egypt and Saudi Arabia. The conflict between Arabs and Jews over Palestine simmered until 1987, when a popular uprising known as the Intifada erupted in the West Bank and Gaza Strip. The war between Iraq and Iran, which raged from 1980 to 1988, featured Muslims killing Muslims as secular and religious Sunnis and Shiites battled for regional dominance.

Compounding these geopolitical fissures were two other issues. First, the terrorism sponsored by countries like Libya and groups like Hezbollah made the murder of civilians, whether Christian, Jewish, or Muslim, a commonplace event, adding to the instability and volatility of the Middle

East. Second, the weight of the past added to the turmoil of the present. "It's a region where hate has roots reaching back to the dawn of history," observed a rueful Reagan in his memoir. "It's a place where the senseless spilling of blood in the name of religious faith has gone on since biblical times, and where modern events are forever being shaped by momentous events of the past, from the Exodus to the Holocaust."[39] The Middle East was a place where for centuries dreams of peace had died, replaced by visions of martyrdom. The 1980s would prove no exception.

The cycle of violence escalated in June 1982, when the Israeli army under the command of General Ariel Sharon invaded Lebanon. Since the 1970s the Palestinian Liberation Organization (PLO), led by Yasser Arafat, had used Lebanon as a base of operations from which to launch raids and fire mortars on Israel. In 1981, the United States brokered a ceasefire between the combatants, but a year later it collapsed after the Israeli ambassador to Great Britain was assassinated in London. The Israeli army then occupied southern Lebanon and bombarded West Beirut, inflicting heavy casualties on Palestinian fighters but also harming many civilians and inciting widespread criticism. In August 1982, the Reagan administration announced that Israel had agreed to a truce. The White House also declared that eight hundred Marines would join a multinational force (MNF) to keep the peace, oversee the evacuation of the PLO from Beirut, and ensure the security of civilians living in refugee camps. After Arafat departed, the MNF withdrew from Lebanon.

The White House next sought to seize the diplomatic initiative. After prior consultation with Egypt, Jordan, and Saudi Arabia, the Reagan administration in September 1982 unveiled a peace plan carefully calibrated to strike a balance between the security needs of the Israelis and the political aspirations of the Palestinians. The Israelis would freeze all settlements in the West Bank and Gaza Strip—the occupied territories—and abandon any plans to annex them. The Palestinians would reject the authority of the PLO—which would play no role in the negotiations—and abandon any ambitions of independent statehood. Instead, the West Bank and Gaza Strip would become part of Jordan, which in turn would grant the Palestinians some degree of political autonomy. In the United States, the plan won praise from most liberals and moderates, who saw it as a fair and just solution.

But in the Middle East the Reagan proposal was dead on arrival. Both the Palestinians and the Israelis—who were not consulted in advance—were outraged. Neither side viewed the compromises as acceptable or reasonable. "We have been betrayed by the Americans," fumed Israeli Prime Minister

Menachem Begin, who had exchanged many personal letters with the president. "It's the biggest betrayal since the State was established. They have stabbed us in the back. We now have a completely different fight on our hands."[40] The initiative went nowhere and the administration elected to put the Palestinian question on the back burner, where it remained for the next five years, until the Intifada brought renewed attention to the plight of the Palestinians in the occupied territories.

Meanwhile, the crisis in Lebanon simmered. In September 1982, President-elect Bashir Gemayel, a conservative Christian with whom Israel hoped to have good relations, was assassinated, probably by agents of Syria, whose forces were also stationed in Lebanon. In response, Christian militia entered the Sabra and Shatila refugee camps—with Israeli permission—and massacred hundreds if not thousands of Palestinian men, women, and children. The exact number remains a matter of dispute. Later in the month, Gemayel's brother was elected president and the MNF returned to Lebanon in an effort to restore order. Nevertheless, tensions remained high and the situation remained tenuous.

In April 1983, a suicide bomber believed to have ties to Hezbollah and Iran drove a delivery van loaded with high explosives into the American Embassy in Beirut. More than sixty people were killed, including several of the best Middle East officers in the Central Intelligence Agency (CIA). At the time, it was the deadliest attack on a U.S. diplomatic mission in history. In August, Begin resigned as prime minister, and in September the Israeli army withdrew from the high ground overlooking the Beirut airport. Soon the American compound came under mortar fire from Muslim militia, who objected to American support for the Christian militia. In response, the U.S. battleship *New Jersey* shelled the Muslim positions, killing Lebanese civilians, reinforcing the perception that the Marines were not neutral peacekeepers, and making them prime targets for revenge.

By the end of September 1983, polls indicated that a majority of the public approved of Reagan's performance in office—except when it came to Lebanon. "The people just don't know why we're there," the president noted in his diary.[41] After the barracks bombing in late October, the answer became even less clear. In an editorial, the *New York Times* agreed with Reagan that there were no words to express the grief Americans felt at the death of the Marines. "But where are the words that express their purpose and the conditions under which they would finally depart?" it asked.[42]

In the days after the disaster, Reagan spoke of how stability in Lebanon was vital to the credibility of the United States in the region and the world. In the months to come, he also vowed that the Marines would complete their mission, not withdraw or cut and run under fire. "[Democratic Speaker of the House Tip O'Neill of Massachusetts] may be ready to surrender," Reagan claimed on February 3, 1984, "but I'm not." An outraged O'Neill replied, "The deaths of the U.S. Marines are the responsibility of the president of the United States. He is looking for a scapegoat. The deaths lie on him and the defeat in Lebanon lies on him and him alone."[43] The relationship between the two men was never fully repaired. Four days later, Reagan publicly ordered a phased redeployment to naval ships offshore, an act that Weinberger had privately urged for months. By April 1984 the last of the Marines had departed. It was a popular move—more than 60 percent of Americans approved, according to *Newsweek*—but one editor wondered "what the press would have done if Jimmy Carter had stationed Marines in a combat zone with unloaded rifles to defend themselves against terrorists."[44]

Reagan may have received less media criticism because of his image as a firm and decisive leader. But reaction to the tragedy in Lebanon was also muted because of events simultaneously taking place in Grenada, a tiny Caribbean island more than six thousand miles from Beirut and more than one thousand miles from Washington. In 1979, a Marxist leader named Maurice Bishop launched a revolution and overthrew the government. Once in power, Bishop suspended the constitution, banned all political parties, and established close ties with the Communist world. With the assistance of military engineers and construction workers from Cuba, he also began to build a new international airport. Bishop claimed that it was to boost tourism by facilitating the landing of commercial jet planes; Reagan believed that it was to promote Communism by facilitating the landing of military cargo planes. The White House feared the transformation of Grenada into a base of operations comparable to Cuba, which the United States saw as a major source of Communist subversion in Central America.

In October 1983, a small group of Bishop's followers deposed and executed him. In the chaos and confusion that followed, the Reagan administration became increasingly concerned for the safety of several hundred American students at St. George's School of Medicine. The Organization of Eastern Caribbean States also appealed to the United States to intervene. On October 22—the day before the bombing of the Marines in Beirut—Reagan secretly gave the green light to a military invasion, which had the support of Weinberger as well as Secretary of State George Shultz and CIA director William Casey. On October 25, Operation Urgent Fury began. In the first major overseas action by the U.S. military since the Vietnam War, more than seven thousand American troops landed on the island. With overwhelming land, sea, and air superiority, they soon took control and airlifted the students to safety. A total of 19 Americans were killed and 116 were injured. Most of the American casualties were due to accidents or friendly fire.[45]

The Grenada invasion nonetheless attracted harsh foreign criticism. The United Nations General Assembly overwhelmingly voted to condemn the operation, which it termed a "flagrant violation of international law."[46] The leaders of France and West Germany were also critical. Even Prime Minister Margaret Thatcher of Great Britain, a staunch U.S. ally and close personal friend of Reagan, expressed disapproval. On the eve of the invasion, she called the president and made a personal appeal. "She's upset and doesn't think we should do it," wrote Reagan in his diary. "I couldn't tell her it had started. This was one secret we really managed to keep."[47]

In the United States, the reaction was mixed. Liberals in general were sharply critical of the Grenada invasion. "We can't go the way of gunboat diplomacy," declared O'Neill. "[Reagan's] policy is wrong. His policy is frightening." Democratic Senator Daniel Patrick Moynihan of New York added that "I don't know how you restore democracy at the point of a bayonet." Seven House Democrats even initiated impeachment proceedings. The *New York Times* opined that it was "a reverberating demonstration to the

President Reagan monitors the situation in Grenada in the early morning of October 22, 1983. (Courtesy of the Ronald Reagan Library.)

world that America has no more respect for laws and borders, for the codes of civilization, than the Soviet Union."[48]

But public opinion—especially among conservatives—was strongly supportive. Reagan appeared to have restored American pride, power, and patriotism. "We got there just in time," he said on national television, two days after the invasion began. "The events in Lebanon and Grenada, though oceans apart, are clearly related," he added, because the Soviet Union had encouraged "the violence in both countries . . . through a network of surrogates and terrorists." The evidence was weak at best. As a former CIA analyst wrote, "The heart of Reagan's case was not even circumstantial; it was mythical and ideological." But the euphoria of the moment dispelled most doubts. As a headline in the *Washington Post* put it: "TIDY UNITED STATES WAR ENDS: 'WE BLEW THEM AWAY.'"[49]

Grenada eased, if not erased, the memories of Lebanon. On television, images of the medical students kissing the tarmac when they landed in Charleston replaced images of rescue teams digging through the rubble in Beirut. The invasion also had two other important consequences according to conservatives. For one, it helped to exorcise the ghost of Vietnam. "For the first time since the Vietnam War," observed author Dinesh D'Souza, "the United States had committed ground troops abroad, sustained casualties, emerged victorious and won the support of the American people." For another, Reagan had reversed the Brezhnev Doctrine—for the first time, the United States had liberated a Communist nation from the Soviet empire.[50] The tide had turned in a portent of what was to come, although at the moment few could see it.

What some could see was that terrorism was emerging as a threat at least as serious as Communism, especially in the Middle East. The threat had two general sources, although they often overlapped. The first came from rogue states like Libya, where Col. Muammar Qaddafi had became dictator after a coup in 1969. A quixotic figure who preached a strange brew of Arab nationalism and Islamic socialism, Qaddafi was a firm ally of the PLO and other terrorist organizations. In the late 1970s, he also developed a relationship with the Soviet Union, which made him an even greater menace in the eyes of the Reagan administration. The second source was radical groups like Islamic Jihad, Abu Nidal, and Hezbollah, which tended to operate independently but typically had close ties to patron states like Iran, Syria, or Libya. In 1984 and 1985, for example, terrorists in Lebanon with links to Iran kidnapped seven Americans. Among them was William Buckley, the CIA station chief in Beirut, who was tortured and later died when denied medical treatment by his captors. His fate and that of the other hostages would become a fixation with Reagan, as the Iran-Contra scandal would demonstrate.

From the start, Reagan took a firm stand against terrorism and drew a clear contrast between what Carter had done and what he would do. "I believe it is high time that the civilized countries of the world made it plain that there is no room worldwide for terrorism," Reagan stated in October 1980 during the presidential debate. "There will be no negotiation with terrorists of any kind."[51] In January 1981, the new president welcomed home from Tehran the embassy hostages with these words: "Let terrorists be aware that when the rules of international behavior are violated, our policy will be one of swift and effective retribution."[52] That same month, Alexander Haig, the new secretary of state, underlined Reagan's policy and offered a sharp rebuke to the Carter administration. "International terrorism," he said, "will take the place of human rights in our concern because it is the ultimate abuse of human rights."[53]

The first test of Reagan's resolve came in August 1981. For years the U.S. Navy had conducted routine training exercises in the Gulf of Sidra, which Qaddafi now claimed as Libyan territory and termed the "Zone of Death." Unintimidated, Reagan ordered the Sixth Fleet into the Gulf. Two Libyan fighter jets were subsequently shot down when they unwisely elected to fire on American F-14s accompanying the fleet. "Let friend and foe alike know that America has the muscle to back up its words," Reagan said as conservatives beamed with pride and pleasure.[54] Liberals were less effusive and more willing to invoke the Vietnam analogy whenever possible. Among them was former Democratic Senator William Fulbright of Arkansas, chair of the Foreign Relations Committee when President Lyndon Johnson had used a similar pretext to escalate U.S. involvement in South Vietnam. "The recent incident in the Gulf of Sidra is reminiscent of the Gulf of Tonkin on August 4, 1964," he warned. "We should remind ourselves of the ultimate consequences of that small incident in the Bay of Tonkin seventeen years ago."[55]

History did not repeat itself in 1981 because Qaddafi opted not to provoke further retaliation for the moment. But in 1985, a series of terrorist incidents rocked the Middle East and Mediterranean world. Two in particular drew international attention. The first incident came in June, when Lebanese Shiites hijacked a Trans World Airlines flight from Athens to Rome and rerouted it to Beirut, where they murdered Navy diver Robert Stethem and dumped his body on the tarmac. Chanting the words "New Jersey"—a reference to the battleship that had shelled Lebanon in February 1984—the kidnappers also threatened to kill the remaining thirty-nine

Americans on board if Israel refused to release more than seven hundred Shiite prisoners. In public, Reagan was resolute. "The United States gives terrorists no rewards and no guarantees," he vowed. "We make no concessions. We make no deals."[56] In private, he pressured Israel to make the exchange, which it did with reluctance. The result was a mixed message at best. It was also a measure of Reagan's determination, even obsession, to free the hostages and avoid the fate of Carter.

The second incident came in October 1985, when four Palestinians hijacked the *Achille Lauro*, an Italian cruise ship. After demanding the release of fifty prisoners in Israeli jails, they shot an elderly, wheelchair-bound Jewish American passenger named Leon Klinghoffer and dumped his body into the Mediterranean Sea. In a complicated arrangement, the terrorists eventually surrendered to the PLO and were aboard an Egyptian plane en route to Tunisia to greet Arafat when Reagan authorized four Navy F-14s to intercept it. Soon the Palestinians were in custody in Italy. The "terrorists may run, but they cannot hide," boasted Reagan.[57] He received powerful praise from the conservative publisher of the *Union Leader* in Manchester, New Hampshire. "You are to be congratulated for [your] courageous action in the war against terrorism," she wrote. "At last, the evil forces of terrorism must reckon with our willingness to react to crimes against American citizens."[58]

Two months later, in December 1985, the White House chose to take further action against Qaddafi when intelligence officials uncovered evidence that linked him to simultaneous attacks at airports in Rome and Vienna. Among the twenty dead were five Americans. In response, the United States cut economic ties with Libya in January 1986. Then in April Qaddafi was suspected in the deadly bombing of a West Berlin disco popular with American servicemen. In retaliation, U.S. jets bombed Tripoli in what the administration justified as an act of self-defense. Among the 150 dead was the dictator's two-year-old adopted daughter. "Despite our repeated warnings," declared a defiant Reagan, "Qaddafi continued his reckless policy of intimidation, his relentless pursuit of terror. He counted on America to be passive. He counted wrong."[59] Most Americans—more than 75 percent—expressed approval, but not all. "If someone had killed Amy it would have been the worst blow that could be delivered to me," said former President Jimmy Carter of his daughter. "I would have sworn as long as my life existed, I would retaliate."[60]

Whether preemptive retaliation might constitute an effective deterrent to international terrorism remained a matter of debate within the White House. In a major speech in October 1984, Shultz asserted that "our responses should go beyond passive defense to consider means of active prevention, preemption, and retaliation." The secretary of state added that although "we may never have the kind of evidence that can stand up in an American court of law . . . we will need the flexibility to respond to terrorist attacks in a variety of ways, at times and places of our choosing."[61] In essence, Shultz sought to create a new strategy for the struggle against terrorism.

Others disagreed with the strategy. Weinberger contended that "preemptive . . . retaliation would be analogous to firing a gun in a crowded theater in the slim hope of hitting the guilty party."[62] Moreover, it was unclear to the secretary of defense how to define what type of terrorism—state, state-sponsored, or random—would warrant deterrent action. What about states that unwittingly or unwillingly harbored terrorists? And how would other nations in turn perceive unilateral American measures—and the American soldiers who carried them out? Would the International Court of Justice or other international tribunals have the authority to judge and punish them? Not until after the attacks on the World Trade Center and the Pentagon in September 2001 would the administration of George W. Bush settle the debate, at least for the moment, by taking the Shultz position and arguing that preemptive retaliation was essential as well as justifiable in the war on terror regardless of international criticism or opposition.

Whether the Reagan record on terrorism was positive also remains a matter of controversy. In the wake of the Lebanon debacle, the administration in April 1984 issued National Security Decision Directive (NSDD) 138, a watershed in counterterrorism policy. The directive called for coordinated intelligence and military operations aimed directly at terrorists and those countries that provided them with support or sanctuary. It also outlined the need to have in place diplomatic measures to encourage international cooperation and economic sanctions to punish those nations that helped or harbored terrorists. And NSDD 138 aided efforts to strengthen the federal criminal code in regard to the promotion, funding, planning, or implementation of terrorist acts, both at home and abroad.

Reagan's supporters point to a number of achievements. The president increased American awareness of the terrorist threat. He also helped shift the international climate of opinion toward terrorism from tolerance to revulsion. As evidence, the United Nations General Assembly made history when it unequivocally and by consensus condemned terrorism for the first time in December 1985. Better intelligence operations prevented possible incidents, and aggressive military operations deterred potential actions. Finally, Reagan restored the power of the presidency in the eyes of a majority of Americans, who gave him high marks for his resolute handling of the terrorist threat.

Reagan's critics point to a number of failures. They note that the number of anti-American terrorist incidents continued to rise even after NSDD 138. They also observe that 1988, the president's final year in office, was the bloodiest ever due mainly to the sabotage of a Pan Am flight over Lockerbie, Scotland, which led to the deaths of 270 passengers, 189 of whom were Americans. The military force used in Lebanon and Libya, detractors contend, was disproportionate and in possible violation of international law. Moreover, it may have escalated the cycle of violence and fed the hunger for revenge against the United States. Finally, the Iran-Contra scandal, which revealed that the White House had in effect traded arms for hostages, damaged American credibility and demonstrated that U.S. policy on terrorism was at best inconsistent and at worst hypocritical.

The roots of that scandal, which a separate section will explore in greater detail, lie in the history of American-Iranian relations. In 1953, President Dwight Eisenhower secretly authorized the CIA to overthrow Dr. Mohammed Mossadeq, the elected leader of Iran, who opposed the foreign exploitation of Iran's wealth and had nationalized the holdings of the Anglo-Iranian oil company. The coup was a success and resulted in the restoration to power of Shah Mohammed Reza Pahlevi, who for the next quarter century ruled as an absolute dictator with the staunch support of the United States. Billions of dollars in aid flowed to him because president after president saw the shah as a crucial bulwark against Soviet aggression and a vital protector of oil resources. He also was a force for moderation and modernization in the Middle East. In 1973, for instance, he opposed the Arab oil embargo imposed on the United States in the wake of the war between Egypt, Syria, and Israel. In 1978, Reagan had visited Iran and met with the shah, whom he praised for granting educational opportunities to women and extending religious freedom to Christians and Jews.

The next year, mass demonstrations erupted against the shah. Many Iranians resented his repressive regime. Others—especially Islamic clergymen and their followers—objected to his efforts to promote liberal reform in a fundamentalist society. In January 1979, the shah fled the country as a powerful revolutionary movement emerged. Amid the chaos, the Ayatollah Ruhollah Khomeini, a fiery religious leader with a visceral hatred of the United States, returned from exile in France and rose to power. By October the shah was living in Mexico but dying from cancer. He appealed to Carter for permission to come to New York for medical treatment. The president granted the request despite threats of reprisal from Iran. In November, militant students seized the American Embassy in Tehran and took sixty-six Americans hostage. The crisis would last for 444 days. Reagan nevertheless was in full agreement with Carter's decision. The shah was a loyal ally, Reagan wrote, and "our country had every moral reason and right to offer him sanctuary from the very beginning and not just as a patient after he became ill in Mexico."[63]

The Iranian revolution had important implications. It highlighted the danger—as in South Vietnam—of basing a policy on a leader or regime that might not enjoy mass support. In a sense, what happened in Tehran was similar to what happened in Saigon. In both instances, the political foundations of American policy were built on quicksand, on governments that ultimately had little or no popular appeal. The Desert One debacle—Carter's abortive effort to rescue the embassy hostages in April 1980—also compounded the military's sense of failure that had lingered since January 1973, when the United States had hastily abandoned South Vietnam. Finally, the Iranian revolution marked the death knell for the Nixon Doctrine, which had required allies to provide for their own military protection. No longer could the United States afford to rely on other nations to defend themselves—particularly not in critical areas like the Persian Gulf, where the stakes were so high. Instead, the United States had to reclaim the role of global or regional policeman, if only to ensure access to oil. It was a role and a challenge that conservatives like Reagan welcomed.

The fall of the shah in 1979 affected domestic politics as well. Above all, it deepened the divide between liberals and neoconservatives within the Democratic Party. Liberals viewed the shah as a corrupt and brutal dictator whose time had passed. On the whole, they were part of a younger generation that had come of age in the 1960s as part of the New Left and counterculture. Neoconservatives saw the shah as a valuable ally in the global confrontation with the Soviet Union. On the whole, they were part of an older generation that had come of age during the New Deal of Franklin Roosevelt or the Cold War of Harry Truman and John Kennedy. Now they were alienated from a majority of their fellow Democrats largely—although certainly not exclusively—as a result of the Vietnam War, which most neoconservatives had strongly supported and most liberals had eventually opposed.

Among the most prominent neoconservatives was Jeane Kirkpatrick, a Georgetown University political scientist and dedicated Democrat who was deeply disenchanted with the Carter administration. Shortly after the Iranian revolution, she published a seminal article on "Dictatorships and Double Standards" in *Commentary*, a neoconservative journal. In brief, Kirkpatrick maintained that liberals were wrong to force democratic reforms on autocratic allies of the United States, especially when Communist leaders were not held to similar standards. The unintended consequence of this "double standard" was the fall of friendly rulers like the shah in Iran and Somoza in Nicaragua and, in their place, the rise of hostile regimes even less committed to personal freedom or human rights. Therefore, she concluded, the United States should demonstrate more tolerance of anti-Communist dictators, who might in time accept democratic principles, and less tolerance of Communist dictators, who were unlikely ever to promote political liberalization. Among the many conservative readers and admirers of the article was Reagan, who asked to meet Kirkpatrick in 1979, invited her to join his campaign in 1980, and named her U.S. ambassador to the United Nations in 1981. Soon most of her fellow neoconservatives would chart a similar course from the Democrats to the Republicans—a development with enormous import for foreign policy in the years and decades to come.

In the Middle East, the Iranian revolution signaled the emergence of Islamic fundamentalism, which would pose an eventual challenge to regimes from Riyadh to Cairo to Damascus. But the chaos in Tehran also seemed to present an immediate opportunity to Saddam Hussein, a secular Sunni with grandiose ambitions who ruled neighboring Iraq. Now he believed he could dominate the region as a whole. In September 1980, Hussein launched a full-scale invasion of Iran after a series of border clashes. His objectives were to secure control of the Shatt al-Arab waterway and seize the oil fields in a nearby province. Moreover, he wanted to suppress any thoughts of rebellion on the part of Iraq's repressed Shiite majority, which might have drawn inspiration from the Islamic revolution in Shiite Iran. At first Iraq made some progress, but Iran soon recovered and by June 1982 it had regained virtually all of the land it had lost at the outset of the war.

For the next six years, Iran was on the offensive, although the war effectively became a brutal stalemate and perhaps the bloodiest conflict since World War II, with more than one million casualties. The trench warfare, massed charges, and gas masks were reminiscent of World War I. So too were the chemical weapons (mustard, cyanide, and nerve gas) employed by Hussein against Iranian soldiers and civilians in direct violation of the Geneva Convention. In an effort at "ethnic cleansing," if not genocide, he also gassed, imprisoned, tortured, and executed almost one hundred thousand Iraqi Kurds, whom he feared might seek independence or collaborate with the enemy. Many of the victims were women and children. But the Reagan administration turned a blind eye toward Hussein's atrocities, which were deemed either an internal matter or collateral damage from the war. Not until September 1988—after the conflict had ended—would the

White House even denounce publicly the Iraqi leader's decision to use poison gas against his own people.

Meanwhile, Iran used whatever tactics it could to turn the tide of battle. It recruited tens of thousands of unarmed children to clear minefields protected by machine guns. The children were roped together, ordered to advance under fire, and given plastic keys to unlock the gates of paradise in case of their deaths, which were virtually certain. In August 1988, the exhausted combatants agreed to a ceasefire that left the border unchanged. By then both nations were deeply in debt (Hussein in particular owed $14 billion to Kuwait, which he would invade two years later), and both leaders were deeply disappointed. "Making this decision was more deadly than taking poison," said a bitter Khomeini, perhaps in reference to Iraq's use of chemical weapons. "I have sold my honor. I have swallowed the poison of defeat."[64]

In Washington, the ayatollah's words engendered little sympathy. Nevertheless, the United States had initially tried to remain neutral in the conflict. On the one hand, it had no diplomatic ties with Iraq, which had attacked Israel in 1967 and was the aggressor in 1980. On the other, the Reagan administration was determined to halt the spread of Islamic extremism in the Middle East, which could threaten the oil supply. A strategy based on balance of power—or shared bloodletting—therefore seemed most appropriate. But once Iran seized the initiative the White House believed it had to tilt toward Iraq. In short order, the Reagan administration restored diplomatic relations, removed Iraq from the list of terrorist nations, and shared vital military intelligence. The United States also extended billions of dollars in economic credits, which enabled Iraq to purchase agricultural products from American farmers. "Our long-term hope," recalled a former ambassador to Baghdad, "was that Hussein's government would become less repressive and more responsible."[65] The hope was in vain.

Reagan made two critical moves in November 1983, a month after the death of the Marines in Beirut. The first came when he issued NSDD 114, which placed the United States firmly on the side of Iraq despite ample evidence that Hussein had deployed chemical weapons against soldiers and civilians in clear violation of international law. The directive pledged that the United States would take whatever measures were necessary and legal to prevent an Iranian victory and protect oil traffic in the Persian Gulf. After Iran and Iraq began to target oil tankers and storage facilities, the U.S. Navy interceded to provide Kuwaiti ships with military escorts. The consequences were tragic. In May 1987, an Iraqi fighter by mistake fired a missile at an American destroyer, the USS *Stark*, killing thirty-seven sailors. In

July 1988, the USS *Vincennes*, an American cruiser, by mistake shot down an Iranian airliner, killing 290 passengers.

The second important event of November 1983 came when Reagan named Donald Rumsfeld as his new special envoy to the Middle East. "I can't think of a better individual in whom to entrust the coordination of our role in the Middle East peace process," the president said of his appointee, who a decade earlier had served as defense secretary in the administration of Gerald Ford and two decades later would serve as defense secretary in the administration of George W. Bush. In December, Rumsfeld flew to Iraq—the first senior American official to visit in six years—and met with Hussein, who greeted him in uniform and armed with a pistol. The meeting apparently went well. In a cable to Washington, the special envoy wrote that it "marked [a] positive milestone in development of U.S.-Iraqi relations and will prove to be of wider benefit to U.S. posture in the region."[66]

In the December 1983 meeting, Hussein agreed that cooperation between the two nations was essential if Iraq was to play the role of strategic counterbalance to Iran. But he also requested that the Reagan administration, which had maintained the arms embargo the Carter administration had placed on Iran during the hostage crisis, now urge its friends and allies to honor the ban as well. In response, Rumsfeld indicated that it was not a problem—the White House had already launched Operation Staunch, which was intended to halt illicit sales of American weapons by other nations to Iran. What he could not have known at the time was that, less than two years later, the first shipment of tube-launched, optically tracked, wire-guided (TOW) anti-tank missiles would arrive in Tehran from the United States via Israel as part of what would become the worst scandal of the Reagan years.

CENTRAL AMERICA AND THE REAGAN DOCTRINE

The mood in the White House was tense on June 25, 1984, as the members of the National Security Planning Group (NSPG) gathered in the Situation Room. Present for the meeting were President Reagan and his top foreign policy aides, including Secretary of State George Shultz, Secretary of Defense Caspar Weinberger, Central Intelligence Agency (CIA) director William Casey, and National Security Council (NSC) adviser Robert "Bud" McFarlane. The topic on the table was how, in the face of growing opposition in Congress, to sustain support for the Contras in their fight against the leftist government of Nicaragua, which was sending weapons to the leftist rebels in El Salvador. All agreed that the United States had a moral and strategic duty to support the Contras, whose confrontation with the Sandinistas placed them on the frontlines of the battle against Communism in Central America. As Reagan put it, "We must obtain the funds to help these freedom fighters." (See "Excerpts from Minutes, National Security Planning Group Meeting.")

Opposition in Congress to aid for the Contras had grown because of two recent developments. In April 1984, the *Wall Street Journal* had reported that mercenaries trained by the CIA had illegally mined the harbors of Nicaragua on behalf of the Contras. The action was in clear violation of national law (there was no prior Congressional notification) and international law (as the World Court would later rule). Then, in June, *CBS News* described how the CIA had secretly used a private cargo company called Southern Air Transport to ship arms and supplies to the Contras via Honduras, a neutral nation that bordered Nicaragua and served as a staging area for covert operations. Now it was virtually certain that the House of Representatives, which Democrats controlled, would soon ban all U.S. military assistance to the anti-Sandinista movement.

In the Situation Room, the president and his advisers agreed that pressure from the Contras was essential if negotiations with Nicaragua were to succeed. Few were optimistic that they would—Shultz saw the odds as no better than 20 percent, and Reagan said it was "far-fetched to imagine that a Communist government like that would make any reasonable deal with us." Nevertheless, diplomacy was critical if only to reassure allies in the region and place the burden of failure on the Sandinistas. Above all, the prospect of peace might convince Congress to continue to aid the Contras, who might eventually overthrow the government of Nicaragua. "We need to hold the Democrats accountable," said Weinberger, who observed that Sandinista leader Daniel Ortega had recently visited Havana and Moscow. "We should ask the Democrats whether they want a second Cuba." (See "Excerpts from Minutes, National Security Planning Group Meeting.")

But what if Congress nonetheless opted (as it would in August 1984) to cut off all aid to the Contras and directed the White House not to take any more steps on their behalf? Casey contended—with the support of Weinberger and Vice President George H. W. Bush—that the administration had the legal authority to solicit assistance from other countries. But Shultz, relying on the legal opinion of White House Chief of Staff James Baker, counseled Reagan that seeking funding for the Contras from a third party without Congressional knowledge or approval was "an impeachable offense." With no clear consensus, McFarlane concluded the meeting by warning that no one should act until the legal issue was resolved. "I certainly hope none of this discussion will be made public in any way," he added and Reagan concurred. "If such a story gets out," the president said, "we'll all be hanging by our thumbs in front of the White House until we find out who did it." (See "Excerpts from Minutes, National Security Planning Group Meeting.") That very same day, Lt. Col. Oliver North, a military aide to the NSC, secretly informed a Contra leader that Saudi Arabia would transfer funds to his private bank account within twenty-four hours. North also told him to keep the information confidential—not even the CIA could know, although it soon would.

The NSPG meeting of June 1984 was a pivotal moment. It revealed three characteristics of the Reagan administration that would ultimately contribute significantly to the Iran-Contra affair. First, the president and his top aides were determined to aid the Contras by virtually any means necessary. Second, the White House was willing to circumvent or reinterpret the law as it saw fit. Third, the administration tended to view Congressional oversight as an unwarranted and unconstitutional intrusion on presidential authority, not as a legitimate check on presidential power. When combined with Reagan's hands-off management style—his tendency to focus on broad policy objectives and delegate specific operational details—the final result was a serious lack of institutional control, with disastrous consequences for the bipartisan consensus in foreign policy that the administration had hoped to forge.

The emergence of Central America as a vital battleground was unexpected. For decades the United States had treated the region with malign neglect, permitting social inequality and political repression to fester and foment. But in the 1980s it became what Jeane Kirkpatrick, U.S. ambassador to the United Nations, termed "the most important place in the world."[67] For the White House, the campaign to defeat the Marxist rebels in El Salvador and destroy the radical regime in Nicaragua was not a sideshow—it was the main front in the Cold War against Communist aggression. El Salvador was, wrote Reagan in his diary, a "must win"—the administration had to keep the pro-U.S. government in power.[68] The stakes were high in large part because the president saw Central America through the East-West prism of Communism versus democracy, not the North-South prism of affluence versus poverty.

At the same time, Reagan was a firm believer in the domino theory, which assumed that defeat in El Salvador and Nicaragua would inevitably endanger Mexico and, by extension, the United States. "El Salvador is nearer to Texas than Texas is to Massachusetts," the president lectured Congress in April 1983. "Nicaragua is just as close to Miami, San Antonio, San Diego, and Tucson as those cities are to Washington."[69] Reagan also liked to quote (or misquote) Vladimir Lenin, the Communist leader of the Russian Revolution, who supposedly stated: "Once we have Latin America, we won't have to take the United States, the last bastion of capitalism, because it will fall into our outstretched hands like overripe fruit."[70] Whether the quote was accurate mattered less than the faith the president placed in it.

In Reagan's mind, the international credibility of the United States was at stake. Failure in Central America would ultimately lead to failure in Western Europe because America's friends would no longer trust him and America's foes—in particular the Soviet Union—would no longer fear him. The U.S. nuclear deterrent that had shielded Britain, France, and West Germany since the late 1940s might not hold in the face of Soviet conventional superiority. Fortunately, success seemed certain in El Salvador and Nicaragua. "Mr. President," assured Alexander Haig, his first secretary of state, "this is one you can win."[71] Unfortunately, Central America became the source of the most significant political scandal since Watergate as well as the most heated political debates since Vietnam.

The complicated and controversial legacies of the Vietnam War haunted American policy in Central America. On the one hand, Reagan was determined to dispel the "Vietnam syndrome" once and for all by demonstrating that the United States had regained the will to win and the power to prevail no matter the mission. On the other, he was conscious that the American people remained scarred by the experience and reluctant to have American soldiers deployed in a guerrilla war on behalf of corrupt governments and dubious objectives. In his memoir, the president was adamant: "I *never* considered sending U.S. troops to fight in Latin America." The record supports his claim—at no time was armed intervention given serious consideration within the White House, in part because Reagan understood that it would generate a popular backlash against the "Great Colossus of the North" by the residents of the region.[72]

The historical reference reveals how the weight of the past also affected American policy in Central America. Time after time the United States had intervened on behalf of corrupt dictators and interfered in the internal affairs of other nations on behalf of American corporations. In Western Europe, the United States had earned a reputation as a defender and advocate of freedom that was, for the most part, deserved. In the Western Hemisphere—and especially in Central America—it had earned a reputation as a bully and a hypocrite whose interests almost always seemed to rest with the prosperous and powerful, not the poor and powerless. Certainly that was the case in both El Salvador and Nicaragua, where the historical record of the United States was dismal.

El Salvador had suffered from extreme repression and poverty since the 1930s as the result of an unholy alliance between wealthy elites and army leaders, who used right-wing death squads to intimidate or assassinate both moderate and radical critics of the regime. After decades of support, the United States during the Carter years had at last severed military aid to El Salvador in the name of human rights. A political coalition of leftist revolutionaries (including Communists) called the Farabundo Marti National Liberation Front (FMLN) also emerged. But in 1980 the popular, American-educated Jose Napoleon Duarte, a moderate Christian Democrat, returned to the capital of San Salvador to become the leader of the government. Duarte, who was elected president in 1972, went into exile after the military deposed, imprisoned, and tortured him.

Duarte sought to halt the violence with renewed assistance from the Carter administration. But in March 1980, death squads with ties to the military murdered Archbishop Oscar Romero, an outspoken opponent of political violence, in the middle of Mass. Then in December—after the election of Reagan—they kidnapped and murdered four American Catholic nuns, who were blindfolded and executed with shots to the back of the head. One of the women was raped first. Two of the nuns were in the Maryknoll order, which included the elderly aunt of House Speaker Tip O'Neill, a liberal Democrat. He was outraged by the killings—and enraged when top officials in the new administration implied that the victims were activists who had somehow provoked their attackers. Under pressure, a lame-duck Carter now suspended aid to El Salvador once again, only to reinstate it when the FMLN announced plans for a "final" offensive (with support from the Sandinistas in Nicaragua). In early 1981, it failed and the conflict settled into a low-intensity, high-brutality civil war, as seventeen thousand soldiers battled four thousand guerrillas. Between 1979 and 1981 both sides committed countless atrocities as an estimated thirty thousand people died, many of them civilians caught in the crossfire.

Perhaps the worst atrocity took place in December 1981 in the village of El Mozote, where a battalion of solders trained by American advisers and armed with American weapons massacred hundreds of El Salvadoran peasants, whose bodies were left unburied as a warning to others. Many of the victims were women and children, including some who had taken refuge in a church. Torture and rape (even of girls as young as twelve) were also reported. The soldiers believed the villagers gave aid and comfort to FMLN guerrillas, who operated in the area and had recently clashed with the battalion. In January 1982, the *New York Times* published a front-page article based on interviews with survivors, photos, and forensic evidence. The reporter wrote that he witnessed "the charred skulls and bones of dozens of bodies buried under burned-out roofs, beams, and shattered tiles."[73]

The White House immediately denied the allegations. The next day the president certified to Congress (as he was required to do, against his wishes, every six months) that El Salvador had made satisfactory progress on political reforms and human rights—a critical step in ensuring that the United States would continue to provide military aid. Top officials in the State Department also testified in February 1982 that the reports from El Mozote were not credible, that the number of victims was exaggerated, and that there was no evidence of a massacre, only of a firefight between soldiers and rebels. It was all, in essence, FMLN propaganda uncritically disseminated by the liberal media, which the *Wall Street Journal* and other conservative publications took to task for deliberate or inadvertent bias. But a decade later, a United Nations Truth Commission ruled that the massacre had taken place—a finding which subsequent forensic research has corroborated.

In 1982, El Salvador held free elections for a constituent assembly with the support and encouragement of the United States. The purpose of the assembly was to implement the political reforms Duarte had proposed and lay the groundwork for a presidential election in 1984. But after the Reagan administration rejected a power-sharing arrangement, the FMLN boycotted the 1982 elections. As a result, they were dominated by the right-wing Nationalist Republican Alliance (ARENA) party led by Roberto D'Aubuisson, a former intelligence officer with ties to the death squads and the assassination of Archbishop Romero. The United States had to pressure D'Aubuisson to yield the presidency to a less controversial and more moderate figure. The civil war nevertheless escalated as U.S. military and economic aid increased. Fears of U.S. intervention also mounted.

But Reagan firmly resisted any suggestion of ground forces in Central America, even when it came from fellow conservatives. "Those sonsof-bitches won't be happy until we have 25,000 troops in Managua [Nicaragua] and I'm not going to do it," he said.[74] In part the president's opposition was based on the polls—Gallup in March 1982 reported that more than 70 percent of Americans opposed sending soldiers to El Salvador even if meant that the FMLN would win.[75] But in part it was based on his acute sensitivity to the painful memories of Vietnam—and perhaps his implicit understanding that the stakes in Central America, while high, were not high enough to warrant the sacrifice of American lives. "We have no intention of sending American combat forces there," Reagan wrote in a letter to a reverend. "You spoke of the lesson of Vietnam. In my view the immorality of Vietnam was asking young men to fight and die for a cause our government had no intention of winning."[76]

In 1984, Duarte won the presidential election, which the United States supervised and financed with more than $1 million in CIA funds. But despite his calls for a negotiated settlement the civil war continued. Five years later, with Duarte forbidden by law from seeking reelection, the new leader of the ARENA party came to power. Although conservative, he too was committed to a peaceful resolution of the conflict, especially now that Reagan had left office. Meanwhile, the FMLN was losing international support—the Soviets were consumed by the fall of the Berlin Wall and the Sandinistas would shortly lose power in Nicaragua. A final rebel offensive again failed to ignite a popular uprising, and in 1992 the guerrillas and the government agreed to a peace treaty, formally ending the bitter and bloody war that had lasted twelve years and claimed the lives of seventy-five thousand El Salvadorans.

Whether Reagan had played a decisive role in the outcome remains a matter of debate. Conservatives contend that U.S. support for the government of El Salvador kept it in power and enabled it to pressure the FMLN to come to the bargaining table. The White House also used the Contras to block weapons shipments from Nicaragua and promoted democratic elections that eroded the political legitimacy of the rebel movement. The administration regularly warned the Duarte government that it had to curb the death squads, if only to retain the goodwill of the American people. Finally, the Caribbean Basin Initiative, a temporary program launched in 1983, expanded U.S. trade with, and investment in, El Salvador and other countries in non-Communist Central America. In sum, conservatives maintain that Reagan's "four Ds" policy of democracy, development, defense, and dialogue worked, albeit more slowly and expensively in terms of dollars spent and lives lost than some might have hoped.[77]

By contrast, liberals contend that the White House's cynical and cavalier attitude toward human rights emboldened the death squads, which escalated the violence and triggered reprisals from the guerrillas. It was Congress—not the administration—that deserved credit for the certification process, which eventually forced the Duarte government and army leaders to take steps to control the death squads and reduce the chronic abuse of human rights in return for continued aid. Military assistance may have pressured the rebels, but it also contributed to atrocities by the army at El Mozote and elsewhere. Finally, had the White House agreed to the proposal made by the FMLN in 1982—or at least offered a constructive counterproposal—the civil war might have ended a decade earlier. In sum, liberals maintain that Reagan's policies unnecessarily deepened the grief and extended the suffering of the people of El Salvador.[78]

For the people of Nicaragua, the historical record of the United States was synonymous with oppression. From 1912 to 1925, U.S. Marines were stationed in the capital of Managua, first to place in power Adolfo Diaz, a former clerk with an American company, and then to keep him in power. After a brief hiatus, the Marines returned to help Diaz defeat a rebellion led by Augusto Sandino, an anticolonialist whose followers were known as Sandinistas. In 1933, the Marines departed but left in place a National Guard trained by American officers and armed with American weapons. The commander was Anastasio "Tacho" Somoza, who loved baseball and could swear in English—traits that apparently endeared him to the American government. He promised Sandino amnesty if he agreed to negotiations—then had the rebel leader arrested and executed. Three years later, Somoza seized control of the country.

For the next four decades, Somoza and his son "Tachito" ruled with an iron hand and sticky fingers, repressing the opposition and enriching their family and friends at the expense of the peasants and middle class. Meanwhile, the United States looked the other way and provided military aid to the anti-Communist dictatorship. But in June 1979 ABC-TV broadcast the brutal murder by Nicaraguan soldiers of an American reporter in cold blood (he was unarmed and kneeling on the ground). A month later, the Sandinistas, a rebel movement composed of moderates and radicals, marched into Managua. Tachito then fled the country and flew to Miami with his mistress as well as most of Nicaragua's hard currency. Left behind were an estimated fifty thousand victims of the war between the government and the insurgents.

With the country bankrupt and in ruins, the Sandinistas immediately asked the United States for assistance. President Carter responded by requesting that Congress send $75 million in economic aid. But Congress delayed and the Sandinistas turned to Cuban leader Fidel Castro, a long-time friend and patron, for help with health clinics and literacy programs. Nicaragua also established diplomatic relations with the Soviet bloc and began to send weapons to the rebels in El Salvador. Revolutionaries drove moderates from office and nationalized the banks. Nicaragua was not yet a Communist country—most property remained in private hands and the Catholic Church was free to criticize the government. But the nation was on the road to radicalism and a collision course with the new administration in Washington, which was determined to make Nicaragua a test case for the Reagan Doctrine.

From the outset, the White House viewed the Sandinistas as a dangerous threat to regional stability and security. Peaceful coexistence was out of the question given the geopolitical logic of the Cold War. As the director of the CIA put it, "If we can't stop Soviet expansionism in a place like Nicaragua, where the hell can we?"[79] Like the Cubans and their patrons, the Soviets, the Sandinistas would soon seek to export revolution throughout Central America. "There is no question," said Reagan in 1979, "that the rebels are Cuban trained, Cuban armed and dedicated to creating another communist country in this hemisphere."[80] If necessary, some officials were even prepared to go directly to what they saw as the root of the problem in Central America—Cuba. "Just give me the word," a defiant Haig told the president in March 1981, "and I'll make that fucking island a parking lot."[81] A discomfited Reagan instead asked for his resignation a year later and replaced him with the more moderate Shultz.

In the short run, the president wanted to interdict the flow of weapons from Nicaragua to El Salvador. In the long run, the White House was determined to overthrow the government in Managua or force it to share power with the Contras, some of whom were former Sandinistas disillusioned by the radical turn. Some were also indigenous peoples mistreated by the new regime. Others were former soldiers or officials in the Somoza regime, while still others were hired guns or drug dealers. But most were directly or indirectly on the payroll of the United States, which armed, trained, and encouraged them to seize control in Nicaragua. In the eyes of the president, the Contras were "freedom fighters" and the "moral equivalent of our founding fathers."[82] Liberal critics were less complimentary. O'Neill, for example, described them as a "sorry group of mercenaries" whose main interest was drug smuggling. (Many of the planes that transported weapons to the Contras returned loaded with cocaine from Colombia, reportedly with the knowledge of U.S. officials and under the direction of Panama ruler Manuel Noriega, a drug trafficker with close connections to the Cali cartel.)[83]

Relations between the White House and the Sandinista regime deteriorated rapidly in 1981. Days after the inauguration, the Reagan administration halted $15 million in economic aid to Nicaragua as breadlines formed in Managua. The Sandinistas reacted by closing down opposition newspapers and beating up opposition leaders. The government also veered sharply to the left by imposing state controls on private businesses and seeking foreign aid from Cuba, Libya, and the Soviet Union. In November, Reagan formally approved a plan to send almost $20 million in covert aid to the Contras in Honduras, which provided base camps and staging areas in return for U.S. support. In December, the president signed an official intelligence finding, as required by law, declaring that the covert aid was vital to national security. Then, again as required by law, he informed the appropriate Congressional intelligence committees of the finding and the rationale behind it, which was to block the flow of weapons to El Salvador, not overthrow the regime in Nicaragua.

Pressure mounted from all sides in 1982. In Managua, the Sandinistas confiscated the property of more than twenty Catholic Churches on the pretext that they had disseminated counterrevolutionary propaganda. In Washington, the State Department promoted the idea of negotiations with Nicaragua while the White House promoted the threat of intervention despite resistance from the Pentagon. The CIA meanwhile proceeded with clandestine operations, which soon became the main focus of U.S. policy. At the same time, liberals in Congress argued for an end to aid as they became more fearful of another Vietnam, more convinced that the administration was not acting in good faith, and more antagonistic toward the Contras. They were, declared Democrat Tom Harkin of Iowa, "vicious cutthroat murderers . . . remnants of the evil, murderous National Guard. In the name of all that is right and decent, we should end our involvement with this group."[84]

Few were prepared to go so far so soon. But in December 1982 Democratic Congressman Edward Boland of Massachusetts, chair of the House Intelligence Committee, offered a compromise. He proposed an amendment to the defense appropriation bill prohibiting the use of funds "for the purpose of overthrowing the government of Nicaragua." The measure won overwhelming support (the vote was 411–0 in the House) and became famous as the first Boland Amendment. At the CIA, Casey was contemptuous of the provision, which he saw as legally meaningless even though Congress had now put into law the limitations the president had imposed earlier. But his general counsel was concerned about the growing threat of congressional scrutiny. "This thing," he predicted, "is going to come back and bite us in the ass like nothing you've ever seen."[85] In retrospect, he understated the impact.

The bite came from an unexpected source in April 1984. In response to the revelation that the CIA had illegally scattered mines off the coast of Nicaragua, Senator Barry Goldwater of Arizona, a conservative Republican who served on the Senate Intelligence Committee, exploded. Outraged that Casey had not bothered to inform the committee in advance, as he was required to do by law, Goldwater wrote to the CIA director that he was "pissed off." How, the senator asked, could he defend the president's foreign policies "when we don't know what the hell he is doing? Lebanon, yes, we all knew that he sent troops over there. But mine the harbors in Nicaragua? This is an act violating international law. It is an act of war. For the life of me, I don't see how we are going to explain it."[86] He was not alone.

In August 1984, Boland proposed another amendment. The measure, which again passed easily and became known as the second Boland Amendment, prohibited aid to the Contras for any reason. "During fiscal year 1985," it specified, "no funds available to the CIA, the Department of Defense, or any other agency or entity of the United States involved in intelligence activities may be obligated or expended for the purpose or which would have the effect of supporting, directly or indirectly, military or paramilitary operations in Nicaragua by any nation, group, organization, movement, or individual."[87] In October 1984, Reagan signed the second Boland Amendment. Nevertheless, Casey and others maintained that the NSC was not an intelligence agency since it had no operational responsibilities. They also continued to claim that the United States could legally solicit aid to the Contras from other countries. Trouble was on the horizon even as Reagan cruised to reelection in November 1984.

That same month, the Sandinistas chose to hold elections originally scheduled for the following year. In preparation, the government lowered the voting age to sixteen. It also took no chances—opposition demonstrations were suppressed and opposition newspapers were censored. In response, the major opposition parties boycotted the election and Ortega won with two-thirds of the votes. But in 1985, with the economy in crisis due largely to Nicaraguan mismanagement and American strangulation, he imposed martial law and jailed thousands of political prisoners. As Ortega's popularity fell, the ranks of the Contras swelled with new recruits. By playing the Communism card and invoking the domino theory, the Reagan administration was even able to persuade Congress to restore $100 million in aid to the rebels in 1986. "Using Nicaragua as a base," warned the president, "the Soviets and Cubans can become the dominant power in the crucial corridor between North and South America. Established there they will be in a position to threaten the Panama Canal, interdict our sea lanes and ultimately move against Mexico."[88] But the likelihood of a Contra victory over the better trained and more experienced Sandinista army remained slim.

Prospects for peace were also slim until 1987, when President Oscar Arias Sanchez of Costa Rica convinced Ortega and the Central American leaders to accept his Contadora Plan. It included four major provisions: a ceasefire across the region; an end to foreign aid (by both the United States and Soviet bloc) to rebel forces in Central America; negotiations between the rebels and the government in both Nicaragua and El Salvador; and free elections in both countries. The Reagan administration objected because the plan would permit the Soviet Union to continue to assist Nicaragua, although the United States could continue to assist El Salvador as well. Nevertheless, Arias—who won the Nobel Peace Prize for his efforts—persisted, and in 1988 the war between the Contras and the Sandinistas ended after the deaths of more than forty thousand Nicaraguans. Two years later, free and fair elections were held. This time Ortega lost to opposition leader Violeta Chamorro, owner of *La Prensa* and widow of Pedro Chamorro, former publisher of the newspaper and an outspoken critic of the Somoza regime until it assassinated him in 1978. After some initial resistance, the Sandinistas accepted the results and a peaceful transition of power took place.

The outcome generated a debate over who should receive credit. Liberals argued that Reagan's policies needlessly exacerbated the conflict and that the settlement was the result of a number of factors. The Cold War had faded, lessening the stakes for the United States and the Soviet Union. Both the Sandinistas and the Contras were exhausted from years of bloodshed. Regional pressure—not the covert actions of the White House—had laid the political foundations for peace negotiations, which ultimately were what brought the two sides together. "President Reagan sought ceaselessly to crush the Sandinistas through a proxy insurgency," asserted the *New York Times*. "The war divided Americans without resolving the argument over its wisdom or morality. It produced the Iran-Contra scandal. And it left Nicaragua's economy in ruins."[89]

By contrast, conservatives argued that the Reagan administration orchestrated the outcome by placing military, economic, and political pressure on the Sandinistas, who ultimately had no choice but to accept the Contadora Plan. "American policy in Nicaragua has worked," asserted *National Review*. "The Contras have been vindicated. Only the threat of escalated war forced the Sandinistas to accept open elections, which then spun out of control."[90] In the end, the defeat of Ortega was a victory for Reagan, who had made the cause his own at great political expense. But whether his temporary triumph—the Sandinistas returned to power when Ortega was reelected president in 2006—would permanently erase the dark shadows of the Iran-Contra scandal remains a historical question.

THE IRAN-CONTRA AFFAIR

In May 1986, a group of Americans with Irish passports, false identities, and suicide pills (in case of discovery) arrived in Tehran and checked into what was once the Hilton hotel. The group included Robert "Bud" McFarlane, Reagan's former national security adviser, and Marine Lt. Col. Oliver North, a staff member of the National Security Council (NSC). The purpose of the clandestine visit was to meet with "moderate" officials in the Iranian government, which was in desperate need of American weapons to defeat the Iraqi army. The hope was that, in return for the sale of arms, the moderates might expedite the release of seven Americans held hostage in Lebanon by terrorists with ties to Tehran. If the officials came to power, Iran might also resume the role it had assumed under the shah, when it was a strategic barrier to Soviet influence in the Middle East. To facilitate the deal, the Americans brought personal gifts for the Ayatollah Khomeini. But in a stunning display of cultural ignorance or insensitivity, the gifts included a chocolate cake from a Jewish bakery in Tel Aviv and a Christian Bible that President Reagan had inscribed with a favorite passage from the New Testament.

Not surprisingly, perhaps, the meetings went poorly. After three days of fruitless discussions, the Americans departed hastily when they learned that their mission was no longer secret. News of the rendezvous had leaked, and within months thousands of leaflets with photos of McFarlane were circulating in Tehran. In November 1986, a Lebanese magazine made international headlines when it reported what had happened and the speaker of Iran's parliament confirmed most of the details. Within forty-eight hours, dramatic accounts of the failed mission were on the front pages of virtually every major newspaper in the United States. The first—but certainly not the last—media bombshell exploded as what eventually became known as the Iran-Contra affair erupted into public view. Soon talk of impeachment was in the air. By the time the dust had settled, the collateral damage to Reagan's popularity and American credibility was extensive, even though liberal Democrats and conservative Republicans continued to debate the meaning and significance of the scandal.

The Iran-Contra affair contained three main storylines. The first was that the Reagan administration had arranged for private donors and foreign nations to channel funds to the Contras in probable violation of the 1984 Boland Amendment, which banned aid or assistance from the United States to the Contras. The second storyline was that the White House, in probable violation of U.S. law, U.S. policy against deals for terrorists, and the U.S.

arms embargo imposed upon Iran in 1983, had sold weapons to Tehran in return for the release of American hostages, among other considerations. The third was that NSC staffers, in association with private individuals, had overcharged the Iranians for the weapons and diverted the proceeds to the Contras, in clear violation of U.S. law and policy, although most likely without the direct knowledge of the president. None of the administration's actions was disclosed to Congress as required by law. Ultimately, no fewer than three investigations—by a presidential commission, a joint House-Senate select committee, and a special prosecutor—would attempt to uncover the full story, but many questions would remain unanswered and unanswerable, at least in any sort of definitive manner.

The scandal had three main players. William Casey, director of the Central Intelligence Agency (CIA), was a conservative Republican with a reputation for impatience and arrogance. He also had a penchant for mumbling inaudibly, which at times made it difficult for Reagan and others to hear or understand him. A lawyer by profession, Casey had overseen clandestine operations for the Office of Strategic Services—the precursor to the CIA—in World War II and served in both the Nixon and Ford administrations. McFarlane was a mild-mannered but ambitious former Marine who had served two tours of duty in Vietnam and joined the NSC in 1982. Afflicted with self-doubts, he had a tendency to defer to others in moments of crisis. North was a bold and brash former Marine who had also served in Vietnam. Shortly after his return in 1974 he had suffered a mental breakdown, probably due to "emotional distress" (his medical records mysteriously disappeared from Bethesda Naval Hospital). But North had returned to active duty, become a born-again Christian, and gone to work at the NSC in 1981. He then recruited former U.S. Air Force general Richard Secord, now an arms dealer, and Iranian-born Albert Hakim, now in the import-export business, for what North called "the Enterprise."

The Contra part of the affair began in the spring of 1984, when it was apparent that Congress would soon restrict aid to the anti-Sandinistas. "Bud," an anxious Reagan told McFarlane after a meeting in the Oval Office, "I want you to do whatever you have to do to help these people keep body and soul together. Do everything you can." With the knowledge and support of Casey, McFarlane went in May—two days after the House had voted to end all aid to the "freedom fighters"—to the Virginia mansion of Prince Bandar, the Saudi ambassador to the United States. Bandar told the NSC official that his government would contribute $1 million a month to the Contra cause. McFarlane told the prince to wire the funds directly to the Miami bank account of a prominent Contra leader. Then, over Memorial Day weekend, the White House quietly announced an "emergency" sale of four hundred Stinger ground-to-air missiles and two hundred launchers to Saudi Arabia. The use of the word "emergency" enabled the administration to bypass Congress, which otherwise would have had thirty days to delay or void the sale. The next time McFarlane saw Reagan, he placed a note card about the Saudi donation in the president's daily briefing book. "Mum's the word," wrote Reagan, who returned the note to Mc-Farlane.[91]

Meanwhile, North was busy on two fronts. First, he was raising money for the Contras from wealthy conservatives through the National Endowment for the Preservation of Liberty (NEPL), a tax-exempt non-profit foundation supposedly dedicated to educational activities. North informed donors that the organization had the president's full support—a perception Reagan encouraged by attending numerous photo opportunities arranged by the foundation, which raised millions of dollars for the Contras and spent millions of dollars on "overhead"—salaries, commissions, and expenses—for NEPL officials. Second, North built the Enterprise to boldly go wherever was necessary. With the help of Secord and Hakim, it soon consisted of a private fleet of ships and planes, piloted by a motley crew of arms dealers and drug traffickers, Cuban exiles and hired mercenaries. To facilitate secrecy, the operation used a network of dummy corporations and Swiss banks.

The Iran part of the affair began in the summer of 1985, after terrorists (some affiliated with Hezbollah) had taken seven Americans hostage in Lebanon the previous year. In June, three days after Reagan had vowed never to negotiate with terrorists, an Israeli official came to McFarlane with an interesting proposition. Israel had developed close ties to Iran when the shah was in power and had maintained a working relationship with the Ayatollah Khomeini based on mutual interests. For their war with Iraq, the Iranians needed Israeli weapons. For their security, the Israelis needed Iran to serve as a strategic check on Saddam Hussein. The official claimed that Iranian moderates opposed to the Khomeini regime had promised that they could arrange the release of the hostages in return for weapons, which Israel would supply if the United States agreed to replace them.

McFarlane was intrigued. On the one hand, if the Reagan administration could convert Iran from a foe to a friend it could transform the strategic balance in the Middle East and strengthen the global leverage of the United States in relation to the Soviet Union. In historical terms, a diplomatic rapprochement between America and Iran might even prove as significant as Richard Nixon's 1972 visit to Communist China, which opened the door to mutual recognition and improved relations between two countries who conveniently shared a common adversary in the Soviet Union. On the other, the Israeli proposal at bottom involved the exchange of arms for hostages, a potential repudiation of U.S. policy on international terrorism and a political risk of the highest magnitude (neither Congress nor the American people would ever support the sale of weapons to Iran if it became public knowledge). The plan was also in violation of Operation Staunch, the arms embargo against Iran that the United States had organized and lobbied other nations to join. It also seemingly contradicted U.S. efforts to curry favor with Iraqi leader Saddam Hussein, who would undoubtedly feel betrayed by a sudden shift to Iran's side. Finally, permitting another country (Israel) to sell American weapons to a third party (Iran) without Congressional notification was a formal breach of the Arms Control Export Act.

In the White House, the Israeli offer met with a mixed response. Secretary of State George Shultz and Secretary of Defense Caspar Weinberger were dubious and expressed reservations. When McFarlane drafted and circulated a secret presidential directive outlining the proposed new Iran policy in June 1985, Weinberger was withering in his assessment. "This is almost too absurd to comment on," he wrote in the margins. "It's like asking [Libyan dictator Muammar] Qaddafi to Washington for a cozy chat."[92] But McFarlane and Casey were enthusiastic. Both men were unrepentant and unreconstructed cold warriors who saw the plan as an ideal way to block Soviet ambitions in the Persian Gulf and improve diplomatic relations with Iran after Khomeini died. For his part, Reagan was also excited because, as he wrote in his diary after a meeting in July, it "could be a breakthrough on getting our seven kidnap victims back."[93] But Casey neglected to inform the president that the middle man allegedly in contact with the Iranian moderates was Manucher Ghorbanifar, an arms dealer of questionable character whom the CIA had previously labeled an "intelligence fabricator" because he had twice failed lie-detector tests.[94]

Why Casey ignored the warning light in plain sight remains unclear. What is clear is that he and McFarlane cleverly crafted anti-Communist arguments designed to appeal to Reagan, a fellow cold warrior. But it is also evident that the president was motivated above all by the plight of the Americans held in captivity in Lebanon. "It is just undeniable that Reagan's obsession with freeing the hostages overrode anything else," admitted McFarlane later. Shultz concurred, although he placed partial blame on the president's aides. "I believe [they] did exactly what . . . staff people shouldn't do," he said. "They knew he had a soft spot for the hostages. And they exploited him." Whether Reagan was primarily an exploited or eager player in the arms-for-hostages game remains a matter of debate. But without question he was a willing participant and, as a biographer has noted, the result was that U.S. policy ironically became a prisoner of the American hostages in the Middle East.[95]

The next critical meeting took place in early August 1985. With the Israelis anxious for a decision, Shultz and Weinberger continued to voice doubts. The secretary of state later said that he had declared that "we were just falling into the arms-for-hostages business and we shouldn't do it."[96] McFarlane and White House chief of staff Donald Regan were in favor of the Iran initiative. Reagan was noncommittal. Clad in pajamas and a bathrobe, he was recovering from intestinal surgery. When the meeting ended, both sides assumed that the president was in agreement with their position. Soon after, according to McFarlane, Reagan gave him an "oral authorization" to transfer one hundred anti-tank missiles to Israel. By law the president should have informed Congress, but he took no action. When later asked by investigators, Reagan first stated that he had approved the transfer in advance. Then he said he had not. Finally he said he could not recall. In any event, Israel went ahead and shipped ninety-six of the missiles to Iran in late August. Who received them is unknown, although it is doubtful it was the so-called moderates.

The shipment led to fresh demands from the Iranians, not the immediate release of any hostages. In response to a request from Washington, Israel in September 1985 sent more than four hundred missiles to Iran and an American missionary received his freedom. Two months later, the Israelis temporarily withdrew from the operation, perhaps because they feared exposure. Into the breach stepped North and the Enterprise, which shipped eighteen Homing All the Way Killer (HAWK) missiles to Tehran via Portugal, only to have the Iranians reject them for technical reasons. Nevertheless, Reagan remained optimistic about the hostages. "We have an undercover thing going by way of an Iranian," he wrote in his diary in November, "which could get them sprung momentarily."[97] In the president's heart, hope sprang eternal.

But in December 1985, Reagan had a dose of reality. First, McFarlane resigned from the NSC and was replaced by Admiral John Poindexter, a brilliant but blinkered bureaucrat who was a close ally of Casey and North. Second, under pressure from CIA lawyers, the president signed an official finding on December 5 that retroactively authorized the three missile shipments made to date. Attached to the finding was a background summary titled "Hostage Rescue—Middle East," which stated that the sole purpose of the covert operation was to "obtain the release of Americans being held hostage in the Middle East." No longer was there any doubt about the main motive behind the Iran initiative. The finding also ordered Casey to disregard his legal obligation to report to Congress "in a timely fashion" unless explicitly ordered to do so by the president.[98] In his journal that night, Reagan wrote that the operation was "our undercover effort to free our five hostages held by terrorists in Lebanon." Then he discretely revealed how informed and involved he was: "It is a complex undertaking with only a few of us in on it. I won't even write in the diary what we're up to."[99]

Two days later, on December 7, Reagan again met with his national security team. The same individuals offered the same arguments with the same result—the president vowed to ship missiles to Iran and free the hostages despite vocal opposition from Shultz and Weinberger. "The weapons will go to the moderate leaders in the army who are essential if there's to be a change to a more stable government," wrote Reagan in his diary, returning to the original justification. "None of this is a gift—the Iranians pay cash for the weapons—so does Israel."[100] A month later, the team (minus McFarlane) reassembled and reenacted the drama. Once again, Casey and Poindexter won the argument, although the outcome was never in doubt. The Iran initiative would continue. But by January 1986, it had degenerated into a straight arms-for-cash deal with Tehran. To authorize the covert sales, Reagan signed two additional presidential findings without bothering to notify either the secretary of state or the secretary of defense, who remained opposed to the operation. Henceforth Shultz and Weinberger, who contemplated resigning, would find themselves "out of the loop," uninformed and unconsulted.

In the spring and summer of 1986, Iran received thousands of missiles despite the fiasco in May, when McFarlane and North were unable to meet face-to-face in Tehran with the supposed moderates—a "heartbreaking disappointment" according to Reagan. In August, the president outlawed weapons sales to terrorist nations, Iran included, but he would not abandon the secret program. Thus far the "rug merchants"—as Reagan described them in his diary—had freed a single hostage, only to murder another and kidnap three more.[101] From that perspective, the covert operation was a failure. But in a different sense it was a success, for North had discovered what he termed a "neat idea"—that he could overcharge for the missiles and divert the proceeds to the Contras, who eventually received tens of millions of dollars from the Enterprise, whose coconspirators also profited handsomely. The separate storylines had now merged into a single scandal, whose exposure was imminent.

The plot was uncovered in October 1986 when a cargo plane leased by the CIA and laden with supplies for the Contras crashed in a hail of gunfire in Nicaragua. North had paid for the supplies with funds diverted from the arms sales to Iran. The plane was piloted by an American mercenary, former Marine Eugene Hasenfus, who survived the crash, was captured by the Sandinistas, and confessed to his role in what he believed was a CIA operation. The White House instantly went into denial mode, asserting that the administration was not involved and that Hasenfus was a private citizen acting on his own. Then in November the administration received more bad news as the Republican Party lost control of the Senate in the congressional elections, followed the next day by the shocking account of the Tehran trip by McFarlane and North. Again, the White House discounted the disclosure.

But despite the denials, the clamor for answers continued. On November 13, the president gave a televised address. Placing his credibility on the line, Reagan contended that the secret initiative was intended to improve relations with Iran, end the war with Iraq, reduce terrorism and, almost as an afterthought, bring home the hostages. The weapons transfers were not ransom payments. "The United States has not made concessions to those who hold our people captive in Lebanon. And we will not," said Reagan. "The United States has not swapped boatloads or planeloads of American weapons for the return of American hostages. And we will not." Both assertions were either half-truths or partial lies—the White House had not negotiated with the kidnappers themselves or traded missiles for hostages directly. The president added that he had "authorized the transfer of small amounts of defensive weapons and spare parts for defensive systems to Iran" which, "taken together, could easily fit into a single cargo plane." Both assertions were false—the missiles had offensive capabilities and could not fit into a single plane. In his summary, Reagan offered these words: "We did not—repeat—did not trade weapons or anything else for hostages, nor will we."[102] This assertion was a technical truth—Iran had paid for the weapons. But left unmentioned were the larger issues as well as the laws evaded and trusts violated.

Panic and confusion engulfed the White House in November 1986. Casey and Poindexter prepared cover stories with false chronologies and offered false testimony under oath to the House and Senate intelligence committees. Both men blamed Israel for having delivered the initial proposition (Reagan in hindsight also said he felt misled). At a press conference on November 19, the president announced that "to eliminate the widespread but mistaken perception that we have been exchanging arms for hostages I have directed that no further sales of any kind be sent to Iran." He also claimed that the United States had not condoned "the shipment of arms by other countries" to Tehran. Later Reagan issued a clarification acknowledging that "there was a third country involved in our secret project with Iran."[103] The next day Shultz informed the president that he had made many false or misleading public statements.

Attorney General Edwin Meese III then asked for and received permission from the president to conduct an internal inquiry. He notified Poindexter on Friday, November 21, that he wanted to see all materials relevant to the Iran initiative. Poindexter in turn contacted North and the two men immediately began to destroy as many documents as possible in what North termed "a shredding party." During the Watergate crisis of 1973–1974, Richard Nixon had obstructed justice by withholding evidence (the famous White House tapes); now top officials were destroying evidence. But on Saturday an aide to Meese found a memo detailing the diversion of funds to the Contras, and on Monday the attorney general revealed the smoking gun to the president after a two-hour meeting in the Situation Room. "This may call for resignations," wrote Reagan in his diary, upset that neither North nor Poindexter had, apparently, told him.[104]

At another press conference on Tuesday, November 25, a shaken Reagan read a four-paragraph prepared statement. Although he continued to defend the Iran operation in broad terms, he stated that he was not "fully informed" and admitted that "in one aspect implementation of that policy was seriously flawed." He then announced the resignation of Poindexter and the reassignment of North from the NSC. The president also promised to appoint a special review board (soon known as the Tower Commission because it was chaired by former Republican Senator John Tower of Texas) to investigate the matter.[105] At that point, Reagan declined to answer questions and surrendered the podium to Meese, who divulged the details of the diversion to reporters.

The revelations shocked and stunned the media. Conservatives were surprised and speechless at first. Liberals reacted with outrage. "The whole affair, from Israeli arms shipments through Swiss bank accounts to subsidizing the Contras, smacks of a pattern of lawlessness," asserted the *New York Times* on November 26. How was Reagan not aware of what the "White House cowboys"—Poindexter and North—were doing? "It's hard to know which would be more alarming, Presidential ignorance or arrogance," added the paper, which endorsed an immediate and complete investigation by Congress because "little serious business can be done at home or abroad

President Reagan meets on November 25, 1986, with (from left to right) Secretary of Defense Caspar Weinberger, Secretary of State George Shultz, Attorney General Edwin Meese, and Chief of Staff Donald Regan to discuss the Iran-Contra affair. (Courtesy of the Ronald Reagan Library.)

until the truth is fully explored and the Administration reaffirms sound judgment and respect for law."[106]

News of the diversion also led to deep public dismay. To millions it seemed as though Reagan had broken his word and his bond with the American people. In the Gallup Poll, the president's approval rating dropped in December 1986 by more than twenty points (from 67 to 46 percent)—the largest one-month decline in the survey's history. Meanwhile, the Justice Department named Lawrence Walsh, a well-regarded Republican lawyer and judge, as a special prosecutor to conduct an independent investigation. Congress prepared to hold joint hearings by House and Senate select committees. The greatest political crisis since the Watergate scandal had begun. But in the end the Iran-Contra affair would not lead to the impeachment or resignation of the president. Unlike Nixon, Reagan would survive his trial by inquiry for a number of reasons.

Historical precedent and the political calendar both worked in Reagan's favor. The Watergate scandal had conditioned the press and the public to look for the smoking gun. In the Iran–Contra affair, the most startling revelation was the diversion of profits by North to the Contras, which became the focus of the inquiries. But it was the charge that the president could most plausibly deny knowledge of—and in many respects the diversion was less significant than the original commitment to trade arms for hostages or the subsequent cover-up. Watergate had also come at the start of Nixon's second term, after a landslide reelection in which he had earned a true mandate from the American people. By contrast, Reagan was a lame duck with little more than a year left in the White House. Moreover, if he was impeached and removed from office it might affect the presidential election by painting Democrats as partisan prosecutors of Republicans and giving Vice President George H. W. Bush the chance to run as the incumbent in 1988. Neither prospect filled Democrats with pleasure.

Above all, Reagan retained a personal appeal and reservoir of trust that served him well, as would the wave of sympathy he received after he underwent prostate surgery in January 1987. In the months after the scandal erupted, many Americans simply wanted to believe him when he claimed, over and over again, that he had not traded arms for hostages, regardless of what some officials might claim or what some documents might reveal. What the public correctly sensed was that in stark contrast to Nixon, who had acted from purely political motives, Reagan had acted from a sincere personal desire to free the Americans held captive. Ironically, he also benefited from the perception that he was an incompetent or inattentive administrator. The popular image of the president as a disengaged and forgetful leader with a touch of senility made the explanation that he was either unaware or manipulated by aides both plausible to liberals and opportune for conservatives. Of course, Reagan's diaries reveal the contrary—that from the start he was an active and assertive participant in the plan to sell arms to Iran, as *Saturday Night Live* had suggested, albeit for laughs.

The Tower Commission finished its investigation in February 1987. The review board was a creation of the executive branch, not an independent body. It also had a limited mandate—to examine how well the NSC had functioned—and a short deadline. Most important, by law it could not subpoena documents or compel witnesses to testify under oath. Nevertheless, the Tower Commission somehow acquired the mantle of impartiality and the final report somehow assumed an air of authority. As a result, the main findings—that the president's detached management style had permitted the original Iran initiative to degenerate into an arms-for-hostages deal and that he had "no knowledge" of the diversion of funds until informed by Meese in November 1986—became the conventional wisdom and a convenient excuse for Reagan, who received great credit for his stated desire to let "all the facts . . . come out."[107]

The Tower Commission was critical of the covert operation, which it termed flawed and unprofessional, an illustration of "the perils of policy pursued outside the constraints of orderly process." The sale of weapons to Iran "rewarded a regime that clearly supported terrorism and hostage-taking." It also fed the perception in the Middle East that the United States was a "creature of Israel" and an enemy of Iraq. The report also pointed to the failure of the president to demand accountability from his subordinates. "Had the President chosen to drive the NSC system, the outcome could well have been different," it noted. Finally, the Tower Commission pointed fingers of blame at most of the principals, including Casey, McFarlane, Poindexter, and Regan, who resigned shortly thereafter. Even Shultz and Weinberger came in for criticism, primarily because they had "distanced themselves from the march of events" and denied the president the full benefit of their counsel. (See "Excerpts from 'The Tower Commission Report.'") Not surprisingly, the secretary of state and secretary of defense were displeased with the report.

But the Tower Commission provided Reagan with political cover, even if it was not readily apparent. In March 1987, he spoke to the nation, embraced the report's recommendations, and accepted "full responsibility"—though not the blame—for what had happened "on my watch." The pundits praised the president—the *New York Times* complimented the candid words and "spirit of contrition," although it observed that the speech contained no apology, formal or otherwise.[108] Instead, Reagan remained resolute, sticking to his story that he was not informed when "what began as a strategic opening to Iran deteriorated, in its implementation, into trading arms for hostages." He also defended his management style, implying that the problems were mostly a matter of personnel, not process, and promising that he had made appropriate changes in the NSC staff. (See "Excerpts from 'Address to the Nation on the Iran Arms and Contra Aid Controversy.'")

In the speech, Reagan admitted that he had falsely claimed that the United States had not traded arms for hostages. Now he conceded he was mistaken, although for understandable and forgivable reasons. "My heart and my best intentions still tell me that's true," the president said, "but the facts and the evidence tell me it is not." If anything, he added, he was guilty of caring too much for the hostages and their families. As Reagan put it, "I asked so many questions about the hostages' welfare that I didn't ask enough about the specifics of the total Iran plan." (See "Excerpts from 'Address to the Nation on the Iran Arms and Contra Aid Controversy.'") It was a masterful touch by a gifted politician. In his diary that night, the president noted proudly that a record 93 percent of the phone calls to the White House after the televised address were strongly positive. "Even the TV bone pickers who follow the speech with their commentaries said nice things about it," he wrote.[109]

The speech was a great success. But many questions remained and liberal critics of the White House expected that the joint hearings in Congress would provide some answers. Unlike the Tower Commission, the House and Senate select committees would have the legal authority to subpoena documents and compel witnesses to testify under oath. With Democrats in charge of Congress, it was assumed by allies and enemies of the administration that they would leave no stone unturned in an effort to find incriminating evidence. As the televised hearings began in May 1987, the level of excitement and anticipation in Washington was at a height not seen since Watergate. But when the hearings came to an end after forty days and twenty-eight witnesses, the hero of the hour was North and the attention of the nation was no longer on impeachment.

The outcome was largely the result of a series of major and minor miscalculations by the majority party. In the spirit of efficiency, Democrats elected to hold joint hearings with eleven senators, fifteen congressmen, and numerous staffers, which proved unwieldy, required a two-tiered seating arrangement, and created the impression on television that it was the lone hero (North) versus the lynch mob (Congress). The joint hearings also led to a clash of political cultures, as the more genteel style of Senate Democrats collided with the take-no-prisoners attitude of House Republicans. In the spirit of bipartisanship, Democrats opted not to subpoena Reagan or Bush, who was present at many of the critical meetings. Also, in the spirit of cooperation, they granted North and Poindexter immunity from criminal prosecution in return for limited testimony and no depositions, which meant the committees had little idea of what to expect from the witnesses in advance. Finally, Democrats selected two intelligent and capable men as lead attorneys. But Arthur Liman was a New York Jew with bad hair and John Nields resembled a 1960s student radical with long hair. Under the bright lights of the television cameras, neither could compete with the handsome and heroic North, a paragon of patriotism who testified in a uniform adorned with medals. It was yet another mistake by Democrats, who could have insisted that he wear a suit instead.

North was the star of the hearings, in part because he offered a simple and stirring defense. We live in a dangerous world, he asserted. In a dangerous world, covert operations are necessary and proper. They also require secrecy and deception. Therefore his actions—whether they involved destroying documents or lying to Congress—were necessary and proper. North also offered three additional justifications. First, in defense of national security it was often essential and acceptable to resort to a higher law beyond the Constitution. Second, in foreign affairs the executive branch had the constitutional right and duty to act without interference from the legislative branch. Finally, free from fear of prosecution for perjury, North alleged that Reagan had known and approved of what he was doing. He was a Marine and he had followed orders—that was it. North had no evidence for this allegation and none was ever found.

But it made little difference. Olliemania swept the nation. Women swooned. Men cheered. Liberals muttered about how the rule of law had to supersede a higher law, but most conservatives hailed the hero without reservation. North posed for pictures with the Senate police force while Liman received death threats, many of them anti-Semitic. After the North performance it was all anticlimactic. Poindexter testified that he had not notified Reagan about the diversion and that to maintain "plausible deniability" he had shielded the president from knowledge of the operation. The role of the CIA and Casey remained obscure because he had died of brain cancer in May 1987, six weeks after suffering a serious stroke and before he could testify to Congress. Of what he had known, of what he had informed Reagan, and of what he had wanted to do—whether for instance he had sought to create a shadow CIA within the regular agency—were and would remain matters of speculation without resolution.

The reports issued by Democrats and Republicans after the hearings mirrored the liberal-conservative split on Iran-Contra. The majority report echoed the liberal line. The scandal was a constitutional crisis—the most serious since Watergate. In a return to the "imperial presidency" of the Vietnam era, the executive branch had defied the legislative branch in abuse of the balance of powers. The president had also committed the second-worst offense possible—he had failed "to take care that the laws be faithfully executed." In particular, Reagan had permitted officials in the administration—regardless of whether he knew or not—to violate the letter and spirit of the Boland Amendment of 1984 by soliciting funds from other nations for the Contras and diverting profits from the Enterprise to them. It was more than a management failure—it was a "gross default of moral leadership," commented the *New York Times*. "At last the committees took the spotlight off the unprovable smoking gun and put it on the smoking cannon."[110]

The minority report echoed the conservative claim. The scandal was above all a political dispute over policy differences. The administration's actions—with the exception of the diversion—were justified and legal. The NSC was not an intelligence agency and the Boland Amendment of 1984 (regardless of the intent of Congress) was not applicable to third parties. "President Reagan drew the line in the dirt and told the Communists they would not be permitted to establish a Soviet beachhead on the mainland of the Americas," declared conservative commentator Patrick Buchanan, a former speechwriter in the Nixon administration. "Make no mistake. That is what the furor in Washington is all about, not whether technicalities of the law were circumvented."[111] Moreover, in constitutional context it was the legislative branch that had tilted the balance of powers by infringing upon the diplomatic prerogatives of the executive branch. The real threat for many conservatives was a return to the "imperiled presidency" of the 1970s, which one of the minority report's main authors, Republican Representative Dick Cheney of Wyoming, was determined to prevent. Later, as vice president in the George W. Bush administration, he was a consistent and forceful advocate of greatly expanded executive authority, especially after the terrorist attacks of September 2001 and the start of the Second Gulf War with Iraq in March 2003.

Others sought to put the Contra scandal in historical context. In the 1930s, Democratic President Franklin Roosevelt had faced the threat of Fascism. Despite isolationism in Congress and the country, he had responded by secretly taking naval action against German submarines in the North Atlantic. Yet he received little condemnation. In the 1980s, Reagan had faced the dual threats of Communism and terrorism. Despite opposition in Congress and the country, he had responded by secretly launching covert operations in Latin America and selling weapons to Iran. Yet he received harsh criticism. It was, some argued, a double standard with little fairness given the historical parallels.

After the hearings had concluded, the wheels of justice or injustice continued to turn, albeit slowly. Although Congress took no action against Reagan, who dismissed the majority report, it brought indictments against North and Poindexter as well as Secord and Hakim, the Enterprise coconspirators. McFarlane pleaded guilty to four counts of withholding information from Congress. Meanwhile, the special prosecutor spent eight years and $40 million investigating the affair. In the end, Walsh added little to the historical record. But he charged fourteen administration officials, including Weinberger, with criminal acts related to either the operation or the cover up. Of those charged, eleven were convicted or pleaded guilty. The convictions of North and Poindexter were overturned on appeal due to technicalities. Weinberger avoided trial when President Bush pardoned him, McFarlane, and four others in December 1992, shortly after he lost his bid for reelection to Arkansas Governor Bill Clinton.

In retrospect, Reagan had few regrets. "If I could do it over again," he reflected, "I would bring both of them [Poindexter and North] into the Oval Office and say, 'Okay, John and Ollie, level with me. Tell me what really happened and what it is that you have been hiding from me. Tell me everything.' If I had done that, at least I wouldn't be sitting here, writing this book, still ignorant of some of the things that went on during the Iran-Contra affair."[112] Others have wondered if his 1984 landslide reelection made the president overconfident. It is also possible that Reagan's more pragmatic and astute first-term aides, such as White House chief of staff James Baker, might have kept in check the president's instinct to free the hostages at all costs and given him better counsel than McFarlane or Regan, who succeeded Baker when he became Treasury secretary.

These and many other questions continue to resist definitive answers and likely will for the foreseeable future. Many documents were destroyed, many remain classified, and many were never kept in the first place. The incomplete and inaccessible archival record, combined with the unexpected death of Casey and the contradictory testimony of Poindexter and North, make it difficult, if not impossible, to learn for certain what Reagan knew and when he knew it. But beyond doubt, the Iran-Contra scandal has contributed significantly to three decades of increasingly bitter partisan strife and a cycle of crises in which many conservatives viewed the 1998 impeachment of President Clinton as political payback for the liberal vendettas against Nixon and Reagan.

Iran-Contra was the low point of the Reagan presidency. "He will never again be the Reagan that he was before he blew it," said Republican Congressman Newt Gingrich of Georgia in February 1987. "He is not going to regain our trust and our faith so easily."[113] The assessment was premature. Although the president's image and reputation suffered—he never again enjoyed the goodwill he had possessed prior to the scandal—his approval ratings rebounded until, when he left the White House in January 1989, he had the highest rating (68 percent) of any chief executive since Roosevelt's death in April 1945. As with Lebanon and Grenada, Reagan benefited from good fortune and good timing, as the emergence of the Iran-Contra affair coincided with the emergence of a new relationship with the Soviet Union. Inside the White House, the scandal also weakened the influence of the ideologues and strengthened the influence of the pragmatists, who supported the new direction. Ironically, what had led the president into the arms-for-hostages fiasco in the first place—his faith in his instincts—would become the foundation of his successful partnership with Mikhail Gorbachev, the Soviet leader. Together, in what was the high point of the Reagan era, they would defy the doubters and detractors to bring the Cold War to a peaceful resolution.

THE COLD WAR—SECOND TERM

In August 1984, Ronald Reagan offered some unscripted and unsettling remarks prior to a national radio address. "My fellow Americans," he quipped, not realizing that he was speaking into a live microphone, "I am pleased to tell you today I've just signed legislation that will outlaw the Soviet Union forever. We begin bombing in five minutes."[114] The weak joke may have amused conservative listeners during the summer heat of the presidential campaign, but it angered liberal critics and alarmed Soviet officials, who anxiously searched for any indications of impending war. Yet in December 1991 legislation to outlaw the Soviet Union was signed—by Mikhail Gorbachev, general secretary of the Communist Party, who on Christmas Day officially acknowledged the formal end of the "evil empire" that had once seemed so menacing and omnipotent.

A decade earlier, the outcome would have shocked and surprised almost everyone on either side of the Iron Curtain, which had divided Eastern and Western Europe since the mid-1940s. When Reagan took office in 1981, the Cold War seemed like a permanent and perilous reality. Few expected any sudden shift in the status quo. Most believed that the United States and the Soviet Union would continue to wage a global struggle for political and military influence and dominance. "The dictatorship of the Communist Party remains untouched and untouchable," predicted Robert Gates, a Central Intelligence Agency (CIA) deputy director, in 1988. "A long, competitive struggle with the Soviet Union still lies before us."[115] But a year later, the fall of the Berlin Wall—only months after Reagan left office—foreshadowed the imminent demise of the Soviet Union.

The unforeseen unraveling of the Soviet empire marked the peaceful conclusion of the superpower rivalry. Unlike his predecessors, Gorbachev opted not to use force when confronted with independence movements in Eastern Europe and the Baltic States. But the end of the Cold War also marked the beginning of a heated debate over whether the outcome was inevitable and, if not, who was most responsible. In hindsight, it seems clear that the Soviet Union was destined to disintegrate at some point under the weight of defense spending and an economic system that stifled individual initiative and could not meet the basic needs of most citizens. "How long will our military-industrial complex keep devouring our economy, our agriculture, and our consumer goods?" complained a Soviet official in the mid-1980s. "How long are we going to take this ogre, how long are we going to throw into its mouth the food of our children?"[116] But when the final chapter would arrive was not clear—certainly 1991 was by no means preordained.

At the center of the political and historical controversy are the relative importance of Gorbachev and Reagan. Many scholars and most liberals credit the Soviet leader, who took office in 1985 and began to implement major reforms almost immediately. Through his policy of *glasnost*, Gorbachev wanted to reorient the Soviet government by making it more transparent. No longer would secrecy and mystery dominate every official action. Through his policy of *perestroika*, Gorbachev wanted to restructure the Soviet economy by spending less on weapons for the military and more on products for consumers. Consequently, he sought to improve relations with the United States and end the arms race that had lasted for decades and cost hundreds of billions of dollars. Through his policy of "new thinking," Gorbachev wanted to promote the revisionist idea that class struggle could no longer serve as the objective basis for the Cold War. Whether his ultimate intent was to strengthen or weaken Communist control remains a matter of some political debate, although few scholars now doubt that he was a genuine reformer. Nevertheless, this interpretation stresses the primary role played by the Soviet leader, who had to overcome the suspicion and distrust of both Kremlin officials and the Reagan administration, which played a secondary role.

By contrast, some scholars and most conservatives view the collapse of Communism as a personal triumph for Reagan. In the words of British Prime Minister Margaret Thatcher, a friend and ally, he "won the Cold War without firing a shot."[117] From the start, the president had a clear vision. Unlike most White House officials and foreign-policy experts, he foresaw a world free of the threat of Communist coercion and nuclear war. Reagan also had a clear plan—he sought to roll back, not contain, the Soviet empire, which he saw as a transitory menace that was vulnerable to economic pressure. Consequently, he launched a historic military buildup because he knew that the technologically inferior and financially strapped Soviets could not afford to keep pace. Reagan moreover applied moral pressure by denying the legitimacy of Communism, which inspired opposition in places like

Poland. Finally, to put military pressure on Moscow, Washington provided covert aid to anti-Communist fighters such as the mujahideen in Afghanistan and the Contras in Nicaragua. Whether the president believed that his actions would lead to dramatic and rapid change in the Soviet Union remains controversial. Nevertheless, this interpretation stresses the deliberate intent and direct impact of Reagan's hard-line policies, which forced Gorbachev—out of despair, not desire—to steer the course that he chose.

Other scholars offer a third explanation, in which Gorbachev and Reagan are costars who share equal billing and warrant equal accolades for ending forty years of bitter hostilities. To his credit, Gorbachev was willing to risk political suicide at home in pursuit of real reform, which led to the eventual dissolution of the Soviet Union and downfall of the Communist Party, whether intentional or not. To his credit, Reagan was willing to disregard harsh criticism from his conservative allies and accept the Soviet leader as a sincere partner for peaceful progress. What this interpretation emphasizes is that Reagan does not deserve praise for the belligerent actions of his first term, which may have prolonged the Cold War by increasing Politburo resistance to Gorbachev's policies. Instead, the president merits applause for the conciliatory actions of his second term, when he and his Soviet counterpart built a strong relationship based on mutual respect and achieved remarkable reductions in nuclear stockpiles.

In retrospect, the Reagan presidency was a tale of two terms. From 1981 to 1984, the United States and the Soviet Union were adversaries. At every public turn, the White House pursued a policy of confrontation and isolation, challenging the "evil empire" and refusing to hold a single summit with Soviet leaders. From 1985 to 1988, Reagan and Gorbachev achieved a remarkable rapprochement as they met five times in four years. The motivation for the shift in policy is ambiguous. Skeptics observe that the turning point, 1984, was an election year when the president or his advisers may have felt he had to pose as a peacemaker. They add that by 1987 the administration needed to deflect attention from the Iran-Contra scandal. By contrast, supporters contend that Reagan was always willing to negotiate—but only from a position of strength and with a partner for peace. Gorbachev, they note, was not in charge until 1985. In any event, the dramatic accomplishments of the final years of the Reagan administration were historic landmarks. The geopolitical landscape was transformed as dreams of a better world replaced nightmares of a nuclear holocaust.

The first of five summits between Reagan and Gorbachev that would change the course of history took place in Geneva in November 1985. The

White House was split on the merits of a meeting—ideologues like CIA director William Casey and Secretary of Defense Caspar Weinberger were opposed, while pragmatists like Secretary of State George Shultz saw an opportunity. Former President Richard Nixon was in favor of a summit, but he warned that it would not solve the irreconcilable differences between the United States and the Soviet Union. There was, he wrote in *Foreign Affairs*, only "one absolute certainty about the Soviet-American relationship," which was that "the struggle in which we are engaged will last not just for years but for decades." Reagan nevertheless prepared diligently by reading two dozen position papers as part of what a senior specialist on the National Security Council (NSC) staff termed the equivalent of "Soviet Union 101." Meanwhile, American diplomats generated briefing books and memoranda on IBM computers while their Soviet counterparts made do with electric typewriters—a revealing comparison of the state of technology in both nations.[118]

The preparation yielded mixed results in Geneva. Reagan earned an edge in style by braving the weather without a coat or hat and by towering over the bundled Gorbachev, who seemed to shiver in the cold. The Soviet leader also revealed, when he removed his hat, that he had less hair than Reagan, who was twenty years older. But the summit achieved little of substance as both leaders sparred over the Strategic Defense Initiative (SDI). It would, warned Gorbachev, inevitably lead to an arms race in outer space. "We will not help you in your plans," he told Reagan. "We will build up in order to smash your shield." The president was not intimidated, however, and soon broke the ice. With stories and jokes, he began to cultivate a personal relationship with Gorbachev, aided by the unprecedented use of simultaneous translation, which permitted the two men to gain a better sense of body language and verbal tone. "This has been a good meeting," commented Reagan. "I think I can work with this guy. I can't just keep poking him in the eye." For his part, Gorbachev described the president as "stubborn and very conservative," but "not as hopeless as some believed."[119] It was a promising, if limited, start.

In the coming months, two developments increased the pressure on Gorbachev. The first came in April 1986, when a nuclear reactor in Chernobyl exploded, releasing an enormous cloud of radioactive fallout that drifted hundreds of miles across Europe. It was the worst nuclear power plant accident in history—more than three hundred thousand residents of the Ukraine had to evacuate their homes. Yet the radiation released was less than what a single nuclear warhead would produce, which led Reagan to wonder whether Gorbachev had contemplated the impact of a single missile with multiple warheads. The second development was a worsening economic crisis aggravated by falling oil prices. "Our goal is to prevent the next round of the arms race," Gorbachev warned the Politburo. "If we do not accomplish it . . . we will lose it because we are already at the limits of our capabilities."[120] In September, frustrated with the lack of progress on the intermediate-range nuclear forces (INF) treaty and other issues, he invited Reagan to meet in Iceland the following month for a brief and frank discussion.

As Reagan awaited his second summit with Gorbachev, some of the president's aides were concerned that he was unprepared given the short lead time and would succumb to the charm or vigor of the Soviet leader. "I don't want you to ever worry," replied Reagan. "I still have the scars on my back from the fights with the communists in Hollywood. I am not going to give away *anything*."[121] Nevertheless, even old friends like the conservative actor Charlton Heston had doubts. He urged the president to "resist the temptations of a Yalta waltz with the Soviet bear." In response, Reagan again stressed that he was ready for the meeting: "I'm willing to dance but intend to lead."[122] He would make no concessions to the Soviet Union, unlike Franklin Roosevelt, whom conservatives had frequently blamed for having conceded Eastern Europe to Joseph Stalin at the Yalta Conference as World War II drew to a close.

The two-day summit in Reykjavik, Iceland, in October 1986 was the most dramatic of the Reagan era. At the start of the first day, Gorbachev submitted a proposal for a new INF treaty and a 50 percent reduction in nuclear arsenals. By the end of the second day, both sides had agreed in principle on a stunning package. It included an INF treaty based on the "zero-zero option" originally presented by Reagan in 1981 and a 50 percent reduction in nuclear weapons (bombers and submarines included) over five years, followed by the complete elimination of land-based nuclear missiles over the next five years. Finally, the United States and the Soviet Union would continue to comply with the ABM treaty for ten years, which meant no deployment of SDI until 1996 at the earliest. But Gorbachev was not satisfied with the two-stage concept, which would have left the Soviet Union at a considerable disadvantage since the United States had more bombers and submarines and fewer missiles. "It would be fine with me if we eliminate all nuclear weapons," said Reagan, who may not have grasped the important technical distinction between weapons and missiles. "We can do that," said Gorbachev as Shultz listened.

At that moment, Gorbachev raised the deal breaker—he wanted SDI research restricted to the laboratory so that the Americans could not develop a defensive shield and then deploy it in 1996 when the Soviets had no more nuclear missiles. "I cannot give in," said Reagan. "This is my last word," replied Gorbachev, who refused to accept assurances that the United States would share SDI technology with the Soviet Union. "I have done everything I could." The president stood. "The meeting is over," he said to Shultz. "Let's go, George, we're leaving." On the way to their cars, the Soviet leader said, "I don't know what else I could have done." To which Reagan heatedly replied, "I do. You could have said yes." Later the president expressed his anger in his diary. "He wanted language that would have killed SDI," Reagan wrote. "The price was high but I wouldn't sell and that's how the day ended."[123]

In the aftermath, confusion and controversy reigned. "At Reykjavik," Reagan recalled in his memoir, "my hopes for a nuclear-free world soared briefly, then fell during one of the longest, most disappointing—and ultimately angriest—days of my presidency."[124] Most liberals shared his sentiments, but their anger was reserved for the president, who had refused to abandon his SDI fantasy in return for the reality of a world rid of nuclear weapons. For their part, most conservatives were appalled that Reagan had casually offered to eliminate all nuclear weapons and nearly surrendered military superiority to the Soviet Union, whose conventional forces (soldiers, tanks, and artillery) outnumbered those of the United States. "Reagan's Suicide Pact" is how *National Review* termed it. "No summit since Yalta has threatened Western interests so much as the two days at Reykjavik," maintained Nixon, who was aghast.[125] "Something like Reykjavik never could happen again, never would happen again, and never *should* happen again," stated an administration official. "That meeting may forever be enshrined in world consciousness as a toss of nuclear dice."[126]

The Iceland summit was a bitter failure, but after emotions had cooled both Reagan and Gorbachev were able to appreciate the compromises the other had made. They also could see new possibilities and new opportunities. Above all, beneath the rhetoric each now understood the other better and sympathized with his desire to bring the Cold War to a peaceful end. In November 1986, the Iran-Contra scandal erupted, giving Reagan every incentive to shift the topic of discussion. Meanwhile, as part of his commitment to glasnost, Gorbachev granted more religious freedom, encouraged greater cultural tolerance, permitted open emigration by Russian Jews, and freed most political prisoners. In December, the Soviet leader even permitted dissident scientist Andrei Sakharov to return to Moscow from exile. The moves won Gorbachev international acclaim—*Time* eventually named him Man of the Decade—and enabled him to abandon his focus on SDI when Sakharov, a nuclear physicist by training and recipient of the Nobel Peace Prize in 1975, declared that the missile shield would not work and was not worth the expense or trouble.

The road to the next summit was now clear. In February 1987, the Soviet Union announced that it would unilaterally and unconditionally agree to the withdrawal of all intermediate-range nuclear missiles in Europe—news welcomed by Reagan, who used it to distract attention from the critical findings of the Tower Commission. Then in June he issued his famous challenge from the Brandenburg Gate in West Berlin: "Come here to this gate! Mr. Gorbachev, open this gate! Mr. Gorbachev, tear down this wall!"[127] Reagan next invited the Soviet leader to Washington, and in December he arrived. It was the first superpower summit on American soil in fourteen years and only the third in the long history of the Cold War. Amid smiles and handshakes, Reagan and Gorbachev signed the INF treaty, which affected less than 5 percent of all nuclear weapons. But it represented a real reduction—not a potential limitation—and eliminated an entire category of nuclear weapons. Although the meeting left unresolved the issue of SDI, it included provisions for on-site inspections—something the secretive Soviets had always opposed.

The Washington summit was nonetheless controversial. Conservatives, who blocked ratification of the treaty in the Senate until May 1988, saw it

President Reagan and Soviet General Secretary Mikhail Gorbachev meet at the White House in December 1987. (Courtesy of the Ronald Reagan Library.)

as a sellout and appeasement. The editor of the *Manchester Union-Leader* argued that "Ronald Reagan is promoting an agreement that will give Communism the advantage, accompanied by a Hollywood show of smiles and handshakes with the leader of what the original Reagan called 'the evil empire.'" In his defense, the president replied that "I'm still the Ronald Reagan I was and the evil empire is still just that." But, he added, the potential for nuclear war was "too great to accept without making an effort."[128] Liberals not surprisingly praised both the effort and the outcome. "These are not the flashiest of summit results," extolled the *New York Times*, "but they are among the soundest." Now it was on to the Moscow summit and regular meetings, where "both sides can explore opportunities in a climate neither of hope nor despair but of self-interest and equilibrium."[129] Adding to the sense of opportunity was Gorbachev's announcement that he would withdraw all Soviet troops from Afghanistan by the end of the year.

At the Moscow summit in June 1988, Reagan and Gorbachev formally completed the INF treaty. Although Soviet security officials brutally disrupted the president's bid to mingle with ordinary citizens, they were unable to prevent him from attending a reception in honor of former political prisoners and human rights activists. "Coming here, being with you, looking into your faces," Reagan told the guests in a voice filled with emotion, "I have to believe the history of this troubled century will indeed be redeemed in the eyes of God and man, and that freedom will truly come for all." Afterward, a dissident put the remarks in perspective: "His words gave us the feeling that our fight is not something trivial but something important, which we should redouble our efforts to continue."[130]

The next morning, the visit was highlighted by an eloquent speech Reagan delivered to selected students at Moscow State University, Gorbachev's alma mater. The president first discussed the rise of the personal computer and the information revolution. "We're breaking through the material conditions of existence to a world where man creates his own destiny," he said. Then Reagan declared that freedom—economic, political, religious, and personal— was the foundation of the revolution. "Freedom," he stated, "is the recognition that no single person, no single authority or government, has a monopoly on the truth, but that every individual life is infinitely precious, that every one of us put on this world has been put there for a reason and has something to offer." Finally, Reagan expressed his hope that the changes in the Soviet Union would prove permanent and lead to lasting peace. "People do not make wars; governments do," he observed. "And . . . a people free to choose will always choose peace." (See "Excerpts from 'Remarks . . . at Moscow State University.'") In essence, it was the Reagan Doctrine restated in human terms.

President Reagan and First Lady Nancy Reagan greet Soviet citizens on Arbat Street during the Moscow summit in May 1988. (Courtesy of the Ronald Reagan Library)

The fifth and final summit between Reagan and Gorbachev was held in New York in December 1988. In a curtain call staged in front of the Statue of Liberty, the president took a last bow and yielded the spotlight to Gorbachev, who at the United Nations pledged to shrink the Red Army by five hundred thousand troops and remove fifty thousand troops from Eastern Europe. The Soviet leader even echoed the words of Reagan in Moscow. "The compelling necessity of the principle of freedom of choice is also clear to us," said Gorbachev, who then offered a remarkable repudiation of the intellectual foundation of the Communist Party. "We are, of course, far from claiming to have infallible truth," he conceded in direct contradiction to Marxist-Leninist theory, "but having subjected the previous realities—realities that have arisen again—to strict analysis, we have come to the conclusion that it is by precisely such approaches that we must search jointly for a way to achieve the supremacy of the common human idea." (See "Excerpts from 'Address by Mikhail Gorbachev at the 43rd U.N. General Assembly Session.'") For the moment, the war of ideas was at an end, although not everyone was ready or willing to acknowledge it.

Conservatives in particular continued to question Gorbachev's motives and mistrust the Soviet Union. "Just because General Secretary Gorbachev wears a smile and dresses fashionably does not mean there is any fundamental change in Soviet goals," warned Weinberger in 1988.[131] "Reagan has accelerated the moral disarmament of the West—actual disarmament will follow—by elevating wishful thinking to the status of political philosophy," wrote columnist George Will, who was otherwise a supporter of the president.[132] But liberals could find little fault with Reagan's performance. By 1991, when the Soviet Union ceased to exist, the Doomsday Clock was back at seventeen minutes to midnight—the safest setting since the atomic age had dawned in 1945.

Reagan could not—nor would he ever—claim all of the credit for the outcome. Before Gorbachev took power, European leaders like Margaret Thatcher in Great Britain and Helmut Schmidt in West Germany had stood by the president, even when it was not popular. Tens of thousands of dissidents across Eastern Europe had also lent their courage to the cause, adding to the political pressure on the Soviet Union, and military alliances like the North Atlantic Treaty Organization (NATO) were always prepared to back Reagan's words with action if necessary. Finally, it is important to remember that in the United States the policy of containment had enjoyed bipartisan support since the 1940s, although markedly less after the Vietnam War. As Republican President Gerald Ford put it, "I feel very strongly that our country's policies, starting with [Democratic President] Harry Truman and those who followed him—Democratic and Republican presidents and Democratic and Republican Congresses—brought about the collapse of the Soviet Union."[133]

The collapse would have come sooner or later. But Reagan—in partnership with Gorbachev—ensured that it would come sooner by striking the right balance between principle and expediency. The president was firm when necessary, which reassured the American people (as perhaps no one else could have) and convinced the Soviet leader that he would not bend on vital issues. Reagan was also flexible when necessary, which enabled him to appreciate who Gorbachev was and break the stalemate on nuclear weapons. What Reagan offered above all was moral clarity and conviction, not intellectual complexity—he was largely unaware of, and uninterested in, the technical details of nuclear policy. But although he never wavered from the end he sought—a world free of the threats of Communist tyranny and nuclear war—he was adjustable and adaptable about the means to reach it. It is an irony of history that Reagan achieved his greatest success when he was pragmatic, not dogmatic, when he allowed reality to trump ideology. It is also an irony that, in the end, the confident and committed cold warrior won his greatest victory through peaceful negotiation, albeit from a position of military and economic strength.

Back in 1978, when Reagan was a senior citizen with lofty ambitions but limited prospects, he had met with a foreign policy adviser to discuss nuclear arms control. "My idea of American policy toward the Soviet Union is simple, and some would say simplistic," said the former governor and future president. "It is this: We win and they lose. What do you think of that?"[134] A decade later, the world had changed for the better. No longer was the Cold War a permanent presence, a fixed feature of the global map. As Reagan and Gorbachev strolled through Red Square in Moscow in 1988, the president was asked if he still considered the Soviet Union an evil empire. After a moment of reflection, he replied that "I was talking about another time, another era."[135] So he was—and so it was.

LEGACIES

Early in Ronald Reagan's second term, a close adviser inquired if he had given any thought to his place in history. The president was dismissive. "First of all," he said, "the history will probably get distorted when it's written. And I won't be around to read it."[136] Reagan's response was a casual blend of false humility and true insight. On the one hand, he was a firm believer in the ultimate power of a single person to make history. In his mind, he was a figure of destiny and he reveled in the role, which led him to bring his official biographer to the Geneva summit. On the other, Reagan knew that presidential history often becomes highly politicized. Scholars may allow contemporary concerns to cloud their historical judgment, while partisans or participants may offer slanted accounts intended to advance the current interests of Republicans or Democrats. The president also anticipated—correctly—that the policies of his administration would remain controversial, as they certainly have in the two decades since he left office.

The legacies of the Reagan era are likewise a matter of debate. Although many conservatives were dubious, the extraordinary thaw in the Cold War reduced the risk of nuclear destruction. Yet the superpower rivalry with the Soviet Union was no longer the only threat faced by the United States or other nations. With the rise of global terrorism and the resurgence of ethnic nationalism—especially in Central Europe after the rapid disintegration of the Soviet empire—the world suddenly seemed more, not less, dangerous in the 1990s. In many other regions, the emergence of new perils and the persistence of old problems also negated the progress made on the Communist front and revealed the inconsistencies, if not contradictions, inherent in the Reagan Doctrine. In particular, liberals highlighted the struggle for freedom in the Philippine Islands and the oppression of blacks in South Africa as well as the plight of Palestinians in the Middle East and the plague of poverty in Latin America.

In the Philippines, the future of democracy seemed uncertain, especially when the United States announced in 1991 that it intended to abandon the Subic Bay Naval Station and Clark Air Force Base, two crucial pillars of local economic prosperity and American defense strategy in the Pacific. The decision marked the end of a tumultuous decade that began with a firm pledge of U.S. support for the corrupt dictator Ferdinand Marcos, a staunch anti-Communist and longtime friend. "We love your adherence to democratic principles and democratic processes," toasted Vice President George H. W. Bush at a banquet in Manila in 1981.[137] Two years later, however, Marcos was implicated in the assassination of opposition leader Benigno Aquino when he returned to the Philippines from exile. Then in 1985, under growing pressure for political reforms from street demonstrators, Communist insurgents, and the Reagan administration, Marcos called for a sudden election—only to withhold the returns and claim victory after it appeared that he had lost to Corazon Aquino, the widow of Benigno.

The political crisis threatened the military bases and led to an intense debate within the White House. The president asserted that the Cold War dictated American support for a loyal ally. But Secretary of State George Shultz argued that continued allegiance to the Marcos regime might lead to a Communist takeover. Ultimately, the secretary prevailed and, after Reagan reluctantly convinced Marcos to relocate to Hawaii and certified the triumph of Aquino, the Philippines made the transition from dictatorship to democracy in 1986. The result demonstrated that, contrary to what some neoconservatives like Jeane Kirkpatrick had predicted, the United States could dump dictators and deliver democracy without creating another Iran or Nicaragua. It also emboldened other neoconservatives who had sided with Shultz and now interpreted the result as proof that promoting freedom in other countries was the right option regardless of whether the leader was a friend or foe. "The best antidote to communism is democracy," explained Paul Wolfowitz, an assistant secretary of state. It was a simple statement, but it portended a momentous redefinition of the Reagan Doctrine, which in time would transcend the traditional parameters of the Cold War. By 2003 Wolfowitz was deputy secretary of defense in the George W. Bush administration and an ardent proponent of the neoconservative view that the United States should use democracy as an antidote to terrorism by removing Iraqi leader Saddam Hussein from power.[138]

In South Africa, President F. W. de Klerk of the National Party in 1990 lifted the ban on the African National Congress (ANC) and freed Nelson Mandela, a black activist who spent almost three decades in prison. Four years later, the ANC, led by Mandela, won the first multiracial election in the nation's history and brought white rule to an end. The outcome dispelled some—but certainly not all—of the rancor of the early 1980s, when the White House revoked the arms embargo and economic sanctions endorsed by the Carter administration. In their place, the Reagan administration advocated what it termed "constructive engagement"—quiet diplomacy intended to persuade President P. W. Botha, an anti-Communist ally and de Klerk's predecessor, to reform the system of segregation known as apartheid. But in 1984 Botha proposed a new constitution that continued to deny the black majority (72 percent of the population) basic political rights. When the townships erupted in violence in 1985, he imposed martial law and unleashed the security forces, which beat and killed thousands of black residents. In the United States, demands for divestment erupted in churches, on campuses, and in Congress, which in 1986 voted to impose economic sanctions on South Africa and then overrode a presidential veto by overwhelming margins.

What happened in South Africa between 1986 and 1990 remains disputed. Supporters of the Reagan administration contend that economic sanctions had little practical effect and undercut the positive achievements of "constructive engagement," such as Botha's decision to initiate secret negotiations with Mandela in 1985, which the White House had encouraged. Critics counter that the economic sanctions had considerable political effect because they conveyed to the white leaders of the National Party the clear message that the United States abhorred apartheid and would not lend unconditional support to South Africa indefinitely, regardless of what the Reagan administration might suggest. Yet both sides tend to agree that most of the credit for South Africa's peaceful revolution rightfully belongs to Mandela, de Klerk, and their followers of all races. Two unexpected events also paved the road to reconciliation. The first was the stroke Botha suffered in 1989, which enabled de Klerk to take his place. The second was the sudden implosion of the Soviet empire, which removed the Communist threat that the National Party had used to legitimate apartheid, curry favor with the White House, and delegitimize the ANC, a formal ally of the South African Communist Party.

In the Middle East, the Arab-Israeli conflict continued to simmer. In 1988, Shultz ended a thirteen-year ban on official contact with the Palestine Liberation Organization (PLO) and announced that the United States was willing to have a dialogue with Yasser Arafat. In return, the PLO chairman recognized Israel's right to exist, accepted the United Nations framework for peace, and renounced terrorism in a limited sense. The Shultz initiative made it easier for subsequent administrations to act as mediators. But the search for peace remained elusive. While the Israelis built settlements in the occupied territories of the West Bank and Gaza Strip throughout the 1990s, the Palestinians encouraged suicide bombers. The rise of Islamic extremism in the form of Hamas, which vowed it would never accept the existence of a Jewish state, complicated efforts to build a Palestinian state. In 2006, Lebanon again became a battleground when Israel invaded in a failed effort to dislodge Hezbollah forces, halt rocket attacks, and diminish Syrian influence. This time, however, the United States opted not to send peacekeepers as the cycle of violence persisted.

In Iraq, the first Bush administration maintained the Reagan administration's policy of providing Saddam Hussein with economic aid. In October 1989, President George H. W. Bush even signed National Security Decision Directive 26, which concluded that "normal relations between the U.S. and Iraq would serve our longer-term interests and promote stability in both the Persian Gulf and the Middle East." Criticism of Hussein—especially his attacks on the Kurds and threats toward Israel—nevertheless mounted. "It is the smell of oil and the color of money that corrodes our principles," stated Republican Senator William Cohen of Maine.[139] In July 1990, the Senate imposed sanctions on Iraq, which a week later invaded Kuwait. The White House responded by sending four hundred thousand American troops to Saudi Arabia—the largest overseas American contingent since the Vietnam War—and forming a multinational coalition against Hussein. Bush also requested and received authorization from Congress and the United Nations to use military force against Iraq.

Operation Desert Storm began in February 1991 after months of failed negotiations and weeks of intensive bombing. In four days of ground combat, the United States inflicted heavy casualties on Iraq, which agreed to a ceasefire in March. The swift and decisive victory was due in large measure to the arms buildup of the Reagan era. But the first Bush administration, fearing internal chaos and civil war, chose to follow the wishes of the coalition and leave Hussein in power. Hussein in turn consolidated his control and began to develop—or so the second Bush administration later claimed—weapons of mass destruction. After the terrorist attacks by al-Qaeda on the World Trade Center and Pentagon in September 2001, those alleged weapons became the main rationale for the Second Gulf War, which the United States launched in March 2003. At the same time, the infidel presence of American troops in Saudi Arabia—home to Mecca and Medina, the two holiest sites in the world for Muslims—was one of the major reasons cited by al-Qaeda leader Osama bin Laden for 9/11.

Other reasons cited by bin Laden included American support for Israel and the American intervention in Beirut in 1982. "As I was looking at those towers that were destroyed in Lebanon," he later claimed, "it occurred to me that we have to punish the transgressor with the same, and that we had to destroy the towers in America, so that they tasted what we tasted."[140] A wealthy Saudi from a powerful family, bin Laden had first come to prominence in Afghanistan, where he had helped to recruit volunteers and raise funds for the mujahideen resistance. But the training camps organized and operated by the United States and Saudi Arabia fell into the hands of Islamic militants known as the Taliban after the withdrawal of the Soviets in 1989. Despite the efforts of the Central Intelligence Agency (CIA) to buy back as many of the Stinger missiles as possible (at $220,000 apiece), the anti-Soviet jihad soon became an anti-American jihad under the influence of al-Qaeda. This unforeseen and unintended result was what journalists liked to call "blowback"—when intelligence agents or "assets" turned their weapons on their patrons.

The blowback from Afghanistan has had lasting and deadly consequences. But the extent to which Reagan was responsible remains contentious. Detractors assert that, at the very least, he and succeeding presidents must share the blame for allowing and encouraging the spread of Islamic extremism, which the United States nurtured in an effort to defeat the Soviets in Afghanistan and win the Cold War. They also contend that the Lebanon fiasco taught Islamic militants that unconventional or asymmetrical warfare would succeed against the United States, which was reluctant to suffer casualties or inflict punishment. But defenders note that the Reagan administration created neither Islamic extremism nor al-Qaeda. They also stress that the CIA had no contact with bin Laden in the 1980s and that support for the Afghan rebels was bipartisan. "We were fighting the evil empire," recalled Democratic Congressman Charlie Wilson of Texas, who had no regrets over his role in funneling arms and aid to the mujahideen guerrillas. "It would have been like not supplying the Soviets against Hitler in World War II."[141] In hindsight, it is evident that at the time Reagan saw the threat of terrorism as secondary to the threat of Communism, but he was hardly alone in that assessment and he had good reason for it. To blame him for what happened in September 2001 thus seems unfair and ahistorical, especially since subsequent administrations had opportunities to prevent the tragedy.

In Latin America, the Reagan record was similarly mixed and debatable. During the 1980s, ten military dictatorships evolved into democratic governments, including Argentina, Brazil, and Chile as well as El Salvador. It was a wave of democratization not seen since the 1950s. But whether the bulk of the credit should go to President Carter's elevation of human rights or President Reagan's support for democratic freedoms remains difficult to determine. The relative importance of pressure from Congress, the media, the Catholic Church, and local activists in Latin America remains unclear as well. Two larger problems further complicate the rise of democracy—or at least the explanation the Reagan administration preferred to promote. The first was a debt crisis that threatened the financial stability of the region as a whole. As inflation raged, the debt burden initially discredited the military dictatorships, but eventually it eroded political support for the democratic regimes, as when the Sandinistas led by Daniel Ortega returned to power in Nicaragua via the ballot box in 2006. The second problem was the potent combination of poverty and inequality, which seemed beyond the reach of politics. Together, they made "Latin American countries ripe for revolution from the left or the right," observed Reagan in his memoirs. "The only long-term solution was economic development of these countries, a better standard of living for their people, democratic rule, and more social justice."[142]

In the short term, Reagan's determination to reverse a revolution from the left in Nicaragua contributed to the worst debacle of his presidency, which ironically took place during the bicentennial celebration of the U.S. Constitution. But the legacies of the Iran-Contra scandal went beyond whether it was fundamentally a constitutional crisis (the liberal view) or a political dispute (the conservative view). On one level, it illustrated the danger of making secret deals with international terrorists—or creating the perception of doing so. On another, it illustrated the danger of trying to evade Congressional oversight. As veterans of Vietnam, National Security Council officials Robert McFarlane, John Poindexter, and Oliver North vividly recalled the clashes in the 1970s between the executive and legislative branches. Their objective in the 1980s was to defuse Congressional opposition by concealing the administration's actions. Instead, they inflamed it by ignoring the rule of law and the will of Congress. Thus the main lesson learned by future Vice President Dick Cheney and other conservatives in the 1990s was that it was better to confront or co-opt the House and Senate directly. That was precisely the approach the second Bush administration took in the immediate aftermath of 9/11, when it pressured Congress to pass the USA Patriot Act and authorize the use of force against Iraq as part of the war on terror.

The first Bush administration was suspicious initially of the Soviet Union, which remained a formidable foe in January 1989. In the next two years, however, the changes promoted by Reagan and Gorbachev gathered momentum and took on a life of their own. In March, the Soviet Union held free elections, followed in June by free elections in Poland that brought Solidarity to power. As promised, Gorbachev took no action, confirming that he would not use military force to maintain Soviet control over Eastern Europe. The Iron Curtain was doomed. In October, the Communist government of East Germany collapsed, and in November the Berlin Wall came down amid joyous celebration. By December 1989 dictatorships in Hungary, Rumania, and Czechoslovakia had also fallen. In October 1990, East and West Germany reunited after forty-five years of division. Eight months later, the United States and the Soviet Union signed an arms control agreement that reduced their arsenals by an additional 50 percent. Finally, Gorbachev formally dissolved the Soviet Union in December 1991, although the various republics had already withdrawn by then. As Reagan had prophesized, the evil empire was no more.

Peace had come at last—or so many hoped. But with the Soviet Union's nuclear arsenal now divided among Russia and three former republics (Belarus, Ukraine, and Kazakhstan), the risk of nuclear confrontation and proliferation had grown significantly, even though the launch codes remained in Moscow's hands. At the same time, the end of Communism would not mean the end of conflict. On the contrary, Europe soon witnessed the revival of ethnic nationalism and violence, which Communist rule in Eastern Europe had kept in check for half a century. Nowhere was the revival more virulent than in the former nation of Yugoslavia, which rapidly fragmented into the separate states of Slovenia, Bosnia, Serbia, and Croatia. In 1992, civil war erupted between the Christian Serbs, Muslim Bosnians, and Catholic Croats. By the time a peace agreement was reached in 1995, an estimated one hundred thousand were dead and another 1.8 million were displaced, victims of the "ethnic cleansing" practiced by all sides, especially the Serbs. Despite the death toll and the frightening prospect that the regional conflict might escalate into a European war, the United States was slow and hesitant to intervene. A major reason, according to Secretary of State James Baker, was that "we do not have a dog in that fight."[143]

Most top officials in the first Bush administration were realists like Baker. They were willing to use force, but only when the United States had vital national interests at stake—such as access to oil in the war against Iraq in 1991. But by the mid-1990s, the conservative camp had split into two other factions as well. Isolationists believed that the end of the Cold War should mark the end of overseas interventions in all but the most extreme cases. Idealists, better known as neoconservatives, believed that the United States should act to promote American values—like freedom and democracy—regardless of whether national security was at stake or the international community was in agreement. In a sense, idealists were partial heirs to Reagan—many had served under or were inspired by him— and by 2003 they were the leading advocates in the second Bush administration of another war with Saddam Hussein. His overthrow, neoconservatives contended, would lead to the spread of democracy throughout the Middle East—an illusory dream that was in deep doubt by 2009. The Reagan Doctrine nevertheless continued to exert considerable influence and appeal.

Back in 1980, during his debate with Carter, Reagan had posed two rhetorical questions to the American people: "Do you feel that our security is as safe? That we're as strong as we were four years ago?" By 1989 the public response was loud and clear—the United States was safer and stronger, with confidence and pride restored. Little wonder that Reagan left office with the highest approval rating of any president in the last half of the twentieth century, or that in 2007, three years after his death, a Gallup Poll named him the second-greatest president in American history. It appears unlikely that historians will soon render a similar verdict. But what mattered most to Reagan was how the United States remained an inspiration to the world. In his farewell address, he described America as a shining "city upon a hill"—a phrase he often borrowed from Puritan leader John Winthrop. And then Reagan concluded, proudly and poignantly, that the country was still "a magnet for all who must have freedom, for all the pilgrims from all the lost places who are hurtling through the darkness, toward home."[144] After eight extraordinary years of turmoil, tragedy, and triumph, now he too could head home.

NOTES

I wish to thank Vincent Cannato, Richard Combs, Betty Dessants, John Ehrman, Sean Kay, James Patterson, David Stebenne, and Tim Thurber for their constructive comments and criticisms. Any and all errors of fact or interpretation, whether major or minor, of course remain my sole responsibility. Paul Burnam, Bernard Derr, and Jody Forman of Ohio Wesleyan University offered research assistance. The Ronald Reagan Presidential Library contains his public papers, which are also available online at www.reagan.utexas.edu/archives/speeches/publicpapers.html.

1. Quoted in Peter Schweizer, *Reagan's War: The Epic Story of His Forty-Year Struggle and Final Triumph* (New York: Doubleday, 2002), 120.

2. Quoted in Philip Jenkins, *Decade of Nightmares: The End of the Sixties and the Making of Eighties America* (New York: Oxford University Press, 2006), 173.

3. Carter, *State of the Union Address*, January 23, 1980. Jimmy Carter Presidential Library, www.jimmycarterlibrary.org/documents/speeches/su80jec.phtml (accessed September 19, 2008).

4. George F. Will, *Suddenly: The American Idea Abroad and At Home, 1986–1990* (New York: Free Press, 1990), 145.

5. Quoted in George W. Ball, "White House Roulette," *New York Review of Books*, November 8, 1984.

6. Quoted in Kiron K. Skinner, Annelise Anderson, and Martin Anderson, eds., *Reagan: In His Own Hand* (New York: Simon & Schuster, 2001), 12.

7. Ronald Reagan, *An American Life* (New York: Pocket Books, 1990), 267, 548.

8. Quoted in Kiron K. Skinner, Annelise Anderson, and Martin Anderson, eds., *Reagan: A Life in Letters* (New York: Free Press, 2003), 395.

9. Conservative columnist Charles Krauthammer coined the term in *Time* magazine in April 1985.

10. Reagan, *Address before a Joint Session of the Congress on the State of the Union*, February 6, 1985.

11. Quoted in Lou Cannon, *President Reagan: The Role of a Lifetime* (New York: Simon & Schuster, 1991), 195.

12. Quoted in Chester J. Pach Jr., "Sticking to His Guns: Reagan and National Security," in W. Elliot Brownlee and Hugh Davis Graham, eds., *The Reagan Presidency: Pragmatic Conservatism and Its Legacies* (Lawrence: University Press of Kansas, 2003), 85.

13. Cannon, *President Reagan: The Role of a Lifetime*.

14. Reagan, *The President's News Conference*, January 29, 1981.

15. Quoted in Schweizer, *Reagan's War*, 236.

16. Reagan, *Remarks to Members of the National Press Club on Arms Reduction and Nuclear Weapons*, November 18, 1981.

17. James Burnham, "Is Disarmament Possible?" *National Review*, January 30, 1960, 67.

18. Quoted in Beth A. Fischer, "Reagan and the Soviets: Winning the Cold War?" in W. Elliot Brownlee and Hugh Davis Graham, eds., *The Reagan Presidency: Pragmatic Conservatism and Its Legacies* (Lawrence: University Press of Kansas, 2003), 122.

19. Quoted in Jenkins, *Decade of Nightmares*, 211.

20. Reagan, *Remarks to Members of the National Press Club on Arms Reduction and Nuclear Weapons*, November 18, 1981.

21. Quoted in Stephen F. Knott, "Reagan's Critics," *National Interest* (Summer 1996): 66–78.

22. Quoted in Beth A. Fischer, "Reagan and the Soviets: Winning the Cold War?" in *The Reagan Presidency*, 122.

23. Quoted in Robert M. Collins, *Transforming America: Politics and Culture During the Reagan Years* (New York: Columbia University Press, 2007), 212.

24. Anthony Lewis, "Onward Christian Soldiers," *New York Times*, March 10, 1983. See also Jenkins, *Decade of Nightmares*, 212.

25. Reagan, *An American Life*, 547.

26. Regan, *Address to the Nation on Defense and Security*, March 23, 1983.

27. Quoted in Lars-Erik Nelson, "Fantasia," *New York Review of Books*, May 11, 2000, 6.

28. Quoted in Jules Tygiel, *Ronald Reagan and the Triumph of American Conservatism* (New York: Pearson Longman, 2005), 140.

29. Mikhail Gorbachev, *Memoirs* (New York: Doubleday, 1995), 407.

30. "Nuclear Facts, Science Fictions," *New York Times*, March 27, 1983.

31. Quoted in Skinner, Anderson, and Anderson, eds., *Reagan: A Life in Letters*, 427–29.

32. Reagan, *An American Life*, 584.

33. Brinkley, *The Reagan Diaries*, 186.

34. Quoted in Skinner, Anderson, and Anderson, eds., *Reagan: A Life in Letters*, 410.

35. Quoted in David Reynolds, *Summits: Six Meetings that Shaped the Twentieth Century* (New York: Basic Books, 2007), 353.

36. Reagan, *An American Life*, 437.

37. Colin Powell, *My American Journey* (New York: Ballantine Books, 1995), 280–81.

38. Reagan, *An American Life*, 453.

39. Reagan, *An American Life*, 407.

40. Quoted in Sam Segev, "The Reagan Plan," in Eric J. Schmertz, Natalie Datlof, and Alexej Ugrinsky, eds., *President Reagan and the World* (Westport, CT: Greenwood Press, 1997), 47.

41. Douglas Brinkley, ed., *The Reagan Diaries* (New York: HarperCollins, 2007), 184.

42. No headline, *New York Times*, October 24, 1983.

43. John A. Farrell, *Tip O'Neill and the American Century* (Boston: Little Brown & Co., 2001), 618–19.

44. Gil Troy, *Morning in America: How Ronald Reagan Invented the Eighties* (Princeton, NJ: Princeton University Press, 2005), 157.

45. Garry Wills, *Reagan's America* (New York: Penguin Books, 1987), 422.

46. United Nations General Assembly Resolution 38/7.

47. Brinkley, *The Reagan Diaries*, 190.

48. Stephen F. Knott, "Reagan's Critics," *National Interest* (Summer 1996): 66–78.

49. Tygiel, *Ronald Reagan and the Triumph of American Conservatism*, 148; Troy, *Morning in America*, 157.

50. Dinesh D'Souza, "How the West Was Won," *American History* (October 2003): 37.

51. "Transcript of the Presidential Debate between Carter and Reagan in Cleveland," *New York Times*, October 29, 1980.

52. Quoted in Michael M. Gunter, "Dealing with Terrorism: The Reagan Record," in *President Reagan and the World*, 167.

53. Quoted in "Discussant: Diane F. Orentlicher," in *President Reagan and the World*, 411.

54. Quoted in Sean Wilentz, *The Age of Reagan* (New York: HarperCollins, 2008), 158.

55. J. William Fulbright, "Another Gulf of Tonkin?" *Washington Post*, August 23, 1981.

56. Quoted in Tygiel, *Ronald Reagan and the Triumph of American Conservatism*, 159.

57. "Transcript of White House News Conference on the Hijacking," *New York Times*, October 12, 1986.

58. Quoted in Skinner, Anderson, and Anderson, eds., *Reagan: A Life in Letters*, 462.

59. Quoted in George P. Shultz, *Turmoil and Triumph: My Years as Secretary of State* (New York: Charles Scribner's Sons, 1993), 686.

60. Quoted in Walter Shapiro, "Assassination: Is It a Real Option?" *Newsweek*, April 28, 1986, 21.

61. Quoted in Michael M. Gunter, "Dealing with Terrorism: The Reagan Record," in *President Reagan and the World*, 170.

62. Quoted in Michael M. Gunter, "Dealing with Terrorism: The Reagan Record," in *President Reagan and the World*, 170.

63. Quoted in Skinner, Anderson, and Anderson, eds., *Reagan: A Life in Letters*, 435.

64. Quoted in Samantha Power, *"A Problem From Hell": America and the Age of Genocide* (New York: Basic Books, 2002), 200.

65. Quoted in Wilentz, *Age of Reagan*, 159.

66. Quoted in James Mann, *The Rise of the Vulcans: The History of Bush's War Cabinet* (New York: Viking Penguin, 2004), 123–24.

67. Quoted in William M. LeoGrande, *Our Own Backyard: The United States in Central America, 1977–1992* (Chapel Hill: University of North Carolina Press, 1998), 581.

68. Reagan, *An American Life*, 477.

69. Quoted in Troy, *Morning in America*, 139.

70. Reagan, *An American Life*, 474.

71. Quoted in Wills, *Reagan's America*, 411.

72. Reagan, *An American Life*, 475.

73. Raymond Bonner, "Massacre of Hundreds Reported in Salvador Village," *New York Times*, January 27, 1982.

74. Quoted in Cannon, *Ronald Reagan*, 291–92.

75. Quoted in Pach, "Sticking to His Guns: Reagan and National Security," in *The Reagan Presidency*, 97.

76. Quoted in Skinner, Anderson, and Anderson, eds., *Reagan: A Life in Letters*, 490.

77. "Discussant: Otto J. Reich," in *President Reagan and the World*, 422–25.

78. "Discussant: Diane F. Orentlicher," in *President Reagan and the World*, 409–21.

79. Quoted in Troy, *Morning in America*, 243.

80. Quoted in Schweizer, *Reagan's War*, 109.

81. Quoted in Pach, "Sticking to His Guns: Reagan and National Security," in *The Reagan Presidency*, 97.

82. Reagan, "Question-and-Answer Session With Reporters on Domestic and Foreign Policy Issues," May 4, 1983.

83. Quoted in Thomas P. O'Neill, *Man of the House: The Life and Political Memoirs of Speaker Tip O'Neill* (New York: Random House, 1987), 440.

84. Quoted in LeoGrande, *Our Own Backyard*, 303–4.

85. Quoted in LeoGrande, *Our Own Backyard*, 304.

86. Quoted in Haynes Johnson, *Sleepwalking Through History: America in the Reagan Years* (New York: W. W. Norton & Co., 1991), 277.

87. Quoted in LeoGrande, *Our Own Backyard*, 345.

88. Quoted in Tygiel, *Ronald Reagan and the Triumph of American Conservatism*, 166.

89. "Nicaragua's Second Revolution," *New York Times*, April 25, 1990.

90. "Nicaragua Goes for Reagan," *National Review*, March 19, 1990.

91. Quoted in Richard Reeves, *President Reagan: The Triumph of Imagination* (New York: Simon & Schuster, 2005), 221–22.

92. Quoted in Mann, *Rise of the Vulcans*, 153.

93. Brinkley, *The Reagan Diaries*, 343.

94. Quoted in Cannon, *President Reagan*, 613.

95. Quoted in Cannon, *President Reagan*, 610–11, 615.

96. Quoted in Wilentz, *The Age of Reagan*, 219.

97. Brinkley, *The Reagan Diaries*, 371.

98. National Security Archive, *The Iran-Contra Affair 20 Years On*, www.gwu.edu/~nsarchiv/NSAEBB/NSAEBB210/index.htm (accessed October 7, 2008).

99. Brinkley, *The Reagan Diaries*, 374.

100. Brinkley, *The Reagan Diaries*, 375.

101. Brinkley, *The Reagan Diaries*, 415.

102. Reagan, *Address to the Nation on the Iran Arms and Contra Aid Controversy*, November 13, 1986.

103. Reagan, *The President's News Conference*, November 19, 1986.

104. Brinkley, *The Reagan Diaries*, 453.

105. Reagan, *Remarks Announcing the Review of the National Security Council's Role in the Iran Arms and Contra Aid Controversy*, November 25, 1986.

106. "The Facts Roar for Themselves," *New York Times*, November 26, 1986.

107. "The White House Crisis; Excerpts from the Tower Commission's Report, Part I," *New York Times*, February 27, 1987.

108. R. W. Apple Jr., "The Reagan White House: In a Spirit of Contrition," *New York Times*, March 5, 1987.

109. Brinkley, *The Reagan Diaries*, 480.

110. "The Laws, Unfaithfully Executed," *New York Times*, November 19, 1987.

111. Quoted in Troy, *Morning in America*, 247.

112. Reagan, *An American Life*, 543.

113. Quoted in Troy, *Morning in America*, 250.

114. Quoted in Collins, *Transforming America*, 224.

115. Quoted in Nelson, "Fantasia," 4.

116. Quoted in Beth A. Fischer, "Reagan and the Soviets," in *The Reagan Presidency*, 125.

117. Quoted in Dinesh D'Souza, "How the East Was Won," *American History* (October 2003): 39.

118. Quoted in Reynolds, *Summits*, 358, 364.

119. Quoted in Reynolds, *Summits*, 373, 383.

120. Quoted in Jenkins, *Decade of Nightmares*, 224–25.

121. Quoted in Schweizer, *Reagan's War*, 263.

122. Quoted in Troy, *Morning in America*, 262.

123. Quoted in Reynolds, *Summits*, 390–91; Reagan, *An American Life*, 679; and Brinkley, *The Reagan Diaries*, 444.

124. Reagan, *An American Life*, 675.

125. Quoted in Reynolds, *Summits*, 392.

126. Kenneth L. Adelman, "United States and Soviet Relations: Reagan's Real Role in Winning the Cold War," in *President Reagan and the World*, 89.

127. Reagan, *Address on East-West Relations at the Brandenburg Gate in West Berlin*, June 12, 1987.

128. Quoted in Skinner, Anderson, and Anderson, eds., *Reagan: A Life in Letters*, 384.

129. "At the Summit: Two for the Seesaw," *New York Times*, December 12, 1987.

130. Quoted in Schweizer, *Reagan's War*, 274–75.

131. Caspar W. Weinberger, "Arms Reduction and Deterrence," *Foreign Affairs* (Spring 1988), www.foreignaffairs.org/19880301faessay7891/caspar-w-weinberger/arms-reductions-and-deterrence.html (accessed October 15, 2008).

132. Will, *Suddenly*, 148.

133. Quoted in Reeves, *President Reagan*, xv.

134. Quoted in Schweizer, *Reagan's War*, 106.

135. Quoted in Skinner, Anderson, and Anderson, eds., *Reagan: A Life in Letters*, 385–86.

136. Quoted in Reeves, *President Reagan*, xiii.

137. Quoted in Tom Wicker, "An American Dilemma," *New York Times*, December 13, 1985.

138. Quoted in Mann, *Rise of the Vulcans*, 136.

139. Quoted in Powers, *"A Problem from Hell": America in the Age of Genocide*, 235.

140. Quoted in Jenkins, *Decade of Nightmares*, 284.

141. Quoted in Sandra McElwaine, "Charlie Wilson Regrets Nothing," *Time*, December 17, 2007, 79.

142. Reagan, *An American Life*, 474.

143. Quoted in Maureen Dowd, "Chardonnay Diplomacy," *New York Times*, November 15, 2006.

144. Reagan, *Farewell Address to the Nation*, January 11, 1989.

1

EXCERPTS FROM "ADDRESS TO MEMBERS OF THE BRITISH PARLIAMENT" (JUNE 8, 1982)

My Lord Chancellor, Mr. Speaker:

We have not inherited an easy world. . . . There are threats now to our freedom, indeed to our very existence, that other generations could never even have imagined.

There is first the threat of global war. No President, no Congress, no Prime Minister, no Parliament can spend a day entirely free of this threat. And I don't have to tell you that in today's world the existence of nuclear weapons could mean, if not the extinction of mankind, then surely the end of civilization as we know it. That's why negotiations on intermediate-range nuclear forces now underway in Europe and the START talks—Strategic Arms Reduction Talks—which will begin later this month, are not just critical to American or Western policy; they are critical to mankind. . . .

At the same time there is a threat posed to human freedom by the enormous power of the modern state. History teaches the dangers of government that overreaches—political control taking precedence over free economic growth, secret police, mindless bureaucracy, all combining to stifle individual excellence and personal freedom.

Now, I'm aware that among us here and throughout Europe there is legitimate disagreement over the extent to which the public sector should play a role in a nation's economy and life. But on one point all of us are united—our abhorrence of dictatorship in all its forms, but most particularly totalitarianism and the terrible inhumanities it has caused in our time—the great purge, Auschwitz and Dachau, the Gulag, and Cambodia.

Historians looking back at our time will note the consistent restraint and peaceful intentions of the West. They will note that it was the democracies who refused to use the threat of their nuclear monopoly in the forties and early fifties for territorial or imperial gain. Had that nuclear monopoly been in the hands of the Communist world, the map of Europe—indeed, the world—would look very different today. And certainly they will note it was not the democracies that invaded Afghanistan or suppressed Polish Solidarity or used chemical and toxin warfare in Afghanistan and Southeast Asia.

If history teaches anything it teaches self-delusion in the face of unpleasant facts is folly. We see around us today the marks of our terrible dilemma—predictions of doomsday, antinuclear demonstrations, an arms race in which the West must, for its own protection, be an unwilling participant. At the same time we see totalitarian forces in the world who seek subversion and conflict around the globe to further their barbarous assault on the human spirit. What, then, is our course? Must civilization perish in a hail of fiery atoms? Must freedom wither in a quiet, deadening accommodation with totalitarian evil?

. . . In an ironic sense Karl Marx was right. We are witnessing today a great revolutionary crisis, a crisis where the demands of the economic order are conflicting directly with those of the political order. But the crisis is happening not in the free, non-Marxist West, but in the home of Marxist-Leninism, the Soviet Union. It is the Soviet Union that runs against the tide of history by denying human freedom and human dignity to its citizens. It also is in deep economic difficulty. The rate of growth in the national product has been steadily declining since the fifties and is less than half of what it was then. . . .

In the Communist world as well, man's instinctive desire for freedom and self-determination surfaces again and again. To be sure, there are grim reminders of how brutally the police state attempts to snuff out this quest for self-rule—1953 in East Germany, 1956 in Hungary, 1968 in Czechoslovakia, 1981 in Poland. But the struggle continues in Poland. And we know that there are even those who strive and suffer for freedom within the confines of the Soviet Union itself. How we conduct ourselves here in the Western democracies will determine whether this trend continues. . . .

Some argue that we should encourage democratic change in right-wing dictatorships, but not in Communist regimes. Well, to accept this preposterous notion—as some well-meaning people have—is to invite the argument that once countries achieve a nuclear capability, they should be allowed an undisturbed reign of terror over their own citizens. We reject this course. . . .

While we must be cautious about forcing the pace of change, we must not hesitate to declare our ultimate objectives and to take concrete actions to move toward them. We must be staunch in our conviction that freedom is not the sole prerogative of a lucky few, but the inalienable and universal right of all human beings. So states the United Nations Universal Declaration of Human Rights, which, among other things, guarantees free elections. . . .

What I am describing now is a plan and a hope for the long term— the march of freedom and democracy which will leave Marxism-Leninism on the ash-heap of history as it has left other tyrannies which stifle the freedom and muzzle the self-expression of the people. . . .

Our military strength is a prerequisite to peace, but let it be clear we maintain this strength in the hope it will never be used, for the ultimate determinant in the struggle that's now going on in the world will not be bombs and rockets, but a test of wills and ideas, a trial of spiritual resolve, the values we hold, the beliefs we cherish, the ideals to which we are dedicated. . . .

Well, the task I've set forth will long outlive our own generation. But together, we too have come through the worst. Let us now begin a major effort to secure the best—a crusade for freedom that will engage the faith and fortitude of the next generation. For the sake of peace and justice, let us move toward a world in which all people are at last free to determine their own destiny.

The Public Papers of President Ronald W. Reagan, The Reagan Presidential Library, www.reagan.utexas.edu/archives/speeches/1982/60882a.htm (accessed October 10, 2008).

2

EXCERPTS FROM "ADDRESS
TO THE ANNUAL CONVENTION
OF THE NATIONAL ASSOCIATION
OF EVANGELICALS"
(MARCH 8, 1983)

. . . Well, I'm pleased to be here today with you who are keeping America great by keeping her good. Only through your work and prayers and those of millions of others can we hope to survive this perilous century and keep alive this experiment in liberty, this last, best hope of man.

. . . Whatever sad episodes exist in our past, any objective observer must hold a positive view of American history, a history that has been the story of hopes fulfilled and dreams made into reality. Especially in this century, America has kept alight the torch of freedom, but not just for ourselves but for millions of others around the world.

And this brings me to my final point today. During my first press conference as President, in answer to a direct question, I pointed out that, as good Marxist-Leninists, the Soviet leaders have openly and publicly declared that the only morality they recognize is that which will further their cause, which is world revolution. I think I should point out I was only quoting Lenin, their guiding spirit, who said in 1920 that they repudiate all morality that proceeds from supernatural ideas—that's their name for religion—or ideas that are outside class conceptions. Morality is entirely subordinate to the interests of class war. And everything is moral that is necessary for the annihilation of the old, exploiting social order and for uniting the proletariat.

Well, I think the refusal of many influential people to accept this elementary fact of Soviet doctrine illustrates an historical reluctance to see totalitarian powers for what they are. We saw this phenomenon in the 1930s. We see it too often today.

This doesn't mean we should isolate ourselves and refuse to seek an understanding with them. I intend to do everything I can to persuade them of our peaceful intent, to remind them that it was the West that refused to use its nuclear monopoly in the forties and fifties for territorial gain and which now proposes a 50-percent cut in strategic ballistic missiles and the elimination of an entire class of land-based, intermediate-range nuclear missiles.

At the same time, however, they must be made to understand we will never compromise our principles and standards. We will never give away our freedom. We will never abandon our belief in God. And we will never stop searching for a genuine peace. But we can assure none of these things America stands for through the so-called nuclear freeze solutions proposed by some.

The truth is that a freeze now would be a very dangerous fraud, for that is merely the illusion of peace. The reality is that we must find peace through strength.

I would agree to a freeze if only we could freeze the Soviets' global desires. A freeze at current levels of weapons would remove any incentive for the Soviets to negotiate seriously in Geneva and virtually end our chances to achieve the major arms reductions which we have proposed. Instead, they would achieve their objectives through the freeze.

A freeze would reward the Soviet Union for its enormous and unparalleled military buildup. It would prevent the essential and long overdue modernization of United States and allied defenses and would leave our aging forces increasingly vulnerable. And an honest freeze would require extensive prior negotiations on the systems and numbers to be limited and on the measures to ensure effective verification and compliance. And the kind of a freeze that has been suggested would be virtually impossible to verify. Such a major effort would divert us completely from our current negotiations on achieving substantial reductions. . . .

Yes, let us pray for the salvation of all of those who live in that totalitarian darkness—pray they will discover the joy of knowing God. But until they do, let us be aware that while they preach the supremacy of the state, declare its omnipotence over individual man, and predict its eventual domination of all peoples on the Earth, they are the focus of evil in the modern world. . . .

. . . Some would have us accept them at their word and accommodate ourselves to their aggressive impulses. But if history teaches anything, it teaches that simple-minded appeasement or wishful thinking about our adversaries is folly. It means the betrayal of our past, the squandering of our freedom.

So, I urge you to speak out against those who would place the United States in a position of military and moral inferiority. . . . So, in your discussions of the nuclear freeze proposals, I urge you to beware the temptation of pride—the temptation of blithely declaring yourselves above it all and label both sides equally at fault, to ignore the facts of history and the aggressive impulses of an evil empire, to simply call the arms race a giant misunderstanding and thereby remove yourself from the struggle between right and wrong and good and evil.

I ask you to resist the attempts of those who would have you withhold your support for our efforts, this administration's efforts, to keep America strong and free, while we negotiate real and verifiable reductions in the world's nuclear arsenals and one day, with God's help, their total elimination.

While America's military strength is important, let me add here that I've always maintained that the struggle now going on for the world will never be decided by bombs or rockets, by armies or military might. The real crisis we face today is a spiritual one; at root, it is a test of moral will and faith. . . .

I believe we shall rise to the challenge. I believe that Communism is another sad, bizarre chapter in human history whose last pages even now are being written. I believe this because the source of our strength in the quest for human freedom is not material, but spiritual. And because it knows no limitation, it must terrify and ultimately triumph over those who would enslave their fellow man. . . .

The Public Papers of President Ronald W. Reagan, Reagan Presidential Library, www.reagan.utexas.edu/archives/speeches/1983/30883b.htm (accessed October 10, 2008).

3

EXCERPTS FROM "ADDRESS TO THE NATION AND OTHER COUNTRIES ON UNITED STATES-SOVIET RELATIONS" (JANUARY 16, 1984)

During these first days of 1984, I would like to share with you and the people of the world my thoughts on a subject of great importance to the cause of peace—relations between the United States and the Soviet Union. . . .

I believe that 1984 finds the United States in the strongest position in years to establish a constructive and realistic working relationship with the Soviet Union. We've come a long way since the decade of the seventies, years when the United States seemed filled with self-doubt and neglected its defenses, while the Soviet Union increased its military might and sought to expand its influence by armed forces and threat. . . .

History teaches that wars begin when governments believe the price of aggression is cheap. To keep the peace, we and our allies must be strong enough to convince any potential aggressor that war could bring no benefit, only disaster. So, when we neglected our defenses, the risks of serious confrontation grew.

Three years ago, we embraced a mandate from the American people to change course, and we have. With the support of the American people and the Congress we halted America's decline. Our economy is now in the midst of the best recovery since the sixties. Our defenses are being rebuilt, our alliances are solid, and our commitment to defend our values has never been more clear. . . .

Yes, we are safer now, but to say that our restored deterrence has made the world safer is not to say that it's safe enough. We're witnessing tragic conflicts in many parts of the world. Nuclear arsenals are far too high, and our working relationship with the Soviet Union is not what it must be. These are conditions which must be addressed and improved.

Deterrence is essential to preserve peace and protect our way of life, but deterrence is not the beginning and end of our policy toward the Soviet Union. We must and will engage the Soviets in a dialogue as serious and constructive as possible—a dialogue that will serve to promote peace in the troubled regions of the world, reduce the level of arms, and build a constructive working relationship.

Neither we nor the Soviet Union can wish away the differences between our two societies and our philosophies, but we should always remember that we do have common interests and the foremost among them is to avoid war and reduce the level of arms.

There is no rational alternative but to steer a course which I would call credible deterrence and peaceful competition. . . . That's why 1984 is a year of opportunities for peace.

But if the United States and the Soviet Union are to rise to the challenges facing us and seize the opportunities for peace, we must do more to find areas of mutual interest and then build on them.

. . . Today there are armed conflicts in the Middle East, Afghanistan, Southeast Asia, Central America, and Africa. In other regions, independent nations are confronted by heavily armed neighbors seeking to dominate by threatening attack or subversion. Most of these conflicts have their origins in local problems, but many have been exploited by the Soviet Union and its surrogates. And, of course, Afghanistan has suffered an outright Soviet invasion. . . .

Would it not be better and safer if we could work together to assist people in areas of conflict in finding peaceful solutions to their problems? That should be our mutual goal. . . .

Our second task should be to find ways to reduce the vast stockpiles of armaments in the world. It's tragic to see the world's developing nations spending more than $150 billion a year on armed forces—some 20 percent of their national budgets. We must find ways to reverse the vicious cycle of threat and response which drives arms races everywhere it occurs. . . .

Our third task is to establish a better working relationship with each other, one marked by greater cooperation and understanding. Cooperation and understanding are built on deeds, not words. . . . Cooperation and understanding are especially important to arms control. In recent years we've had serious concerns about Soviet compliance with agreements and treaties. Compliance is important because we seek truly effective arms control. . . .

In working on these tasks, our approach is based on three guiding principles—realism, strength, and dialogue. Realism means we must start with a clear-eyed understanding of the world we live in. We must recognize that we are in a long-term competition with a government that does not share our notions of individual liberties at home and peaceful change abroad. We must be frank in acknowledging our differences and unafraid to promote our values.

Strength is essential to negotiate successfully and protect our interests. If we're weak, we can do neither. Strength is more than military power. Economic strength is crucial, and America's economy is leading the world into recovery. Equally important is our strength of spirit and unity among our people at home and with our allies abroad. We're stronger in all these areas than we were three years ago. Our strength is necessary to deter war and to facilitate negotiated solutions. . . .

I have openly expressed my view of the Soviet system. I don't know why this should come as a surprise to Soviet leaders who've never shied from expressing their view of our system. But this doesn't mean that we can't deal with each other. We don't refuse to talk when the Soviets call us imperialist aggressors and worse, or because they cling to the fantasy of a Communist triumph over democracy. The fact that neither of us likes the other system is no reason to refuse to talk. Living in this nuclear age makes it imperative that we do talk. . . .

We will negotiate in good faith. Whenever the Soviet Union is ready to do likewise, we'll meet them halfway. . . .

Our policy toward the Soviet Union—a policy of credible deterrence, peaceful competition, and constructive cooperation—will serve our two nations and people everywhere. It is a policy not just for this year, but for the long term. It's a challenge for Americans; it is also a challenge for the Soviets. If they cannot meet us halfway, we will be prepared to protect our interests and those of our friends and allies. . . .

We can't predict how the Soviet leaders will respond to our challenge. But the people of our two countries share with all mankind the dream of eliminating the risk of nuclear war. It's not an impossible dream, because eliminating these risks is so clearly a vital interest for all of us. Our two countries have never fought each other. There's no reason why we ever should. Indeed, we fought common enemies in World War II. Today our common enemies are poverty, disease, and above all, war. . . .

Just suppose with me for a moment that an Ivan and an Anya could find themselves, oh, say, in a waiting room, or sharing a shelter from the rain or a storm with a Jim and Sally, and there was no language barrier to keep them from getting acquainted. Would they then debate the differences between their respective governments? Or would they find themselves comparing notes about their children and what each other did for a living?

Before they parted company, they would probably have touched on ambitions and hobbies and what they wanted for their children and problems of making ends meet. And as they went their separate ways, maybe Anya would be saying to Ivan, "Wasn't she nice? She also teaches music." Or Jim would be telling Sally what Ivan did or didn't like about his boss. They might even have decided they were all going to get together for dinner some evening soon. Above all, they would have proven that people don't make wars.

People want to raise their children in a world without fear and without war. They want to have some of the good things over and above bare subsistence that make life worth living. They want to work at some craft, trade, or profession that gives them satisfaction and a sense of worth. Their common interests cross all borders.

If the Soviet Government wants peace, then there will be peace. . . . Let us begin now.

The Public Papers of President Ronald W. Reagan, Reagan Presidential Library, www.reagan.utexas.edu/archives/speeches/1984/11684a.htm (accessed October 10, 2008).

4

EXCERPTS FROM MINUTES, NATIONAL SECURITY PLANNING GROUP MEETING (JUNE 25, 1984); 2:00–3:00 P.M.; SITUATION ROOM

SUBJECT: Central America

Mr. McFarlane: The purpose of this meeting is to focus on the political, economic, and military situation in Central America; to offer a status report, and to discuss next steps needed to keep our friends together while continuing to make progress toward our overall political goals. . . .

The key question we need to consider now is what we believe about the prospects for further talks with Nicaragua; do we believe that Nicaragua wants to come to a reasonable agreement? . . .

Secretary Shultz: Mr. President, we would not have gotten the deployment of Pershing missiles in Europe if people had not seen that we had a credible, vigorous negotiation going on. Similarly, you have moved to get yourself in a position with the USSR where we have made credible proposals and they have walked out. This is useful because it shows who is at fault for the lack of progress.

Similarly, in Central America, our basic thrust has to be to generate positive elements of the political and economic situation, and to provide security help so that our efforts to disrupt the Nicaraguan export of subversion are as strong as we can get. An essential ingredient in that strategy is that we can say, if Nicaragua is halfway reasonable, there could be a regional negotiated solution—one which we support as much as we can. It is essential to have something like that going on or else our support on the Hill goes down. . . .

So on our efforts to engage Nicaragua, there is one piece of very bad news. We don't have the votes in the House of Representatives to obtain additional funds for the anti-Sandinistas. . . .

Mr. Casey: The legal position is that CIA is authorized to cooperate and seek support from third countries. In fact, the finding encourages third country participation and support in this entire effort, and we are considering Salvador, Guatemala, Honduras and a South American country. If we notify the oversight committees, we can provide direct assistance to help the FDN [Nicaraguan Democratic Force] and get the money they need from third countries. There will be some criticism, but senior members of the oversight committee recognize that we need to do this. We need a decision to authorize our permitting the FDN to obtain third country support. . . .

Secretary Weinberger: . . . On the anti-Sandinista issue, I think we need to take the offensive against the Democrats in Congress. We need to hold them accountable for not providing the resources needed to defend democracy. We need to hold the Democrats accountable. We should ask the Democrats whether they want a second Cuba. They see Ortega going after the visit of Secretary Shultz to Havana and then to Moscow. Do the American people want this? . . .

President Reagan: It all hangs on support for the anti-Sandinistas. Can we get that support in the Congress? We have to be more active. With respect to your differences on negotiating, our participation is important from that standpoint to get support from Congress. . . . If we are just talking about negotiations with Nicaragua, that is so far-fetched to imagine that a Communist government like that would make any reasonable deal with us, but if it is to get Congress to support the anti-Sandinistas, then that can be helpful.

Amb. Kirkpatrick: If we don't find the money to support the Contras, it will be perceived in the region and the world as our having abandoned them and this will lead to an increase in refugees in the region and it will permit Nicaragua to infiltrate thousands of Nicaraguan trained forces into El Salvador. And this will be an infiltration we could not stop. The Democrats don't want to vote because they don't want to accept the responsibility for their votes against this program. I believe we need to make their responsibility in the Congress clear to the U.S. public. We must require the Democrats to stand up and be counted. If you showed your commitment and the Administration's commitment with more activity it would be a positive factor in Congress. If we can't get the money for the anti-Sandinistas, then we should make the maximum effort to find the money elsewhere . . .

Secretary Shultz: Several points: (1) everyone agrees with the Contra program but there is no way to get a vote this week. If we leave it attached to the bill, we will lose the money we need for El Salvador. (2) We have had a vote on the anti-Sandinista program and the Democrats voted it down. It already is on the record and the Democrats are on the record. (3) I would like to get money for the Contras also, but another lawyer, Jim Baker, said that if we go out and try to get money from third countries, it is an impeachable offense.

Mr. Casey: I am entitled to complete the record. Jim Baker said that if we tried to get money from third countries without notifying the oversight committees, it could be a problem and he was informed that the finding does provide for the participation and cooperation of third countries. Once he learned that the funding does encourage cooperation from third countries, Jim Baker immediately dropped his view that this could be an "impeachable offense," and you heard him say that, George.

Secretary Shultz: Jim Baker's argument is that the U.S. Government may raise and spend funds only through an appropriation of the Congress.

Secretary Weinberger: I am another lawyer who isn't practicing law, but Jim Baker should realize that the United States would not be spending the money for the anti-Sandinista program; it is merely helping the anti-Sandinistas obtain the money from other sources. Therefore, the United States is not, as a government, spending money obtained from other sources.

Secretary Shultz: I think we need to get an opinion from the Attorney General on whether we can help the Contras obtain money from third sources. It would be the prudent thing to do. . . .

President Reagan: I think there is merit to continuing the current negotiating session with the Nicaraguans, which has already begun, because the press is eager to paint us as having failed again, and we don't want to let Nicaragua get off the hook. . . . The Contra funding is like the MX spending. It is what will keep the pressure on Nicaragua, and the only way we are going to get a good Contadora treaty is if we keep the pressure on. . . .

Mr. Casey: It is essential that we tell the Congress what will happen if they fail to provide the funding for the anti-Sandinistas. At the same time, we can go ahead in trying to help obtain funding for the anti-Sandinistas from other sources; the finding does say explicitly "the United States should co-operate with other governments and seek support of other governments." The limitation we have in the Congress is the cap on U.S. spending; we want to get that lifted. We have met no resistance from senior members of the intelligence committees to the idea of getting help with third country funding.

Mr. Meese: As another non-practicing lawyer I want to emphasize that it's important to tell the Department of Justice that we want them to find the proper and legal basis which will permit the United States to assist in obtaining third party resources for the anti-Sandinistas. You have to give lawyers guidance when asking them a question.

Secretary Weinberger: I agree that we should be giving greater emphasis to obtaining funding for the anti-Sandinistas. We should make it a major issue with the Congress, Mr. President. I also agree that we should facilitate third country support for the anti-Sandinista groups. . . .

Mr. Casey: We need the legal opinion which makes clear that the U.S. has the authority to facilitate third country funding for the anti-Sandinistas, and at the same time, we need to find a way to provide humanitarian assistance to any anti-Sandinistas and their families who might be going into Costa Rica or Honduras to escape the Nicaraguan military actions against them. We need this humanitarian assistance to be available right away.

President Reagan: . . . On the anti-Sandinistas, I am behind an all-out push in Congress. We must obtain the funds to help these freedom fighters. . . .

Vice President Bush: How can anyone object to the U.S. encouraging third parties to provide help to the anti-Sandinistas under the finding? The only problem that might come up is if the United States were to promise to give these third parties something in return so that some people could interpret this as some kind of an exchange.

Mr. Casey: Jim Baker changed his mind as soon as he saw the finding and saw the language.

Mr. McFarlane: I propose that there be no authority for anyone to seek third party support for the anti–Sandinistas until we have the information we need, and I certainly hope none of this discussion will be made public in any way.

President Reagan: If such a story gets out, we'll all be hanging by our thumbs in front of the White House until we find out who did it.

The meeting adjourned at 3:50 p.m.

The National Security Archive: The Iran-Contra Affair 20 Years On, www.gwu.edu/~nsarchiv/NSAEBB/NSAEBB210/index.htm (accessed September 14, 2008).

5

EXCERPTS FROM ADDRESSES BY NEW YORK GOVERNOR MARIO CUOMO AND MASSACHUSETTS SENATOR EDWARD KENNEDY, DEMOCRATIC NATIONAL CONVENTION (JULY 16–19, 1984)

KEYNOTE ADDRESS BY GOVERNOR MARIO CUOMO

On behalf of the great Empire State and the whole family of New York, let me thank you for the great privilege of being able to address this convention. Please allow me to skip the stories and the poetry and the temptation to deal in nice but vague rhetoric. Let me instead use this valuable opportunity to deal immediately with the questions that should determine this election and that we all know are vital to the American people. . . .

But what about foreign policy? They said that they would make us and the whole world safer. They say they have. By creating the largest defense budget in history, one that even they now admit is excessive—by escalating to a frenzy the nuclear arms race; by incendiary rhetoric; by refusing to discuss peace with our enemies; by the loss of 279 young Americans in Lebanon in pursuit of a plan and a policy that no one can find or describe.

We give money to Latin American governments that murder nuns, and then we lie about it. We have been less than zealous in support of our only real friend—it seems to me, in the Middle East—the one democracy there, our flesh and blood ally, the state of Israel. Our—Our policy—Our foreign policy drifts with no real direction, other than an hysterical commitment to an arms race that leads nowhere—if we're lucky. And if we're not, it could lead us into bankruptcy or war.

Of course we must have a strong defense! Of course Democrats are for a strong defense. Of course Democrats believe that there are times that we must stand and fight. And we have. Thousands of us have paid for freedom with our lives. But always—when this country has been at its best—our

201

purposes were clear. Now they're not. Now our allies are as confused as our enemies. Now we have no real commitment to our friends or to our ideals—not to human rights, not to the refuseniks, not to Sakharov, not to Bishop Tutu and the others struggling for freedom in South Africa.

We—We have in the last few years spent more than we can afford. We have pounded our chests and made bold speeches. But we lost 279 young Americans in Lebanon and we live behind sand bags in Washington. How can anyone say that we are safer, stronger, or better?

That—That is the Republican record. That its disastrous quality is not more fully understood by the American people I can only attribute to the President's amiability and the failure by some to separate the salesman from the product. . . .

We believe—We believe as Democrats, that a society as blessed as ours, the most affluent democracy in the world's history, one that can spend trillions on instruments of destruction, ought to be able to help the middle class in its struggle, ought to be able to find work for all who can do it, room at the table, shelter for the homeless, care for the elderly and infirm, and hope for the destitute. And we proclaim as loudly as we can the utter insanity of nuclear proliferation and the need for a nuclear freeze, if only to affirm the simple truth that peace is better than war because life is better than death. . . .

INTRODUCTION OF VICE PRESIDENT WALTER F. MONDALE BY SENATOR EDWARD M. KENNEDY

With President Mondale in the White House, instead of slashing essential measures to strengthen our schools, we will cancel that needless missile without a mission, that reckless weapon without a home, the MX missile. We cannot afford wasteful military spending which weakens both our economy and the national security. A just society cannot be tough on poor mothers and easy on Pentagon contractors. . . .

And ever since the bygone days of Herbert Hoover, every president, even Richard Nixon, has negotiated with the leader of the Soviet Union, except Ronald Reagan.

His Deputy Undersecretary of Defense reassures us that we do not have to be too afraid of a nuclear exchange because—and let me quote his preposterous words—"Everybody's going to make it if there are enough shovels to go around." We have a better idea: Everybody is going to make it if the Reagan Administration is no longer around.

For most of his public career, President Reagan has fervently denounced nuclear arms control. Suddenly, in this election year, he endorses it with equal fervor, but, until now, Ronald Reagan has never met an arms control agreement he didn't dislike. . . .

The voters will not forget Ronald Reagan's real and perilous views on the nuclear issue. He intends to spend billions on "Star Wars" in outer space, and that is why we must send him back to Hollywood, which is where both "Star Wars" and Ronald Reagan really belong.

In a second term, President Reagan would proceed even faster with an arms race that could end the human race. President Mondale will negotiate with the Soviet Union for a mutual and verifiable freeze on the production, testing and deployment of nuclear weapons.

President Reagan would stand even closer to right-wing dictatorships abroad and the racist regime in South Africa. He would sell even more sophisticated weapons to the enemies of Israel. President Mondale will stand for democracy, and he will stand against apartheid, and he will stand with Israel for a secure peace in the Middle East.

President Reagan will move nearer to confrontation and conflict in our own hemisphere and around the globe. President Mondale will build a strong America: strong in its nuclear deterrence, stronger than it is now in its conventional forces, and strongest of all in its determination to settle differences—wherever possible—by seeking talks and not by sending troops.

Under President Mondale, there will be no wasteful war in Lebanon, no secret war in Nicaragua, and no wider war in Central America.

S. Perlmutter, R. Boylan, and J. Vaught, eds., *Official Proceedings of the 1984 Democratic National Convention* (Washington, DC: Democratic National Committee, 1984).

6

EXCERPTS FROM
THE TOWER COMMISSION REPORT
(FEBRUARY 26, 1987)

WHAT WAS WRONG

The arms transfers to Iran and the activities of the NSC staff in support of the Contras are case studies in the perils of policy pursued outside the constraints of orderly process.

The Iran initiative ran directly counter to the Administration's own policies on terrorism, the Iran-Iraq war, and military support to Iran. This inconsistency was never resolved, nor were the consequences of this inconsistency fully considered and provided for. The result taken as a whole was a U.S. policy that worked against itself.

The Board believes that failure to deal adequately with these contradictions resulted in large part from the flaws in the manner in which decisions were made. Established procedures for making national security decisions were ignored. Reviews of the initiative by all the NSC principals were too infrequent. The initiatives were not adequately vetted below the Cabinet level. Intelligence resources were underutilized. Applicable legal constraints were not adequately addressed. The whole matter was handled too informally, without adequate written records of what had been considered, discussed, and decided.

This pattern persisted in the implementation of the Iran initiative. The NSC staff assumed direct operational control. The initiative fell within the traditional jurisdictions of the Departments of State, Defense, and CIA. Yet these agencies were largely ignored. Great reliance was placed on a network of private operators and intermediaries. How the initiative was to be carried out never received adequate attention from the NSC

205

principals or a tough working-level review. No periodic evaluation of the progress of the initiative was ever conducted. The result was an unprofessional and, in substantial part, unsatisfactory operation.

In all of this process, Congress was never notified.

A FLAWED PROCESS

The initiative to Iran was a covert operation directly at odds with important and well-publicized policies of the Executive Branch. But the initiative itself embodied a fundamental contradiction. Two objectives were apparent from the outset: a strategic opening to Iran, and release of the U.S. citizens held hostage in Lebanon. The sale of arms to Iran appeared to provide a means to achieve both these objectives. It also played into the hands of those who had other interests—some of them personal financial gain—in engaging the United States in an arms deal with Iran.

In fact, the sale of arms was not equally appropriate for achieving both these objectives. Arms were what Iran wanted. If all the United States sought was to free the hostages, then an arms-for-hostages deal could achieve the immediate objectives of both sides. But if the U.S. objective was a broader strategic relationship, then the sale of arms should have been contingent upon first putting into place the elements of that relationship. An arms-for-hostages deal in this context could become counterproductive to achieving this broader strategic objective. . . .

The Board believes that a strategic opening to Iran may have been in the national interest but that the United States never should have been a party to the arms transfers. As arms-for-hostages trades, they could not help but create an incentive for further hostage-taking. As a violation of the U.S. arms embargo, they could only remove inhibitions on other nations from selling arms to Iran. This threatened to upset the military balance between Iran and Iraq, with consequent jeopardy to the Gulf States and the interests of the West in that region. The arms-for-hostages trades rewarded a regime that clearly supported terrorism and hostage-taking. They increased the risks that the United States would be perceived, especially in the Arab world, as a creature of Israel. They suggested to other U.S. allies and friends in the region that the United States had shifted its policy in favor of Iran. They raised questions as to whether U.S. policy statements could be relied upon. . . .

The Board was unable to reach a conclusive judgment about whether the 1985 shipments of arms to Iran were approved in advance by the President. On balance the Board believes that it is plausible to conclude that he did approve them in advance.

★★★★★★★★★★

FAILURE OF RESPONSIBILITY

The NSC system will not work unless the President makes it work. After all, this system was created to serve the President of the United States in ways of his choosing. By his actions, by his leadership, the President therefore determines the quality of its performance. . . .

The President's management style is to put the principal responsibility for policy review and implementation on the shoulders of his advisors. Nevertheless, with such a complex, high-risk operation and so much at stake, the President should have insured that the NSC system did not fail him. He did not force his policy to undergo the most critical review of which the NSC participants and the process were capable. At no time did he insist upon accountability and performance review. Had the President chosen to drive the NSC system, the outcome could well have been different. . . .

President Reagan's personal management style places an especially heavy responsibility on his key advisors. Knowing his style, they should have been particularly mindful of the need for special attention to the manner in which this arms-sale initiative developed and proceeded. On this score, neither the national security adviser nor the other NSC principals deserve high marks. . . .

In the case of the Iran initiative, the NSC process did not fail, it simply was largely ignored. The national security adviser and the NSC principals all had a duty to raise the issue and insist that orderly process be imposed. None of them did so. . . .

None of the principals called for a serious vetting of the initiative by even a restricted group of disinterested individuals. The intelligence questions do not appear to have been raised, and legal considerations, while raised, were not pressed. No one seemed to have complained about the informality of the process. No one called for a thorough re-examination once the initiative did not meet expectations or the manner of execution changed. While one or another of the NSC principals suspected that something was amiss, none vigorously pursued the issue.

Mr. Regan also shares in this responsibility. More than almost any chief of staff of recent memory, he asserted personal control over the White House staff and sought to extend this control to the national security adviser. He was personally active in national security affairs and attended almost all the relevant meetings regarding the Iran initiative. He, as much as anyone, should have insisted that an orderly process be observed. In addition, he especially should have ensured that plans were made for handling any public disclosure of the initiative. He must bear primary responsibility for the chaos that descended upon the White House when such disclosure did occur.

Mr. McFarlane appeared caught between a President who supported the initiative and the Cabinet officers who strongly opposed it. While he made efforts to keep these Cabinet officers informed, the Board heard complaints from some that he was not always successful. VADM Poindexter on several occasions apparently sought to exclude NSC principals other than the President from knowledge of the initiative. Indeed, on one or more occasions Secretary Shultz may have been actively misled by VADM Poindexter.

VADM Poindexter also failed grievously on the matter of Contra diversion. Evidence indicates that VADM Poindexter knew that a diversion occurred, yet he did not take the steps that were required given the gravity of that prospect. He apparently failed to appreciate or ignored the serious legal and political risks presented. His clear obligation was either to investigate the matter or take it to the President—or both. He did neither. Director Casey shared a similar responsibility. Evidence suggests that he received information about the possible diversion of funds to the Contras almost a month before the story broke. He, too, did not move promptly to raise the matter with the President. Yet his responsibility to do so was clear.

The NSC principals other than the President may be somewhat excused by the insufficient attention on the part of the national security adviser to the need to keep all the principals fully informed. Given the importance of the issue and the sharp policy divergences involved, however, Secretary Shultz and Secretary Weinberger in particular distanced themselves from the march of events. Secretary Shultz specifically requested to be informed only as necessary to perform his job. Secretary Weinberger had access through intelligence to details about the operation. Their obligation was to give the President their full support and continued advice with respect to the program or, if they could not in conscience do that, to so inform the President. Instead, they simply distanced themselves from the program. They protected the record as to their own positions on this issue.

They were not energetic in attempting to protect the President from the consequences of his personal commitment to freeing the hostages.

Director Casey appears to have been informed in considerable detail about the specifics of the Iranian operation. He . . . should have taken the lead in vetting the assumptions presented by the Israelis on which the program was based and in pressing for an early examination of the reliance upon Mr. Ghorbanifar and the second channel as intermediaries. He should also have assumed responsibility for checking out the other intermediaries involved in the operation. Finally, because Congressional restrictions on covert actions are both largely directed at and familiar to the CIA, Director Casey should have taken the lead in keeping the question of Congressional notification active. . . .

Tower Commission Report: Report of the President's Special Review Board. Washington, DC: U.S. Government Printing Office, 1987.

7

EXCERPTS FROM "ADDRESS TO THE NATION ON THE IRAN ARMS AND CONTRA AID CONTROVERSY" (MARCH 4, 1987)

M y fellow Americans:

For the past three months, I've been silent on the revelations about Iran. And you must have been thinking: "Well, why doesn't he tell us what's happening? Why doesn't he just speak to us as he has in the past when we've faced troubles or tragedies?" Others of you, I guess, were thinking: "What's he doing hiding out in the White House?" Well, the reason I haven't spoken to you before now is this: You deserve the truth. And as frustrating as the waiting has been, I felt it was improper to come to you with sketchy reports, or possibly even erroneous statements, which would then have to be corrected, creating even more doubt and confusion. There's been enough of that. I've paid a price for my silence in terms of your trust and confidence. But I've had to wait, as you have, for the complete story. That's why I . . . appointed a Special Review Board, the Tower Board, which took on the chore of pulling the truth together for me and getting to the bottom of things. It has now issued its findings.

I'm often accused of being an optimist, and it's true I had to hunt pretty hard to find any good news in the Board's report. As you know, it's well-stocked with criticisms, which I'll discuss in a moment; but I was very relieved to read this sentence: "The Board is convinced that the President does indeed want the full story to be told." And that will continue to be my pledge to you as the other investigations go forward. . . .

I've studied the Board's report. Its findings are honest, convincing, and highly critical; and I accept them. And tonight I want to share with you my thoughts on these findings and report to you on the actions I'm taking to implement the Board's recommendations. First, let me say I take full responsibility for my own actions and for those of my administration. As angry as I may be about activities undertaken without my knowledge, I am still accountable for those activities. As disappointed as I may be in some who served me, I'm still the one who must answer to the American people for this behavior. And as personally distasteful as I find secret bank accounts and diverted funds—well, as the Navy would say, this happened on my watch.

Let's start with the part that is the most controversial. A few months ago I told the American people I did not trade arms for hostages. My heart and my best intentions still tell me that's true, but the facts and the evidence tell me it is not. As the Tower Board reported, what began as a strategic opening to Iran deteriorated, in its implementation, into trading arms for hostages. This runs counter to my own beliefs, to administration policy, and to the original strategy we had in mind. There are reasons why it happened, but no excuses. It was a mistake. I undertook the original Iran initiative in order to develop relations with those who might assume leadership in a post-Khomeini government.

It's clear from the Board's report, however, that I let my personal concern for the hostages spill over into the geopolitical strategy of reaching out to Iran. I asked so many questions about the hostages' welfare that I didn't ask enough about the specifics of the total Iran plan. Let me say to the hostage families: We have not given up. We never will. And I promise you we'll use every legitimate means to free your loved ones from captivity. But I must also caution that those Americans who freely remain in such dangerous areas must know that they're responsible for their own safety.

Now, another major aspect of the Board's findings regards the transfer of funds to the Nicaraguan Contras. The Tower Board wasn't able to find out what happened to this money, so the facts here will be left to the continuing investigations of the court-appointed Independent Counsel and the two congressional investigating committees. I'm confident the truth will come out about this matter, as well. As I told the Tower Board, I didn't know about any diversion of funds to the Contras. But as President, I cannot escape responsibility.

Much has been said about my management style, a style that's worked successfully for me during eight years as Governor of California and for most of my Presidency. The way I work is to identify the problem, find the right individuals to do the job, and then let them go to it. I've found this invariably brings out the best in people. They seem to rise to their full capability, and in the long run you get more done. When it came to managing the NSC staff, let's face it, my style didn't match its previous track record. . . .

For nearly a week now, I've been studying the Board's report. I want the American people to know that this wrenching ordeal of recent months has not been in vain. I endorse every one of the Tower Board's recommendations. In fact, I'm going beyond its recommendations so as to put the house in even better order. I'm taking action in three basic areas: personnel, national security policy, and the process for making sure that the system works.

First, personnel—I've brought in an accomplished and highly respected new team here at the White House. . . . Second, in the area of national security policy, I have ordered the NSC to begin a comprehensive review of all covert operations. I have also directed that any covert activity be in support of clear policy objectives and in compliance with American values. . . . Third, in terms of the process of reaching national security decisions, I am adopting in total the Tower Report's model of how the NSC process and staff should work. . . .

Now, what should happen when you make a mistake is this: You take your knocks, you learn your lessons, and then you move on. That's the healthiest way to deal with a problem. This in no way diminishes the importance of the other continuing investigations, but the business of our country and our people must proceed. I've gotten this message from Republicans and Democrats in Congress, from allies around the world, and—if we're reading the signals right—even from the Soviets. And of course, I've heard the message from you, the American people. You know, by the time you reach my age, you've made plenty of mistakes. And if you've lived your life properly—so, you learn. You put things in perspective. You pull your energies together. You change. You go forward.

My fellow Americans, I have a great deal that I want to accomplish with you and for you over the next two years. And the Lord willing, that's exactly what I intend to do.

The Public Papers of President Ronald W. Reagan, Reagan Presidential Library, www.reagan.utexas.edu/archives/speeches/1987/030487h.htm (accessed October 10, 2008).

8

EXCERPTS FROM "REMARKS AND QUESTION-AND-ANSWER SESSION WITH THE STUDENTS AND FACULTY AT MOSCOW STATE UNIVERSITY" (MAY 31, 1988)

As you know, I've come to Moscow to meet with one of your most distinguished graduates. In this, our fourth summit, General Secretary Gorbachev and I have spent many hours together, and I feel that we're getting to know each other well. Our discussions, of course, have been focused primarily on many of the important issues of the day, issues I want to touch on with you in a few moments. But first I want to take a little time to talk to you much as I would to any group of university students in the United States. I want to talk not just of the realities of today but of the possibilities of tomorrow.

Standing here before a mural of your revolution, I want to talk about a very different revolution that is taking place right now, quietly sweeping the globe without bloodshed or conflict. Its effects are peaceful, but they will fundamentally alter our world, shatter old assumptions, and reshape our lives. It's easy to underestimate because it's not accompanied by banners or fanfare. It's been called the technological or information revolution, and as its emblem, one might take the tiny silicon chip, no bigger than a fingerprint. One of these chips has more computing power than a roomful of old-style computers. . . .

Like a chrysalis, we're emerging from the economy of the Industrial Revolution—an economy confined to and limited by the Earth's physical resources—into one . . . in which there are no bounds on human imagination and the freedom to create is the most precious natural resource. Think of that little computer chip. Its value isn't in the sand from which it is made but in the microscopic architecture designed into it by ingenious human minds. Or take the example of the satellite relaying this broadcast around

215

the world, which replaces thousands of tons of copper mined from the Earth and molded into wire. In the new economy, human invention increasingly makes physical resources obsolete. We're breaking through the material conditions of existence to a world where man creates his own destiny. Even as we explore the most advanced reaches of science, we're returning to the age-old wisdom of our culture, a wisdom contained in the book of Genesis in the Bible: In the beginning was the spirit, and it was from this spirit that the material abundance of creation issued forth.

But progress is not foreordained. The key is freedom—freedom of thought, freedom of information, freedom of communication. . . .

The explorers of the modern era are the entrepreneurs, men with vision, with the courage to take risks and faith enough to brave the unknown. These entrepreneurs and their small enterprises are responsible for almost all the economic growth in the United States. They are the prime movers of the technological revolution. In fact, one of the largest personal computer firms in the United States was started by two college students, no older than you, in the garage behind their home. Some people, even in my own country, look at the riot of experiment that is the free market and see only waste. What of all the entrepreneurs that fail? Well, many do, particularly the successful ones; often several times. And if you ask them the secret of their success, they'll tell you it's all that they learned in their struggles along the way; yes, it's what they learned from failing. Like an athlete in competition or a scholar in pursuit of the truth, experience is the greatest teacher.

And that's why it's so hard for government planners, no matter how sophisticated, to ever substitute for millions of individuals working night and day to make their dreams come true. The fact is, bureaucracies are a problem around the world. . . .

We are seeing the power of economic freedom spreading around the world. Places such as the Republic of Korea, Singapore, Taiwan have vaulted into the technological era, barely pausing in the industrial age along the way. . . .

At the same time, the growth of democracy has become one of the most powerful political movements of our age. In Latin America in the 1970s, only a third of the population lived under democratic government; today over 90 percent does. In the Philippines, in the Republic of Korea, free, contested, democratic elections are the order of the day. Throughout the world, free markets are the model for growth. Democracy is the standard by which governments are measured. . . .

But freedom doesn't begin or end with elections. Go to any American town, to take just an example, and you'll see dozens of churches, representing many different beliefs—in many places, synagogues and mosques—and you'll see families of every conceivable nationality worshiping together. Go into any schoolroom, and there you will see children being taught the Declaration of Independence, that they are endowed by their Creator with certain unalienable rights—among them life, liberty, and the pursuit of happiness—that no government can justly deny; the guarantees in their Constitution for freedom of speech, freedom of assembly, and freedom of religion. Go into any courtroom, and there will preside an independent judge, beholden to no government power. There every defendant has the right to a trial by a jury of his peers, usually twelve men and women—common citizens; they are the ones, the only ones, who weigh the evidence and decide on guilt or innocence. In that court, the accused is innocent until proven guilty, and the word of a policeman or any official has no greater legal standing than the word of the accused. Go to any university campus, and there you'll find an open, sometimes heated discussion of the problems in American society and what can be done to correct them. Turn on the television, and you'll see the legislature conducting the business of government right there before the camera, debating and voting on the legislation that will become the law of the land. March in any demonstration, and there are many of them; the people's right of assembly is guaranteed in the Constitution and protected by the police. Go into any union hall, where the members know their right to strike is protected by law. . . .

But freedom is more even than this. Freedom is the right to question and change the established way of doing things. It is the continuing revolution of the marketplace. It is the understanding that allows us to recognize shortcomings and seek solutions. It is the right to put forth an idea, scoffed at by the experts, and watch it catch fire among the people. It is the right to dream—to follow your dream or stick to your conscience, even if you're the only one in a sea of doubters. Freedom is the recognition that no single person, no single authority or government has a monopoly on the truth, but that every individual life is infinitely precious, that every one of us put on this world has been put there for a reason and has something to offer. . . .

But I hope you know I go on about these things not simply to extol the virtues of my own country but to speak to the true greatness of the heart and soul of your land. . . . The great culture of your diverse land speaks with a glowing passion to all humanity. Let me cite one of the most eloquent contemporary passages on human freedom. It comes, not from the literature of America, but from this country, from one of the greatest writers of the twentieth century, Boris Pasternak, in the novel *Dr. Zhivago*. He writes: "I think that if the beast who sleeps in man could be held down by threats—any kind of threat, whether of jail or of retribution after death—then the highest emblem of humanity would be the lion tamer in the circus with his whip, not the prophet who sacrificed himself. But this is just the point—what has for centuries raised man above the beast is not the cudgel, but an inward music—the irresistible power of unarmed truth."

The irresistible power of unarmed truth. Today the world looks expectantly to signs of change, steps toward greater freedom in the Soviet Union. We watch and we hope as we see positive changes taking place.
. . .

At the same time, we should remember that reform that is not institutionalized will always be insecure. Such freedom will always be looking over its shoulder. A bird on a tether, no matter how long the rope, can always be pulled back. And that is why, in my conversation with General Secretary Gorbachev, I have spoken of how important it is to institutionalize change—to put guarantees on reform. And we've been talking together about one sad reminder of a divided world: the Berlin Wall. It's time to remove the barriers that keep people apart. . . .

I've been told that there's a popular song in your country—perhaps you know it—whose evocative refrain asks the question, "Do the Russians want a war?" In answer it says: "Go ask that silence lingering in the air, above the birch and poplar there; beneath those trees the soldiers lie. Go ask my mother, ask my wife; then you will have to ask no more, 'Do the Russians want a war?'" But what of your one-time allies? What of those who embraced you on the Elbe? What if we were to ask the watery graves of the Pacific or the European battlefields where America's fallen were buried far from home? What if we were to ask their mothers, sisters, and sons, do Americans want war? Ask us, too, and you'll find the same answer, the same longing in every heart. People do not make wars; governments do. And no mother would ever willingly sacrifice her sons for territorial gain, for economic advantage, for ideology. A people free to choose will always choose peace. . . .

Your generation is living in one of the most exciting, hopeful times in Soviet history. It is a time when the first breath of freedom stirs the air and the heart beats to the accelerated rhythm of hope, when the accumulated spiritual energies of a long silence yearn to break free. . . .

We do not know what the conclusion will be of this journey, but we're hopeful that the promise of reform will be fulfilled. In this Moscow spring, this May 1988, we may be allowed that hope: that freedom, like the fresh green sapling planted over Tolstoy's grave, will blossom forth at last in the rich fertile soil of your people and culture. We may be allowed to hope that the marvelous sound of a new openness will keep rising through, ringing through, leading to a new world of reconciliation, friendship, and peace.

Thank you all very much, and da blagoslovit vas gospod—God bless you.

The Public Papers of President Ronald W. Reagan, Reagan Presidential Library, www.reagan.utexas.edu/archives/speeches/1988/053188b.htm (accessed October 16, 2008).

9

EXCERPTS FROM "ADDRESS BY MIKHAIL GORBACHEV AT THE FORTY-THIRD U.N. GENERAL ASSEMBLY SESSION" (DECEMBER 7, 1988)

Two great revolutions, the French revolution of 1789 and the Russian revolution of 1917, have exerted a powerful influence on the actual nature of the historical process and radically changed the course of world events. Both of them, each in its own way, have given a gigantic impetus to man's progress. They are also the ones that have formed in many respects the way of thinking which is still prevailing in the public consciousness. . . .

Today we have entered an era when progress will be based on the interests of all mankind. Consciousness of this requires that world policy, too, should be determined by the priority of the values of all mankind. . . .

Further world progress is now possible only through the search for a consensus of all mankind, in movement toward a new world order. . . . The formula of development "at another's expense" is becoming outdated. . . . The very tackling of global problems requires a new "volume" and "quality" of cooperation by states and sociopolitical currents regardless of ideological and other differences.

As you ponder all this, you come to the conclusion that if we wish to take account of the lessons of the past and the realities of the present, if we must reckon with the objective logic of world development, it is necessary to seek—and seek jointly—an approach toward improving the international situation and building a new world. . . . It is evident, for example, that force and the threat of force can no longer be, and should not be instruments of foreign policy. . . .

The compelling necessity of the principle of freedom of choice is also clear to us. The failure to recognize this, to recognize it, is fraught with very dire consequences, consequences for world peace. Denying that right to the peoples, no matter what the pretext, no matter what words are used to conceal it, means infringing upon even the unstable balance that is, has been possible to achieve.

Freedom of choice is a universal principle to which there should be no exceptions. . . .

Such are our reflections on the natural order of things in the world on the threshold of the twenty-first century. We are, of course, far from claiming to have infallible truth, but having subjected the previous realities—realities that have arisen again—to strict analysis, we have come to the conclusion that it is by precisely such approaches that we must search jointly for a way to achieve the supremacy of the common human idea . . .

Our country is undergoing a truly revolutionary upsurge. . . . In order to involve society in implementing the plans for restructuring it had to be made more truly democratic. Under the badge of democratization, restructuring has now encompassed politics, the economy, spiritual life, and ideology. We have unfolded a radical economic reform, we have accumulated experience, and from the new year we are transferring the entire national economy to new forms and work methods. . . .

In moving toward such bold revolutionary transformations, we understood that there would be errors, that there would be resistance, that the novelty would bring new problems. We foresaw the possibility of breaking into individual sections. However, the profound democratic reform of the entire system of power and government is the guarantee that the overall process of restructuring will move steadily forward and gather strength. . . .

We are more than fully confident. We have both the theory, the policy and the vanguard force of restructuring a party which is also restructuring itself in accordance with the new tasks and the radical changes throughout society. And the most important thing: all peoples and all generations of citizens in our great country are in favor of restructuring.

We have gone substantially and deeply into the business of constructing a socialist state based on the rule of law. A whole series of new laws has been prepared or is at a completion stage. ... This means such acts as the Law on Freedom of Conscience, on glasnost, on public associations and organizations, and on much else. There are now no people in places of imprisonment in the country who have been sentenced for their political or religious convictions. . . .

Now about the most important topic, without which no problem of the coming century can be resolved: disarmament. ...Today I can inform you of the following: The Soviet Union has made a decision on reducing its armed forces. In the next two years, their numerical strength will be reduced by five hundred thousand persons, and the volume of conventional arms will also be cut considerably. These reductions will be made on a unilateral basis, unconnected with negotiations on the mandate for the Vienna meeting. . . .

Finally, being on U.S. soil, but also for other, understandable reasons, I cannot but turn to the subject of our relations with this great country. . . . Relations between the Soviet Union and the United States of America span five and a half decades. The world has changed, and so have the nature, role, and place of these relations in world politics. For too long they were built under the banner of confrontation, and sometimes of hostility, either open or concealed. But in the last few years, throughout the world people were able to heave a sigh of relief, thanks to the changes for the better in the substance and atmosphere of the relations between Moscow and Washington. . . .

We acknowledge and value the contribution of President Ronald Reagan and the members of his administration, above all Mr. George Shultz. All this is capital that has been invested in a joint undertaking of historic importance. It must not be wasted or left out of circulation. The future U.S. administration headed by newly elected President George Bush will find in us a partner, ready—without long pauses and backward movements—to continue the dialogue in a spirit of realism, openness, and goodwill, and with a striving for concrete results, over an agenda encompassing the key issues of Soviet-U.S. relations and international politics.

. . . One would like to believe that our joint efforts to put an end to the era of wars, confrontation and regional conflicts, aggression against nature, the terror of hunger and poverty, as well as political terrorism, will be comparable with our hopes. This is our common goal, and it is only by acting together that we may attain it.

Mikhail Gorbachev, Forty-Third United Nations General Assembly Session, A/43/PV.72, December 7, 1988.

SELECTED READINGS

GENERAL BACKGROUND

Brownlee, Elliott, and Hugh Davis Graham, eds. *The Reagan Presidency*. Lawrence: University Press of Kansas, 2003.

Busch, Andrew. *Reagan's Victory*. Lawrence: University Press of Kansas, 2005.

Collins, Robert. *Transforming America*. New York: Columbia University Press, 2007.

Critchlow, Donald. *The Conservative Ascendancy*. Cambridge, MA: Harvard University Press, 2007.

Jenkins, Philip. *Decade of Nightmares: The End of the Sixties and the Making of Eighties America*. New York: Oxford University Press, 2006.

Johnson, Haynes. *Sleepwalking Through History*. New York: W. W. Norton, 1991.

Patterson, James. *Restless Giant: The United States from Watergate to Bush v. Gore*. New York: Oxford University Press, 2005.

Pemberton, William. *Exit with Honor: The Life and Presidency of Ronald Reagan*. New York: M. E. Sharpe, 1997.

Troy, Gil. *Morning in America: How Ronald Reagan Invented the 1980s*. Princeton, NJ: Princeton University Press, 2005.

Tygiel, Jules. *Ronald Reagan and the Triumph of American Conservatism*. New York: Pearson, 2006.

Wilentz, Sean. *The Age of Reagan*. New York: HarperCollins, 2008.

Will, George F. *Suddenly: The American Idea at Home and Abroad*. New York: Doubleday, 1987.

BIOGRAPHY AND MEMOIRS

Brinkley, Douglas, ed. *The Reagan Diaries*. New York: HarperCollins, 2007.

Cannon, Lou. *President Reagan: The Role of a Lifetime*. New York: Simon & Schuster, 1991.

————. *Governor Reagan*. New York: Public Affairs, 2003.

Evans, Thomas. *The Education of Ronald Reagan*. New York: Columbia University Press, 2006.

Farrell, John. *Tip O'Neill and the Democratic Century*. Boston: Little, Brown, 2001.

Gorbachev, Mikhail. *Memoirs*. New York: Doubleday, 1995.

Haig, Alexander. *Caveat: Reagan, Realism and Foreign Policy*. New York: Scribner, 1984.

O'Neill, Thomas P. *Man of the House: The Life and Political Memoirs of Speaker Tip O'Neill*. New York: Random House, 1987.

Powell, Colin. *My American Journey*. New York: Random House, 1995.

Reagan, Ronald. *An American Life*. New York: Pocket Books, 1990.

Regan, Donald. *For the Record: From Wall Street to Washington*. New York: Harcourt Brace and Co., 1988.

Shultz, George. *Turmoil and Triumph*. New York: Scribner, 1993.

Skinner, Kiron, and Martin Anderson, eds. *Reagan: A Life in Letters*. New York: Free Press, 2003.

Weinberger, Caspar. *Fighting for Peace*. New York: Grand Central Publishing, 1990.

OVERVIEWS OF THE REAGAN PRESIDENCY AND DOMESTIC ISSUES

Anderson, Martin. *Revolution*. New York: Harcourt, Brace, 1988.

Conley, Richard S., ed. *Reassessing the Reagan Presidency*. Lanham, MD: University Press of America, 2003.

Dallek, Robert. *Ronald Reagan: The Politics of Symbolism*. 2nd ed. Cambridge, MA: Harvard University Press, 1999.

Diggins, John Patrick. *Ronald Reagan: Fate, Freedom, and the Meaning of History*. New York: W. W. Norton, 2007.

Ehrman, John. *The Eighties: America in the Age of Reagan*. New Haven, NJ: Yale University Press, 2005.

Kengor, Paul, and Peter Schweizer, eds. *The Reagan Presidency: Assessing the Man and His Legacy*. Lanham, MD: Rowman & Littlefield, 2005.

Mervin, David. *Ronald Reagan and the American Presidency*. London: Longman Group, 1990.

Morris, Edmund. *Dutch*. New York: Random House: 1999.

Reeves, Richard. *President Reagan: The Triumph of Imagination*. New York: Simon & Schuster, 2005.

Schaller, Michael. *Right Turn*. New York: Oxford University Press, 2007.

Sloan, John. *The Reagan Effect*. Lawrence: University Press of Kansas, 1999.

Stockman, David Alan. *The Triumph of Politics: Why the Reagan Revolution Failed*. New York: HarperCollins, 1986.

FOREIGN AFFAIRS

Burns, E. Bradford. *At War in Nicaragua: The Reagan Doctrine and the Politics of Nostalgia*. New York: Harper & Row, 1987.

Byrne, Malcolm, and Peter Kornbluh, eds. *The Iran-Contra Affair: The Declassified History*. New York: New Press, 1993.

Draper, Theodore. *A Very Thin Line: The Iran-Contra Affairs*. New York: Hill & Wang, 1991.

Ehrman, John. *The Rise of Neoconservatism: Intellectuals and Foreign Affairs, 1945–1994*. New Haven, NJ: Yale University Press, 1995.

Fitzgerald, Frances. *Way Out There in the Blue: Reagan, Star Wars, and the End of the Cold War*. New York: Simon & Schuster, 2000.

Garthoff, Raymond. *The Great Transition: American-Russian Relations and the End of the Cold War*. Washington, DC: Brookings Institution Press, 1994.

———. *Détente and Confrontation: American-Soviet Relations from Nixon to Reagan*. Washington, DC: Brookings Institution Press, 1990.

Jentleson, Bruce W. *With Friends Like These: Reagan, Bush and Saddam*. New York: W. W. Norton & Co., 1994.

Kengor, Paul. *The Crusader: Ronald Reagan and the Fall of Communism*. New York: HarperCollins, 2006.

Kornbluh, Peter. *Nicaragua: The Price of Intervention*. Washington, DC: Institute for Policy Studies, 1987.

Lafeber, Walter. *Inevitable Revolutions: The United States in Central America*. New York: W. W. Norton & Co., 1984.

Leffler, Melvyn P. *For the Soul of Mankind: The United States, the Soviet Union, and the Cold War*. New York: Hill & Wang, 2007.

LeoGrande, William M. *Our Own Backyard: The United States in Central America, 1977–1992*. Chapel Hill: University of North Carolina Press, 1998.

Lowenthal, Abraham F. *Partners in Conflict*. Baltimore: Johns Hopkins University Press, 1990.

Mann, James. *Rise of the Vulcans: The History of Bush's War Cabinet*. New York: Viking Press, 2004.

Matlock Jr., Jack. *Reagan and Gorbachev: How the Cold War Ended*. New York: Random House, 2004.

Oberdorfer, Don. *From the Cold War to a New Era: The United States and the Soviet Union, 1983–1991*. Baltimore: Poseidon Press, 1998.

O'Shaughnessy, Hugh. *Grenada: An Eyewitness Account of the U.S. Invasion and the Caribbean History that Provoked It*. New York: Dodd Mead, 1985.

Powers, Samantha. *"A Problem from Hell": America and the Age of Genocide*. New York: Basic Books, 2002.

Reynolds, David. *Summits: Six Meetings that Shaped the Twentieth Century*. New York: Basic Books, 2007.

Schmertz, Eric, ed. *President Reagan and the World*. Westport, CT: Greenwood Press, 1997.

Schoultz, Lars. *National Security and U.S. Policy Toward Latin America*. Princeton, NJ: Princeton University Press, 1987.

Schweizer, Peter. *Reagan's War: The Epic Story of His Forty-Year Struggle and Final Triumph*. New York: Doubleday, 2002.

Rabinovich, Itamar. *The War for Lebanon, 1970–1983*. Ithaca, NY: Cornell University Press, 1984.

Stares, Paul. *Space and National Security*. Washington, DC: Brookings Institution Press, 1987.

Talbott, Strobe. *Deadly Gambits: The Reagan Administration and the Stalemate in Nuclear Arms Control*. New York: Alfred A. Knopf, 1984.

Tower, John, et al. *The Tower Commission Report*. New York: Bantam, 1987.

Walker, Thomas, ed. *Reagan versus the Sandinistas: The Undeclared War on Nicaragua*. Boulder, CO: Westview Press, 1987.

Walsh, Lawrence. *Firewall: The Iran-Contra Conspiracy and Cover-up*. New York: W. W. Norton & Co., 1997.

Woodward, Bob. *Veil: The Secret Wars of the CIA, 1981–1987*. New York: Simon & Schuster, 1987.

INDEX

ABOUT THE AUTHORS

John Ehrman is a foreign affairs analyst for the federal government and an independent scholar specializing in modern American conservatism. He is the author of *The Rise of Neoconservatism: Intellectuals and Foreign Affairs, 1945–1994, The Eighties: America in the Age of Reagan,* and numerous articles and reviews on conservative politics.

Michael W. Flamm is professor of history at Ohio Wesleyan University. He is author of *Law and Order: Street Crime, Civil Unrest, and the Crisis of Liberalism in the 1960s,* and coauthor of *Debating the 1960s: Liberal, Conservative, and Radical Perspectives* and *The Chicago Handbook for Teachers: A Practical Guide to the College Classroom.*